THE PROFESSIONALIZATION OF ECONOMICS

Classics in Economics Series
Warren J. Samuels, Series Editor

Economic Semantics,
Fritz Machlup. With an introduction by Mark Perlman

The Economy as a System of Power,
Edited by Marc R. Tool and Warren J. Samuels

Essays in Economics,
Joseph A. Schumpeter. With an introduction by Richard Swedberg

Evolutionary Economics,
David Hamilton. With a new introduction by the author

Institutional Economics,
John Commons. With an introduction by Malcolm Rutherford

Inventors and Moneymakers,
Frank W. Taussig. With an introduction by Warren J. Samuels

Main Currents in Modern Economics,
Ben Seligman. With an introduction by E. Ray Canterbery

Methodology of Economic Thought,
Edited by Marc R. Tool and Warren J. Samuels

Political Element in Development of Economic Theory,
Gunnar Myrdal. With an introduction by Richard Swedberg

State, Society, and Corporation Power,
Edited by Marc R. Tool and Warren J. Samuels

The Professionalization of Economics
John Maloney. With a new introduction by the author

THE PROFESSIONALIZATION OF ECONOMICS

Alfred Marshall and the Dominance of Orthodoxy

John Maloney

With a New Introduction by the Author

Routledge
Taylor & Francis Group
LONDON AND NEW YORK

Originally published in 1985 by Cambridge University Press
Published 1991 by Transaction Publishers

Published 2019 by Routledge
2 Park Square, Milton Park, Abingdon, Oxon OX14 4RN
52 Vanderbilt Avenue, New York, NY 10017

Routledge is an imprint of the Taylor & Francis Group, an informa business

Library of Congress Catalog Number: 90-42498

Library of Congress Cataloging-in-Publication Data
Maloney, John, 1948—
The Professionalization of Economics: Alfred Marshall and the Dominance of Orthodoxy / John Maloney.
p. cm.
Reprint, with new introd. Originally published: Cambridge; New York: Cambridge University Press, 1985.
Includes bibliographical references and index.
ISBN 0-88738-345-9
1. Neoclassical school of economics—History. 2. Economics—History. 3. Marshall, Alfred, 1842–1924. I. Title.
HB98.2.M35 1990
330.15'5—dc20 90-42498
CIP

ISBN 13: 978-0-88738-345-8 (pbk)
ISBN 13: 978-1-138-53786-6 (hbk)

To my mother and
in memory of my father

Contents

Contents

Introduction to the Transaction Edition

1990 sees the centenary of the first publication of Marshall's *Principles of Economics*. It also ends a decade in which Marshall's reputation steadily rose. In the 1980s mathematical competence became more essential than ever for an economist's professional standing. (Compare the contents of the *American Economic Review* for 1969 and 1989). And yet, perhaps as a reaction, mathematical virtuosity for its own sake found fewer and fewer defenders. Marshall—who saw mathematical proficiency as a habit of thought and an emblem of sharp thinking but never as an end in itself—would have approved. The rising generation of economists is one that ought to approve of Marshall.

Distorted perspectives on the man and his economics have also gone into eclipse. To attribute this to the decline of the radical left would be unjust to those radicals who pointed out, all along, that Marshall was very much more than another "bourgeois apologist." Nonetheless, the army of those only interested in the great economists of the past for the "apologetic intent" that could be blown into their work has largely trooped off the stage, and scholarship and historical justice alike are the better for it.

Thirdly, it is possible at the time of writing to discern Marshall as a patron of today's environmental fashions. Externalities had to wait for Marshall for rigorous analysis, and insofar as economics is entitled to cast itself as a green science and not a dismal one, that right comes from a tradition that is Marshallian.

Certainly there has been far more Marshalliana in the five years since this book was first published than in any comparable previous period. Pride of place must go to David Reisman's trilogy, *The Economics of Alfred Marshall* (1986), *Alfred Marshall: Progress and Politics* (1987) and *Alfred Marshall's Mission* (1990). The last of these stands out especially as the most shrewd and sympathetic portrait of the man and his goals yet to have been drawn. Yet some of the most original insights into the entire Marshall era have come from Alon Kadish's *Historians, Economists and Economic History* (1989) with its focus on the partition of political economy into (Marshallian) economic analysis on the one hand and economic history on the other. Marshall, in fact, possessed exactly those personal and intellectual qualities needed to keep nineteenth-century political economy intact—assuming it were possible for anyone to do so. Dr Kadish's book, however, starts with the fact that Marshall used his power divisively, and charts his long and (in every sense) devious march through the institutions of Cambridge in quest of an independent and—by the standards of the day—narrowly analytical Cambridge Economics Tripos.

After the reviews of the first edition of *Principles*, Marshall characteristically thanked, for their "goodwill, fairness and generosity of interpretation," those who "on the whole condemned the book" as well as those who on the whole approved of it. The most common criticism of *Marshall, Orthodoxy and the Professionalisation of Economics* has concerned its perhaps excessive fascination with welfare economics as the alleged touchstone of professionalisation. One critic went so far as to say that to make welfare economics the criterion of the subject's maturity is like making physicists' ethical reactions to the atomic bomb the criterion of their professionalisation as physicists. But the entire point about the "professional" welfare economics developed by Marshall and Pigou is that it *exempted* economists from having to reflect on the ethical consequences of changes in what they defined as economic welfare (even if Marshall, for one, did not press his claim to such exemption).

There have also, however, been criticisms of excessive deference towards, or failure to evaluate explicitly enough, the work of Marshall's historicist adversaries and of Hobson. Any such omission arose from my assumption that the two "camps" would be seen on all sides to have had very different objectives regarding the development of economics, and that a comparison of abilities was to that extent beside the point. Nonetheless, I am quite happy to proclaim my own opinion that one Marshall is worth ten Hobsons, thirty Cunninghams and fifty Ashleys! Sententious moralist, devious adversary and frequently infuriating colleague he may have been, but Marshall the economist is what matters, and Marshall the economist for fifty years put his analytical genius to the service of humanity in general and its least fortunate members in particular. What is humanity that it should ask for more?

University of Exeter

Preface

This book is mainly about the years 1885–1908, the period of Marshall's professorship in political economy at Cambridge. The first chapter, however, sets the scene as it stood a few years previously, while the last focuses on the succession of Pigou and developments up to 1914. It also had to be decided how far to consider the post-1914 work of the main economists discussed. In the case of Hobson, in particular, some later work does express important lifelong attitudes more fully and/or unambiguously than anything he wrote before 1914. Consequently it would be wrong to insist on a neat cut-off point here.

I should like to thank Professor A. W. Coats, who supervised the Ph.D. thesis on which this book is based, for his endless enthusiasm, kindness and patience with a sometimes wayward student. So basic and pervasive is his contribution to this book that it would be hard to single out anything of mine within it untouched by his influence. (The faults remain mine.) I should also like to thank Maurice Cowling, both as a source of valuable comments and suggestions on the original draft of this book and, more fundamentally, as one of the great teachers of history; I would never have wished to be other than a Peterhouse man. The staff of Cambridge University Library, the Marshall Library of Economics, Nottingham University Library, the British Library of Economic and Political Science (London School of Economics), the Bodleian Library and Hull University Library have been unfailingly efficient and hospitable. The staff of Cambridge University Press have been most helpful and long-suffering. I have had illuminating conversations with Professor R. D. Collison Black, Dr David Cannadine, the late Professor Philip Sargant Florence, Dr Alon Kadish, Professor Joseph Lee, Professor Austin Robinson, Roy Trinder and Allan Ward. Plymouth Polytechnic gave me a sabbatical term to complete the thesis on which this book is based, and my economist colleagues between them took over my teaching while I was away. Grace Maloney compiled the index for me, and Mary Beard saved me a last-minute journey to London by volunteering to copy out some of Cannan's correspondence for me. To all of these I owe a debt of gratitude.

Tideford, Cornwall

J. M.

Introduction to the First Edition

Two notable events took place in Cambridge in November 1884. The first was the premature death of Henry Fawcett, the blind postmaster-general whose simultaneous tenure of the Cambridge chair of political economy had aroused admiration even in an age much less specialised than our own. The second was the even more premature death of the contest to succeed to Fawcett's chair, once it became known that Alfred Marshall of Balliol College, Oxford, was a candidate.

Marshall's qualifications were unequalled in England. His intellectual excellence had been proved in 1865 when, in a distinguished year for the Mathematical Tripos, he had come second only to the future Lord Rayleigh. His energy and enthusiasm as a young Cambridge lecturer in the 1870s was well remembered. His administrative ability was guaranteed by six years as principal of University College, Bristol. His published work was not only of high quality and originality in itself, but was widely known to be little more than an hors d'œuvre to a massive, slowly gestating work of general principles, much of which had already been disseminated informally to pupils. At forty-two, he was about the right age. He was even married to a former Cambridge economics don of some reputation in her own right.

The initial uncertainty about Fawcett's vacant post, then, was largely uncertainty as to whether Marshall would want it. It was by no means obvious that he would. He had only been a year at Balliol under his 'beloved Master' Benjamin Jowett. He liked Balliol's values, its distinctive mixture of moral earnestness and worldly ambition; he liked being successor to the college lectureship held by Arnold Toynbee; and, in the wider Oxford context, it was a good omen to have taught three outstanding young economists in the first year there. Nevertheless, Balliol was in the business of training missionaries, sacred and secular, and a missionary, in Marshall's eyes, was what Cambridge economics needed.

Marshall disbelieved in a division of labour between different universities. It followed that his main objectives for Cambridge economics were also his objectives when he turned his thoughts to the national scene. First, he wanted economists to be trained in a body of theory which – without excessive grief – he recognised would be inaccessible to laymen. Secondly he sought, via the development of welfare economics, to give the economist a specialist voice in the art of policy-making. Thirdly, he wanted to enhance the scientific authority of his subject by keeping it clear of political partisanship.

Marshall, we shall see, had varying degrees of success in achieving these objectives, both within the Cambridge and the national contexts. But he had a sufficiently sweeping success in *propagating* them as objectives to create a new orthodoxy which spread rapidly across English political economy in the years after 1885. It was, it must be repeated, an orthodoxy of aim. But it was more than a mere aim at an orthodoxy. Marshall spoke freely (though not in public) of 'economic insiders' and 'economic outsiders'; and the status of professional insider depended more than anything else on whether the economist's intentions seemed to be helping or hindering the transformation of economics into a science. To have the right aims counted for more than success in achieving them.

Consequently, the first part of this book, 'Marshall's plans' is, in the main, an extended statement of Marshall's objectives for political economy and an analysis of the technical and ideological orthodoxy which their pursuit imposed. And the *successful* pursuit of these objectives defines a process of professionalisation as the term is often understood. Hence the title of the book, and hence the preoccupations of Parts 2 and 3, to which we now turn.

A profession has been succinctly defined as a vocabulary, an organisation, a journal and a conference. Only the vocabulary mattered very much in Marshall's day. The organisations, the journals and the conferences were – by deliberate design – wide open to people with little training or knowledge. If one imagines hospital orderlies writing in *The Lancet* or village churchwardens addressing the Synod, that hardly conveys an exaggerated picture of the *Economic Journal* in its early days, or the economic section of the British Association for the Advancement of Science throughout the Marshall era.

Why did the majority of academic specialists endorse this democratic approach? It may have been a half-proud, half-embarrassed awareness of how very curious their own activities were. Most emerging academic disciplines need a period of partial retreat from the world. But in economics the gap between academic and public preoccupations was especially glaring. The cause of this will be discussed in the main body of the book. But the consequence was that all economists, with the exception of the uncomplicated Edgeworth, tried in their different ways to court the general public. And, in turn, the consequence of this was that political economy's 'professional' institutions failed to demarcate any important boundaries. A primarily institutional focus would therefore be inappropriate. What we have rather tried to do is to trace the rise of a self-conscious sense of profession among economists and to explain why, intellectually and ideologically, it was dominated by the Marshallian 'paradigm'.

This approach makes much of the sociology of the professions redundant for our purpose. Nevertheless, Marshall's objectives for economics can usefully be correlated with three of the criteria of professionalisation laid down by sociologists, and this provides a framework for parts 2 and 3 of this book.

(1) *The professional is trained in a specialised body of theory.* This was Marshall's first and paramount objective. How, and how far, it penetrated the ranks of his contemporaries is the principal concern of part 2, 'Marshall's peers'.

(2) *He has an effective monopoly of a defined specialist function or functions.* This corresponds to Marshall's second objective. As already mentioned, he looked to an advanced conception of welfare economics to give the economist an authoritative voice in policy discussions. How he, his Oxford 'opposite number' Edgeworth and his Cambridge successor Pigou fared in this quest is described in the first chapter of part 3.

(3) *He observes professional ethics which either institutional sanctions or the force of colleagues' opinions impel him to maintain.* This corresponds to Marshall's third objective, in the sense that political neutrality, and indeed ethical neutrality itself, were the principal professional ethics which Marshall enjoined on his colleagues. How they treated these ideals – and how far Marshall himself lived up to them – is discussed in the second and third chapters of part 3.

It has been suggested in this introduction that success for Marshall in achieving his main aims would have been a sufficient condition for professionalisation as we have defined it. But should it also be seen as a necessary condition? That is to say, given (as we shall see) that Marshall fell far short of complete success in what he was trying to do, how far did this make professionalisation impossible?

To answer this question requires that we distinguish between and relate to one another the objective and subjective determinants of professionalisation. Whatever the occupation we are considering, we need to know how the different subjective assessments, of who is and who is not competent to do what, relate to the reality. And we need to know this primarily because today's assessment, if made convincingly enough, may *become* reality tomorrow. A group of specialists who announce their monopoly of occupational competence may thus achieve a real monopoly if they can secure, on the basis of their claims, the right to decide whom to train and not to train for the occupation, and in what to train them.

The thesis of this book is that this is what happened in economics between 1880 and 1914; that economic orthodoxy, accused on all sides in the 1870s and 80s of both theoretical inadequacy and social irrelevance, resolved this position not by a successful answer to these criticisms, but by capturing a dominant position in which it could largely ignore its critics. At the same time, however, it will be stressed that the nature of economic theory *objectively* and qualitatively changed during our period, and that this change was indispensable to professionalisation. No amount of power politics, of ideological claims, specialist jargon and academic prestige could have compensated for it.

Part 1

MARSHALL'S PLANS

I

Economics in the 1870s

Adam Smith completed the *Wealth of Nations* in 1776, and our Political Economy is therefore just a hundred years old. In that time it has had a wonderful effect. The life of almost every one in England – perhaps every one – is different and better in consequence of it. The whole commercial policy of the country is not so much founded on it as instinct with it. Ideas which are paradoxes everywhere else in the world are accepted axioms here as a result of it. No other form of philosophy has ever had one thousandth part of the influence on us; its teachings have settled down into the common sense of the nation, and have become irreversible.[1]

So begins Bagehot's '*The Postulates of Political Economy*', an essay written on the centenary of the *Wealth of Nations*, and in which celebration runs less than a nose ahead of doubt. Anxiously, Bagehot contrasts the continuing worldly success of Smith's economics with the indifferent reputation of political economy in the 1870s. 'It lies', he says, 'rather dead in the public mind. Not only does it not excite the same interest as formerly, but there is not exactly the same confidence in it. Younger men either do not study it, or do not feel that it comes home to them, and that it matches with their most living ideas.'[2]

The essay, like its companion *The Preliminaries of Political Economy*, is a defensive undertaking. It tries to mitigate the claims of political economy in order to make them more effective. Thirty years later W. J. Ashley was to pronounce the attempt a failure, suggesting that, in trying to rehabilitate orthodox political economy, Bagehot, in the minds of many, had had the effect of further discrediting it.[3] Is this true? Bagehot's iconoclastically modest claim for political economy was that its boundaries were much narrower than the classical economists, especially Smith, had implied. 'We need – not that the authority of our Political Economy should be impugned, but that it should be *minimised*; that we should realise distinctly where it is established, and where not; that its sovereignty should be upheld, but its frontiers marked.'[4]

It is quite possible that, as Ashley implies, many of Bagehot's audience heard these words as something like an admission of defeat, a proclamation that only humdrum labours awaited the political economist. Several of the speakers at the Political Economy Club's dinner for the centenary of the *Wealth of Nations* made this last claim; but in a victorious, if recessional, spirit. Robert Lowe, the former Chancellor of the Exchequer, even envisaged a permanent rest on the oars. 'The great work has been done.'[5] Gladstone appeared to demur at Lowe's summary, but then predicted that the Political Economy Club of 1976 would look back on a century in which economic legislation had been confined to currency questions and economic theory had been largely confined to confining the legislation.[6]

In the context of the general reappraisal of economics that was going on in the 1870s, Bagehot's two essays sound optimistic and the Political Economy Club's celebrations positively complacent. But that is only the measure of the chastened state of the science after 1870. In the space of five years (1869–74) economists had had to absorb Thornton's main attack on classical orthodoxy, Mill's recantation of the wage-fund theory, new heights of invective from the pen of Ruskin, the publication of Jevons' *Theory of Political Economy*, the launching of Cliffe Leslie's assault on deductive economics and the deaths of Mill and Cairnes. It is small wonder that most saw the late 1860s and the early 1870s as a time of decay, not of rebirth. There were exceptions. Bagehot's sensitive ear picked up the lusty cries of both English and Swiss marginalist infants above the noise of the classical house caving in. But Bagehot was not enthusiastic about what he heard:

> Mr Stanley Jevons, and M. Walras of Lausanne, without communication and almost simultaneously, have worked out a 'mathematical' theory of Political Economy; – and anyone who thinks what is ordinarily taught in England objectionable, because it is too little concrete in its method, and looks too unlike life and business, had better try the new doctrine, which he will find to be much worse on these points than the old. ('Postulates of Political Economy', p. 20)

And as late as 1883 Sidgwick could begin his *Principles of Political Economy* with an entirely negative and pessimistic account of political economy's fortunes since the early sixties.

Sidgwick, however, ran the theme of political economy's 'objective' decline alongside the theme of its growing unpopularity in the outside world. He looked longingly back to 1861, when a layman, purely incidentally to an article on English Jurisprudence, could throw in a eulogy to political economy as a true science whose success was on a par with astronomy's.[7] By the late 1870s such praise was long dried up, and economists were fighting off the threatened humiliation of expulsion from the British Association for the Advancement of Science.[8]

It is as well for this book that economics was not so excluded, because the annual meetings of the British Association's Section F (the social science section) between 1870 and 1885 are an indispensable chart of the long debate, never heard before and never wholly silenced since, on the question: whither economics? Continuous public discussion of where a subject should be going is a hallmark of professionalisation: only a sense of belonging to a competent specialist body will produce the collective self-consciousness needed to keep the 'scope, method and destination' issue perpetually on, or near, the boil. But though professionalisation is a sufficient condition for this kind of appraisal to be taking place at any given point of time, it is not a necessary one. Economists between 1870 and 1885 endlessly discussed their subject's future not because of any professional self-consciousness, but because of the consciousness that they were nothing like professional enough, and had no immediate prospect of being so.

There was every reason for this modesty. Leslie Stephen's *Life of Henry Fawcett* describes Cambridge economics in the 1860s and 70s, telling us that when Fawcett became professor of political economy in 1863, 'professors' lectures were considered to be mainly ornamental, and they scarcely formed a part of the real educational system'.[9] Later the university tried to invigorate the atmosphere by making attendance at Fawcett's lectures compulsory for pass degree students. Candidates for honours, however, were exempted on the grounds that their time was too valuable! But even Cambridge fared better than Oxford, where the chair of political economy from 1868 to 1888 ensconced the dim light of Bonamy Price, an old gentleman who was never quite sure whether economic theory was impossible or merely undesirable. With both Oxford and Cambridge effectively out of action, the call to turn economics into a professional discipline came from Manchester. And Jevons' recipe for professionalisation was specialisation.

Jevons himself was a specialist in both pure theory and industrial organisation (as well as statistics, botany, geology, meteorology and the philosophy of science). Other economists have straddled the boundary between pure and applied economics just as successfully as Jevons did – Smith, Marx and Keynes alike would have been much lesser men had they not done so. But Jevons was unique in not being, and apparently not wanting to be, a synthesiser. Instead he was a polymathic specialist who almost made a virtue of disconnectedness. And greater disconnectedness was Jevons' cure for the confusion in which he found economics in 1879.

> the present chaotic state of economics arises from the confusing together of several branches of knowledge. Sub-division is the remedy. We must distinguish the empirical element from the abstract theory, from the applied theory and from the more detailed art of finance and administration. Thus will arise various sciences, such as commercial statistics, the mathematical theory of economics, systematic and descriptive economics, economic sociology and fiscal science.[10]

This, it will be seen later, is the opposite of what Marshall eventually tried to do. It is also contrary to the prevailing spirit in which economics' future was discussed by Section F.

Most speakers at the British Association agreed with Jevons that economics should both aspire to the rigour of the natural sciences and at the same time come closer to poverty, unemployment, industrial unrest, slow growth, the coal question, the agriculture question and the entire social question. But whereas Jevons saw these as objectives whose competing claims could only be satisfied by increased division of labour among economists, the British Association predominantly looked for a single path along which all those who saw themselves as economists could advance together.

Another theme which in the 1870s both linked and divided economists was the need to propagate the subject more effectively. It linked Jevons, who warned that 'if people do not understand a true political economy they will make a false one of their own',[11] with Bonamy Price, who proclaimed the test of a true political economy to be 'that its teaching, its principles, its arguments, and above all its language, shall be intelligible to all'.[12] The divisive issue was what kind of economics should be propagated. Jevons' conviction that economic theory should imitate the natural sciences was, to Bonamy Price, precisely the kind of attitude which robbed economists of practical influence.

Price's antipathy to theory was extreme. To him, the test of 'real economical teaching' was that 'it should land the pupil in the perception that [political economy] is made up of familiar truisms'.[13] Unquestionably, he said, political economy employed analysis; but if the actions it analysed 'were habitually performed before the analysis, and for the very reasons indicated by the analysis, what discovery has been made?' This revolutionary dictum, which abolishes at a stroke the value not only of economic theory but of any kind of explanatory statement about anything, had, we can presume, few supporters among economists. But Cliffe Leslie's hostility to Jevons' conception of economics was every bit as strong as Price's.

Leslie's contribution to economics will be mentioned again in chapter 5. But in the meantime a few facts about him should be noted. Like Thorold Rogers, he paid homage to Adam Smith as an inductive, historically-minded economist whose brand of economics should never have been supplanted by the grotesque abstractions and unbalanced methodology of Ricardo. So far had economics gone along the Ricardian road, building a mountain of deductive generalisations on the pinpoint that was 'economic man', that the only thing to do was to level the whole superstructure to the ground and make a fresh, and cautious, start. The new economics should draw on historical material, not unreal psychological stereotypes. And it should be designed to shed light on the connection between economic and other phases of social evolution. 'If Political Economy, under that name, be not now bent to the task, it will speedily be taken out of the hands of its teachers by Sociology.'[14]

Leslie was particularly hostile to the idea that economics either did, or ever could, mirror the procedures of the natural sciences. To Bagehot's claim that the abstract economist, like Darwin, reasoned, deductively fron one '*vera causa*', he retorted that the desire for wealth 'so far from being a *vera causa*, is an abstraction compounding a great variety of different and heterogeneous motives, which have been mistaken for a single homogeneous force'.[15] Leslie then went on to criticise Cairnes, whose *Character and Logical Method of Political Economy* (1854) had claimed that the economist, by the power of introspection, had a 'knowledge of ultimate causes' such that 'he is already, at the outset of his enterprises, in the position which the physicist only attains after ages of laborious research'. Although Leslie showed no hostility to the idea of introspection as such, he denied that its use could give deduction a place in economics in any way comparable to its place in physics.

Leslie, then, cast doubt on the usefulness of both deductive economics (at least as it then existed) and autonomous economics. A coolness towards deduction and a disbelief in autonomy do normally go together in economics; and this is no coincidence, as we shall argue later in this chapter. But, now the issue of an autonomous economics has been raised, we must ask: autonomous from what? We must look at what was happening, in and around the 1870s, outside the increasingly narrow world of economics.

II

The soil in which nineteenth-century English economics grew was liberal and utilitarian. Although utilitarianism is potentially the most authoritarian of all doctrines – no other contains so total an injunction that the individual should sacrifice his welfare to that of the mass – it is nonetheless linked to liberalism in that both spring from the same rationalist roots. Being a liberal nearly always involves the belief that most people are – at least potentially – reasonable enough, and the consequences of their use of reason predictable enough, to make paternalistic government unnecessary.[16] And being a utilitarian both induces and is induced by a rationalistic attitude to existing institutions; the ethical goal of the greatest happiness translates readily into a touchstone of institutional efficiency.

Or does it? The ethical goal of the greatest happiness yields few if any direct prescriptions. In practice all utilitarians have had to build a transmission mechanism before the felicific engine can turn the legislative wheels:[17] and in practice this transmission mechanism has turned out to be a replacement for, not an appendage to, the engine. Thus when Bentham says that the aim of legislation is the greatest happiness of the greatest number, that security and equality are two of the principal means to be promoted to this end, and that when the two conflict equality should give way, his last statement makes the other two largely redundant. But without the last statement, we have little of use to the legislator.

It is true that there is more to utilitarianism than the ethical criterion of the greatest happiness. Its other main axiom is that actions are motivated by the desire for pleasure and the avoidance of pain. But no one has ever been able to define 'pleasure' and 'pain' in such a way as not to make the axiom either patently false or tautologous. It has also been claimed that, until Sidgwick promulgated the doctrine of altruistic hedonism, utilitarianism *told* people to be selfish. But this is surely incorrect. Utilitarianism told people to do whatever will maximise total happiness: it was the doctrine of the invisible hand, an idea wholly distinct from utilitarianism, which assured them that self-interest often led in this direction.

Utilitarianism, then, was a largely empty box: at the very least, it possessed crippling ambiguities which transcended the mere paradox of its authoritarian implications and liberal adherents. However, like Marxism, it is a hybrid of method and doctrine; and, again like Marxism, it is from this marriage that it derives its proselytising power. Taken as nothing but doctrine it is negative and destructive, scornfully razing the pretensions of moral intuitionists and 'natural rights' philosophers.[18] Taken as nothing but method, it is more positive but less radical – not much more than a blunt tool of rationality for those already disposed to be rationalistic. But, fused into a whole, it created a compelling rhetoric of rebellion, clear-sightedness, practicality and humanitarianism – a rhetoric which, in the hands of confident men who did not doubt they knew what caused pleasure and pain, could invigorate the lazy, arouse the apathetic and reassure the timid.

III

Utilitarianism, rationalism and liberalism have traditionally been seen as loyal and effective allies. And the conventional view has been to see Cambridge as their true home, and Sidgwick as their prime embodiment, in the 1870s and 80s; the 'other place' being the source of an Idealist influence which both turned men's minds towards, and supplied intellectual justification for, the tackling of the 'social problem' in a way that Cambridge utilitarians could not, and probably did not want to, emulate. In recent years, however, two historians[19] have criticised this polar view. C. J. Dewey's portrait of Sidgwick is of a man who

> rendered utilitarianism invulnerable to idealist attack by stealing his opponents' clothes. Beginning his intellectual career as an enthusiast for a single philosophy and a single method, he died an arch eclectic; his personal odyssey reflecting the steadily increasing complexity of the Victorian intellect.[20]

And Dewey gives Sidgwick much more than just a reflexive role. Although he (rightly) presents Sidgwick's *negative* moves – the rejection of sensation-psychology, atomistic sociology and free market economics – as not especially original adjustments of outlook in the context of the times, he also praises the distinctiveness of Sidgwick's positive attempt to revise utilitarianism. In the first place, says Dewey, Sidgwick used his own study *The Development of European Polity* to locate, analyse the nature of and recommend the nurture of, a national solidarity not deducible from atomistic axioms and contract theories of the State. Secondly, Sidgwick treated the Smithian–Benthamite notion of 'sympathy', not as a useful and natural supplement to the invisible hand in dovetailing individual and collective interests, but as a force both more socially necessary and more fragile than Mill had believed it to be. Thirdly – and this follows on from the last point – Sidgwick tried to rejuvenate utilitarian ethics with a massive injection of intuitionism. This he did not only because he saw conscience as a source of good not to be explained in hedonistic terms, but also because he saw it as giving clearer ethical guidance than could the felicific calculus. 'We can see clearly . . . what we ought to do; but we cannot see clearly what will lead to our happiness.'[21]

Dewey's thesis has come in for heavy criticism, both implicit and explicit. J. B. Schneewind, in a massive study of Sidgwick's ethics, makes it clear that Sidgwick was not seeking an even-handed synthesis of utilitarian and intuitionist morality, but rather trying to show that utilitarianism was 'superior in validity' to intuitionism – 'superior in validity' meaning that, when respective prescriptions conflict, the first one's precepts must be accepted as overruling the precepts of the other. Stefan Collini rightly points out that the holistic overtones of *The Development of European Polity* are more than equalled in the work of Mill, and further argues that there is ample evidence in *Methods of Ethics* to show that Sidgwick, far from stealing his opponents' clothes, 'would not have been seen dead in the gaudy finery of the Idealists'.[22]

But even if it is wrong to term Sidgwick an 'Idealist', or even an '"Idealist"', whether or not we do so has little bearing on his, and Cambridge's, orientation towards social legislation. And the *generally* limited importance of Idealism as a stimulus to the social conscience is underlined in the Oxford context by Michael Freeden's *The New Liberalism*:

> Had Green not existed, liberalism would still have become collectivist and favourably oriented to progressive reform . . . Green and Arnold Toynbee were paragons of a social crusading spirit hardly connected by their followers with theoretical conceptualisation . . . Oxford provided the

emotional atmosphere and motivation to study social problems and undertake social work rather than the intellectual justification and framework for social reform.[23]

And as regards the intellectual justification (or lack of it) which Oxford provided for social reform, Melvin Richter's *The Politics of Conscience* shows, perhaps even more than Richter intends, how tenuous was the link between Green's belief that 'the Universe is a single, eternal activity or energy, of which it is the essence to be self-conscious, that is to be itself and not-itself'[24] and his policy prescriptions. Nonetheless there *was* a link; the idea of 'positive liberty'.

Idealism – whether expounded in religious or secular terms – is about the realisation of the kingdom of God within each man. However this consummation is supposed to come about, it must involve a form of liberation other than the mere removal of external restraint. No Idealist therefore has ever been satisfied – no Idealist ever could be satisfied – with the negative concept of liberty. An Idealist can be (and Green was) largely preoccupied with the 'negative' task of removing obstacles to self-realisation; but not only is this task distinct from minimising the coercion of the individual by others; it creates the justification for *increased* coercion where necessary. Idealism both legitimised and necessitated the idea of 'positive liberty', which in turn legitimised and necessitated a more active State.

And yet it is hard to disagree with Freeden's view that Idealism, though a willing attendant to social reform, was not a necessary one. It created neither the initial need nor the sole means to supersede 'negative liberty'. With or without Green, even the minimally philanthropic section of the intelligentsia was cavilling at classical liberalism as an ideology which, logically interpreted, forbade all State help to the poor as being an invasion of the natural rights of the rich. And there were perfectly adequate non-Idealist ways of getting round this difficulty, if difficulty it was. Utilitarianism with its message that there were no rights, only right actions, was one. The – perfectly unproblematic – synthesisation of the liberal position with the tenet that there were no absolute property rights was another. And both Sidgwick and Marshall in large measure adopted both these positions, though Sidgwick, the philosopher, was the more explicit about them.

This is not, however, to deny that a 'social crusading spirit' was fostered, more than anywhere else, at Oxford. As Freeden says even while he is discounting the independent influence of Idealism, Oxford was a powerful emotional armoury of middle-class goodwill – a judgement which is confirmed, and specifically extended to Oxford's young economists, by Alon Kadish.[25] And it was an economist, Toynbee, who ended a lecture to working men with the great pleading peroration which, incontestably, represents the high point of Oxonian generosity and guilt.

> We – the middle classes, I mean, and not merely the very rich – we have neglected you; instead of justice we have offered you charity, and instead of sympathy, we have offered you hard and unreal advice; but I think we are changing. If you would only believe it and trust us, I think that many of us would spend our lives in your service. You have – I say it clearly and advisedly – you have to forgive us, for we have wronged you; we have sinned against you grievously – not knowingly always, but still we have sinned, and let us confess it; but if you will forgive us – nay, whether you will forgive us or not, we will serve you, we will devote our lives to your service, and we cannot do more. It is not that we care about public life, for what is public life but the miserable, arid waste of barren controversies and personal jealousies, and grievous loss of time? Who would live in public life if he could help it? But we students, we would help you if we could. We are willing to give up something much dearer than fame and social position. We are willing to give up the life we care for, the life with books and with those we love. We will do this, and only ask you to remember one thing in return. We will ask you to remember this – that we work for you in the hope and trust that if you get material civilisation, if you get a better life, if you have opened up to you the possibility of a better life, you will lead a better life.[26]

Granted that the difference in outlook of the two universities has sometimes been exaggerated, it is still not possible to imagine this strange moving outburst coming out of Cambridge.

IV

A word is now in place about the influence of evolutionary ideas on social thought. Social evolutionism – a cluster of theories of which Social Darwinism was but one – did not become influential until after 1880. An extended discussion of its nature and effects would therefore be out of place in this chapter. It is, however, a theme which will crop up constantly in this book: first because it had a direct influence on the economics of both Marshall and Hobson; secondly because some of its exponents propagated a bogus 'scientific' ethics which held economists back from ethical neutrality; and thirdly because it pushed erstwhile liberals into collectivism in a way which neither utilitarianism nor Idealism was capable of doing.

And fourthly – and this point must be looked at now – evolutionism and Idealism alike have been seen as substitutes for belief in God. Indeed, more generally, a great deal has been said about this or that doctrine being an emotionally necessary replacement for religious belief – often accompanied by the characterisation of this or that occupation as a 'secular priesthood'. To write off a secular doctrine as a substitute for religious belief is as irrelevant to its validity as to write it off as a rationalisation of economic interest. Nonetheless there is some truth in the view that Idealism and evolutionism acted as replacements for Christian faith.

The issue of evolutionism, however, was complicated by the fact that it also took a part in *dis*placing Christian belief. Darwin's *Origin of the Species*, first published in 1859, was the most important of a series of challenges whose cumulative effect was to persuade a large number of people that God could only be allowed back on terms dictated by science. The controversy over *Essays and Reviews*, published by seven clergymen in 1860, helped to drive this tendency home. *Essays and Reviews* was a provocative attempt to 'illustrate the advantage desirable to the cause of religious and moral truth, from a free handling, in a becoming spirit, of subjects peculiarly liable to suffer by the repetitions of conventional language, and from traditional methods of treatment'.[27]

The questioning, independent spirit of *Essays and Reviews* may have touched off a decline in orthodox religious enthusiasm greater than either its authors intended or its explicit conclusions warranted. Fear of its potential effects was certainly behind the vigorous condemnation of the book by the majority of senior churchmen; condemnation which in turn may, by its unwisely inquisitorial tone, have dealt a further blow to the status of the Church. The battle to prevent the emasculation of holiness by science and liberalism was often effectively, even brilliantly, fought – one of the most brilliant campaigners was a layman, W. H. Mallock,[28] whose *New Republic* (1875) contained a remarkable prefiguration of the satirical treatment some conservative Christians were to hand out to 'progressive' clergymen a century later – but it was from the first to last reactive. It may be that enough of the Church's intellectuals were, albeit privately, themselves experiencing enough of the mid-Victorian crisis of faith to damp the collective fire.

The enforced retreat of Christianity transposed much evangelical fervour into a secular key where it was, on the whole, less effective. The totalitarian streak in evangelicalism – and a movement which enjoins the conscious minute-by-minute subordination of all actions to an exact and exacting code must be owned to have a totalitarian streak – is apt to be found bearable only when irradiated by the spark of faith. The difference between Christian and secular evangelism is captured by the difference between the respective moralisings of Cunningham and Marshall. Stripped of their rhetorical garb, they amounted to very much the same thing. Yet Cunningham, the Christian, still sounds fresh, sincere and wise, whereas Marshall, the agnostic, seldom rises above the kind of dusty headmagisterial waffle which might emanate from a very faded school magazine. To say the Victorian evangelical conscience sounds especially overblown when not accompanied by religious faith is, of course, different from saying that there can be no purely secular morality; it is, however, to assert that a purely secular morality is, in terms of persuasive power, a handicapped morality – the great sad fact that dominated and dogged the ultimately unsatisfactory life of Henry Sidgwick.

Secular economics, however, presented none of the problems of secular ethics. Although Marshall's agnosticism put him in a minority among economists, many of the Christian majority wrote in such a way as to give no clue to their religious beliefs. It is hard to see how the contributions of Jevons (Unitarian), Wicksteed (Unitarian minister) or J. N. Keynes (Nonconformist) would have differed if all three had been atheists. Nicholson tacked an essay about Christianity and economics on to the end of his *Principles*, but it is wholly dispensable to the rest of the book. The one 'religion' which could not fail to affect an economist's work was not Christianity but Comtism.

Comte's influence in England, on the wane in the years after 1870, flared up again after Ingram's presidential address of 1878 to Section F of the British Association. In it, Ingram argued, in Comtist language, for the subordination of economics and statistics to the super-science of Comtist sociology. Repercussions were immediate and prolonged. In Philip Abrams' words:

> [Ingram's] argument was taken up and defended or rebutted in a dozen periodicals and in all the leading intellectual societies during the next two years. It became a point of reference for public lectures, conference papers,

and essays. For the next decade echoes of it reverberate everywhere in the writings of economists, statisticians, anthropologists, reformers and philosophers.[29]

However, considering that Ingram's address dealt, more than anything else, with the future of economics, the specifically economic echoes were not as clear as might have been expected. This is probably because, although most economists in the 1880s spent much time discussing the nature of their subject, the issue of economics' autonomy from other disciplines was never effectively disentangled from the issue of economics' correct methodology. Perhaps this conflation was justified: perhaps, even, the two issues *could* not have been disentangled very successfully.

Yet the correlation between deductive economics and autonomous economics, though strong, is not so obvious that it should be taken for granted. Marxist economics, after all, violates the correlation. It is both primarily deductive, and aggressively historically relativistic: and historical relativism and epistemological autonomy are incompatible. (If there is no timeless 'economic man', economic theory must be steered by economic history.) It is, however, precisely Marx's achievement that he, more than anyone else, managed to construct an economics both relativistic and deductive. Those economists who cannot accept Marxism, to a much greater extent than those who can, have to choose between the rigour of deduction and the realism of relativism – the latter choice putting paid to their pretensions of disciplinary independence.

In the years after 1870, the orthodox school of economics plumped heavily for the first choice – or, rather, those economists who plumped for the first choice succeeded in erecting a formidable, and exclusive, orthodoxy. So formidable was it that it is easy to forget that their choice ran counter to the dominant interdisciplinary trend in the world of scholarship as a whole. The irony was that this interdisciplinary trend was itself given a hefty push by the collapse of classical economics, or, to be more exact, by the collapse of the compulsory pessimism enjoined by the classical theory of wages. If this seems an eccentric claim, or if the reader cannot yet see why we have spoken of an 'irony', we would ask him to imagine himself in 1870, a generous youth unable to argue his way past the curmudgeonly pseudo-Malthusianism of his elders. To wake up one morning and find you no longer had to believe the iron law of wages must have been heady liberation indeed, fit to send idealistic young men and women clambering onto the waiting bandwagons of social reform – Idealism, evolutionism and revisionist utilitarianism. But it was precisely these ideologies which, once rolling, carried the intelligentsia out of the static world of methodological atomism, leaving the assumptions of the marginalists looking deviant and dated. So, when classical economics drank hemlock around 1870, it handed a cup of subtler poison to its successor. We have to investigate why the results, over the next forty years, were anything but fatal.

V

Just before beginning to do so, however, it should be emphasised that the great depression in economists' spirits in the 1870s, like the Great Depression 'out there' in the economy, should not be exaggerated. The speeches at the Adam Smith centenary celebration, when all is said and done, do read like an unforced celebration. Ashley's assertion that Bagehot's defence of political economy merely gave its reputation another downward shove is not supported by any evidence. And if Jevons found economic science 'chaotic' in 1879,[30] the much less critical Cairnes had found it on the brink of chaos in 1854:

> the laws of population, of rent, of foreign trade, the effects of different kinds of expenditure upon distribution, the theory of prices – all fundamental in the science – are still unsettled, and must be regarded as 'open questions' . . . so far from the period of controversy having passed, it seems hardly yet to have begun . . . controversy respecting fundamental principles which lie at the root of its reasonings, and which were regarded as settled when Col. Torrens wrote.[31]

Nor is there any convincing evidence of a decline after 1870 in political economy's reputation outside the ranks of its own practitioners. Doubtless it continued to be unpopular with those among whom it had always been unpopular; but lay presidents of Section F in the 1870s typically addressed the annual gathering with a breezy buoyancy which must have had Jevons fidgeting in his seat and muttering that ignorance was bliss.[32]

If economists in the 1870s were in self-conscious mood, that is a sign of maturity rather than melancholy. If critics (some economists, some not) accused economics both of theoretical weakness and of inapplicability, they went on doing so right up to 1914 and beyond. The disagreements over methodology, admittedly, suffered an abrupt diminuendo after the early 1890s: but, so far as other basic controversies became less conspicuous, that was only because critics of orthodoxy came to look less and less like economists, and non-economists came to look less and less like qualified critics. Why this happened, and what it led to, are the two principal themes of the rest of this book.

2

Marshall's objectives and Marshallian orthodoxy

Our first criterion of professionalism was that the professional is trained in a body of specialised theory inaccessible to laymen.[1] Here, for economics, the crucial interaction was between advancing analysis and the rise of the academic specialist. That academic economists were relatively quick to adopt marginal utility theory has been pointed out by R. S. Howey[2] and G. J. Stigler.[3] And this eventually had major effects on the relative internal status of different economists, for when the slower theorists came round, as most of them did, to recognising and accepting the marginal paradigm, they naturally tended to identify the academics as the creative and progressive element in economics. Equally important was marginalism's tendency to encourage a different kind of recruit into academic economics from previously. It extended a tempting invitation to young academics in other fields – logicians like Neville Keynes, philosopher-mathematicians like Marshall – to walk into an old field of study made new, and to use their trained analytic powers and detachment from particulars to put experienced men right and make their own names.

But the causation was not all one way. For the rise of a self-conscious specialist community of largely academic membership changed the pattern of theoretical progress. Besides attracting a different kind of recruit in the first place, it promoted the ideals of detachment and originality for the practising economist. The question of detachment has been taken up by Stigler, who contrasts the broadly theoretical interests of academics such as Jevons, Marshall, Edgeworth, Sidgwick and Cannan with the more policy-oriented work of non-academics: Bagehot, Bonar, Goschen, Hobson, Macleod, Palgrave and the Webbs. The question of how far the academic community accelerated scientific progress by inculcating the value of theoretical originality is no less important, but in the nature of things is harder to answer.

Why is this so? In one respect it is not a difficult question at all: the expansion of paid academic research made it normal, indeed obligatory, to be original. But there is a more subtle problem which raises basic issues in the sociology of science.

The point is this. The neoclassical doctrine undoubtedly helped to create a scientific community with the appetite to take pains over a long and complex research programme. But to what do we attribute the materialisation of this programme – to the new doctrine or the new community? To phrase the question differently, did marginalism actually provide a programme objectively better at supporting research and development than its predecessors, irrespective of the character of the relevant academic community? Or are all systems of theory potential research programmes which materialise only if the men involved are optimistic enough to recognise their potential and, collectively, skilled enough to develop it? And if the second hypothesis is true, why was marginalism actualised? Did it by its nature attract the kind of individuals who would want to do research in a cumulative way? Or was its arrival on the economic scene purely coincidental with theirs?

Our own view is that the neoclassical paradigm was, in terms of research potential, fundamentally and objectively different from anything that had come before. In the first place, it put forward a universal principle of behaviour which, in most fields of economic activity, was neither too easy nor too hard for the economist to apply. That is to say, it initially postulated an atomistic economy of universal rationality, but was flexible enough not merely to take in but also to provide valuable insights into imperfect competition, indivisibilities, non-rational consumer behaviour and so on. And the question of how far its analysis should be taken in different areas of economics, by allowing no definitive answer, allowed economists of diverse methodological outlook to work together on it. (If this sounds too favourable a picture of marginalism to anyone, let us add that one could make the same point by saying that marginalism is tautological enough to go anywhere, unrealistic enough to make its application an exacting task and untestable enough to allow economists to argue over its limits for ever. But we are not at this stage trying to evaluate the children of the neoclassical research programme; merely to explain its fertility.) In the theory of distribution it provided the key to a generalisation of Ricardo's theory of rent, a critique of the labour theory of value and a bridge into advanced calculus via its application of Euler's theorem. In the theory of the firm it gave the first comprehensive analysis of the differences between monopoly and competition, and eventually led to the theory of imperfect competition. It virtually created the theory of public finance as a branch of economics, and demonstrated its persuasive powers by producing that rare phenomenon, a policy conversion on grounds of pure theory, when Edgeworth abandoned proportional for progressive taxation. And in welfare economics the General Optimum enabled Pigou to rehabilitate as a topic of economic theory the relationship between the State and the individual.

We are not arguing that the size and importance of the neoclassical research programme depended wholly on the inherent qualities of marginal utility theory and that social and personal factors counted for nothing. This would omit a great deal. Above all it would omit the guiding hand of Marshall. Marshall's outstanding achievement was not the sizeable but sometimes overrated direct contribution which he made to economic theory in *Principles of Economics*, but rather his success – gained by tactical skill, eloquence and tenacity – in keeping his colleagues' eyes on the goal of an economics whose range, precision and predictive reliability would compare with that of the natural sciences.

This chapter will look at the professionalisation of British economics during the decades after 1870 through the eyes of the man who dominated it for most of those years. If professionalisation consists, as Weber suggested, of the 'routinisation of charisma', then at least the historian is never in a moment's doubt as to whose charisma stood to be routinised. It will consider his aspirations for a genuinely 'scientific' economics, examine his reasons for holding them and try to establish how far they created a professional orthodoxy. But for a full understanding of Marshall's objectives for economic science, it is necessary briefly to examine his own reasons for becoming an economist.

II

Second Wrangler in 1865, Marshall swung through metaphysics, moral philosophy and psychology in the next seven years, before finally alighting on political economy. The trajectory was consistently away from pleasure towards duty. Psychology, taken up because more 'relevant' than metaphysics, was itself superseded when it led Marshall to examine 'the possibilities of higher and more rapid development of human faculties'. For this in turn brought Marshall up against the contention 'that the resources of production do not suffice for affording to the great body of people the leisure and the opportunity for study'. Fervently hoping that this contention was false but unable to prove or disprove it with his existing knowledge, Marshall turned his attention to political economy. For a time he regarded himself as 'a wanderer in the land of dry facts; looking forward to a speedy return to the luxuriance of pure thought'.

> But the more I studied economic science, the smaller appeared the knowledge which I had of it in proportion to the knowledge which I needed: and now, at the end of nearly half a century of almost exclusive study of it, I am conscious of more ignorance of it than I was at the beginning ...[4]

Obviously however, Marshall was kept in economics by more than just a sense of his own ignorance. Once he had taken it up as his main study, he never swerved from the view that the most urgent question of his age was 'whether it was necessary that there should be any so called "lower classes" at all', whether all could receive the opportunities contingent on freedom from poverty and 'the stagnating influences of excessive mechanical toil'.[5] Yet the pull of 'pure thought' was always there. Writing to James Ward in 1900, Marshall recalled that even as a young man zeal for economics would never have got him out of bed at five o'clock in the morning: 'but philosophy did that till I became ill and my right foot swelled to double its normal size'. And there is the revealing language of an appendix to the *Principles of Economics* (3rd edition onwards, extended in the 5th), entitled 'Uses of Abstract Reasoning in Economics'. 'Academic diversion ... indulged in long chains of deductive reasoning ... no technical responsibility for the material ... edifice of pure crystal ... playful excursions'[6] – hedonism could hardly sound guiltier. Its significance is as complex as the man – a mixture of self-deprecation, self justification and self-rededication to more important things.

The contradiction between analytical and social ends pervaded Marshall's career. His main way of dealing with it, as we shall see, was to deny that it existed. Even so, he still had to decide his policy on the related question of how to divide his time and energy between writing, teaching and intervening in public affairs. Broadly, Marshall chose retirement. He was induced to sit on one Royal Commission and give evidence to four others; he once addressed the Co-operative Congress; he took his turn as president of Section F;

and he occasionally wrote to *The Times*. But that is all. And one of the most striking things about Marshall's story is that an economist should devote himself so single-mindedly to scholarship and yet exert an influence on his subject so difficult to reduce to 'mere' scholarly achievement. The sources of this influence we now begin to examine.

III

Classical economists were seldom preoccupied with the future of their own science. Those who did not assume that their own stage of analysis was the ultimate or penultimate one tended not to see the development of economic theory as a continuous process at all. Not the least of Marshall's achievements was his success in firing colleagues' imaginations with his belief that all were co-operating in something both cumulative and incomplete.

'The economist must stand fast by science' was the message of Marshall's inaugural lecture as Professor of Political Economy at Cambridge (1885). By 'science' he meant the methods, the logical standards, the painstaking analysis of topics of manageable size, which characterised the natural sciences.

> Eloquence and erudition have been lavishly spent in the service of Economics. They are good in their way; but what is most wanted now is the power of keeping the head cool and clear in tracing and analysing the combined action of many combined causes. Exceptional genius being left out of account, this power is rarely found save among those who have gone through a severe course of work in the more advanced sciences. Cambridge has more such men than any other university in the world. But alas! few of them turn to the task![7]

One lesson the physical sciences were particularly qualified to teach. So long as the 'brilliant but impatient Greek genius' had attempted a monist explanation of all physical events, progress had been slow; the modern age owed its progress to 'a breaking up of broad problems into their component parts' (*Principles*, p. 770). Still less could a single intellectual scheme ever suffice to explain all social phenomena. All the undoubted revolutionary genius of Comte and Spencer could hardly be said 'even to have made a commencement with the construction of a unified social science' (*ibid.* p. 770). Economic understanding lay not in that direction, but in the mastery of the engine of analysis, unique among social studies, which economics had itself constructed. In particular, Marshall argued that the pitfalls of excessive historical relativism would thus be avoided. Different countries, different centuries might present economic phenomena with apparently little in common, but underlying differences of form was a unity of substance as fundamental as it was difficult for the layman to detect. By discovering the meaning of 'The Many in One, The One in Many',[8] while at the same time training himself in the common sense so lacking among the Comteans, the economist might steer between a priori dogmatism and haphazard lawlessness. The organon of economic science alone could assess how Ricardian historical reality really was.

Undoubtedly, Marshall believed, the scientific approach was on the increase. But much remained to be done; and Marshall could never discuss the scientific nature of economics for long without slipping in a warning against instant relevance at the expense of thoroughness and long-term gain. The *Principles* (p. 39) criticises those who cannot see further than the immediate topic in hand. Should we adopt this approach, Marshall argues

> the direct pursuit of practical aims leads us to group together bits of all sorts of knowledge, which have no connection with one another except for the immediate purposes of the moment and which throw but little light on one another. Our mental energy is spent on going from one to the other; nothing is thoroughly thought out; no real progress is made.

Even Mill would have avoided the wage-fund pitfall – by putting his main theory of wages before his theory of supply and demand – had he not 'allowed his zeal for giving a more human tone to economics to get the better of his judgement, and to hurry him on the work with an incomplete analysis' (*Principles*, p. 824). Two groups Marshall found particularly susceptible to this kind of haste. One was the historical school, who were 'content with mere facts', not fully appreciating that 'the light of facts will not be thrown directly, it will be reflected and concentrated by science' (*Present Position of Economics*, p. 171). The other was the socialists, of whom more later.

The more analytical parts of the *Principles* were Marshall's monument to the natural-science conception of economics. It is now time to consider in detail three of its subsidiary conceptions: economics as biological science, as business science, and the 'scientific' theory of economic policy which Marshall hoped would result from his researches into welfare economics. In each case we hope first to show

how Marshall's studies added to his intellectual authority over his fellow economists. In the second half of this chapter, this characteristic will be linked to the more general theme of a 'Marshallian orthodoxy'.

IV

In 1898 Marshall proclaimed economic biology as 'the Mecca of economic science'.[9] The entire latter half of Book 4 of the *Principles* discusses the balancing forces in the birth, life and eventual decay of a race or firm, while the Preface even reduces economic statics to the status of a special case. But the work of the economic biologist, Marshall warned the young in 1897, had hardly begun. 'Much remains for your generation to do.'[10]

As evolutionary theory of economics appealed to many sides of Marshall's nature, including the political one. It gave hope of deliberate progress. (The classical economists, says the *Principles*, were perhaps too cautious about what was possible.) But at the same time it cautioned against hasty reform. The evolutionary process must not be overtaken. The economist must 'oppose all plausible shortcuts to that great end, which would sap the springs of energy and initiative' (*Principles*, p. 48).

Economic biology also had a more personal value for Marshall. In its promise of delineating for man a path to perfection which would also be a framework for studying him scientifically, it promised an area of reconciliation for the optimist and the dispassionate scientist in Marshall. This point needs some reflection. What worried Marshall was not just the feasibility of subjecting a perfectible being to a static science of measurable motives and predictive pretensions. The doubtful justifiability of devoting his life to this end must also have given him qualms. With his idealistic view of what man could be, he ached to be required in helping to point the way. An earnest moralist but a diffident young man, is it conceivable that he was unconcerned at his choice of an academic mission widely despised for its gross materialism? To study the science of wealth without ulterior purpose must have seemed very like an insult to the future. Yet none of the existing economic doctrines offered Marshall the way ahead that he wanted. Mill's humanity he admired, but Mill was much besides an economist. The Ricardians he respected, but found pessimistic and unimaginative. Owen and the early socialists were inspiring, but their views were 'based on little historic and scientific study',[11] and they did not always understand the doctrines which they attacked. It is thus not surprising that Marshall adopted the idea of economic biology so enthusiastically. Only economic biology could do justice to the interaction between circumstances and character, and so allow political economy to make not just an ethical contribution, but a unique and indispensable one. The materialist outlook was basically a Christian outlook, the very new economist told fellow members of the Cambridge Reform Club in 1873.[12]

Marshall the paternalist moralist also found his voice in economic biology. Behind its shield he busied himself prescribing what he considered to be the progressive and regressive elements in the working class. Activities were the key. In considering economic changes, the only sure criterion was whether they would promote 'that healthful exercise and development of faculties which yields happiness without pall ... No utilisation of waste gasses in the blast furnace can compare with the triumph of making work for the public good pleasurable in itself.'[13]

What was the human raw material like? During his life Marshall sought out, influenced, learned from, and usually admired a great many working-class leaders. Nor is his respect for the potential of the working man in any doubt. But towards the ordinary labourer as he then was, his attitude was of mistrustful condescension – as he showed when he gave the Commissioners on the Aged Poor an unsolicited lecture on how to examine a working-class witness:

> And then the methods of cross-examination which one naturally applies to an experienced witness should be rather suspended. One can generally get to know whether a man is speaking bona fide or not. If he is not, of course he should be cross-examined sharply; but if he is speaking only what he believes, he should be allowed a very great margin. The ordinary laws of sticking rigidly to the point should not be insisted upon; he should be encouraged to say what he chooses. The members of the Commission should be men of a strongly sympathetic nature, who would abstain from asking any question of a kind that would unnecessarily annoy a working-man witness. They should be much more careful with regard to working men's evidence than with regard to the evidence of educated people.[14]

What the working man believed, then, was a constraint, not a potential contribution, to the range of workable administrative philosophies. What the working man liked was as much a moral obstacle as an economic datum. The immediate pursuit of 'higher', 'inducible' wants, planned for the labourer by the ethical instincts of the elite, was condemned only for its unpracticality.[16] Much of Marshall's writing does not even bother to justify his personal moral evaluation of different forms of consumption, or for that matter to reveal what it is, but takes the reader's knowledge and acquiescence for granted:

Much more than half, possibly even three-quarters of the total income of the nation is devoted to uses which make for happiness and the elevation of life, as nearly as efficiently as is possible with our present limited understanding of the arts of life. ('The Social Possibilities of Economic Chivalry', *Economic Journal*, March 1907, p. 13)

And perhaps more than half of the consumption of the upper classes of society in England is wholly unnecessary. (*Principles*, 1st edn, p. 124)

These economic facts were urgent; so were their redistributive implications. Marshall had little patience with the view that any significant redistribution of income would be followed by a dark age of drink before higher working-class tastes arrived to justify higher working-class incomes. Yet the rank-and-file labourer of whom he wrote remained curiously faceless and passive – pitiable but perfectible, an inefficient pleasure machine with a high-minded future. To assist fully in realising this future the economist must first attain his own maturity at 'the Mecca of economic science ... economic biology'.

But it was not just that the evolutionary idea suited Marshall uncommonly well. More than any other economist he suited it. Even for his time he was an unusually intense moralist, and there were two reasons why evolution, in applying itself to economic thought, was likely to acquire an unwontedly moral slant.

(1) More or less measurable inequalities of income meant that the justification (or lack of it) for middle-class privilege was a more precise, hence less escapable, question for economics than for any other contemporary social study. Mill, Sidgwick and Edgeworth were among those who tried to wed the equalising implications of marginal utility theory to a personal disposition in favour of the characteristic activities of the well-to-do intellectual. Hence successive stages of social evolution could scarcely be considered without asking whether the wants and activities to which they gave rise could morally justify the respective degrees of class privilege by which they were characterised. Thus the ethical consideration of changing activities was unavoidable.

(2) In his book *Evolution and Society*, J. W. Burrow shows how

the idea of evolution, by imposing apparent order on human diversity, allowed historians, anthropologists and lawyers to do justice to both the need for inner certainty and the fact of complexity. Only an ethical conception of evolution could have performed this function for the neoclassical economist without causing him grave intellectual embarrassment. To have turned back to a purely positivistic theory of long-run economic development would have been to create a second body of economic analysis clearly needing, but glaringly devoid of, a well-defined logical relation to the marginal paradigm. So economics needed an ethical dimension – in a way that law and anthropology did not – for it to speak of evolution.

We have tried to show how much 'economic biology' contributed to Marshall's confidence in the future of economic science. No praise was implied for the idea in itself, which amounted to little more than the unrelated fragments of a social dynamics dressed up in Darwinian language to give them a teleological appearance. An agnostic from an early age, Marshall probably continued to hanker for a 'creative purpose'. But in this he was far from alone; and this is why his search for it increased his hegemony over his economist contemporaries. The theory of evolution appealed as much to economists as to any students of society. Its ethical implications (for them) meant that the convinced moralist – provided he were not an unscientific and emotional enthusiast – would be its most imaginative exponent and a source of conviction to the others. But its political connotations were also important. Without making a hard and fast generalisation, it is fair to say that social evolution soon settled down as a liberal's doctrine. Conservative objections to the idea of transcendent historical laws are anything but exclusively twentieth-century phenomena; few socialists have never chafed against the limited role for political action allowed by a set of laws which omits a law of discontinuous change. And with the publication of Darwin's second great book, *The Descent of Man*, evolution became a friend of libertarian ideas in their broadest sense. *Origin of the Species* had been open to Hobbesian misinterpretation. *The Descent of Man* equated survival of the fittest with survival of the most sociable and co-operative towards one another. From this, libertarians drew all kinds of arguments against a need for coercive authority.

Yet liberalism, in both the narrow bourgeois sense and the broader anti-authoritarian one, retained strong links with methodological atomism. Hence the ideal evolutionary propagandist was a rare creature, needing individualist social views and yet the strong personal urge to transcend the changeless human stereotypes of individualistic economic epistemology. Ethically, politically and methodologically, then, Marshall, and Marshall alone, with his distinctive descriptions of evolving wants and activities, looked capable of leading economics where it wanted to be led.

V

Marshall was telling Cambridge of the need for graduate economists in business for many years before the foundation of an Economics Tripos became a public issue. His inaugural lecture demanded a change in spirit, rather than curriculum: 'If more University men looked upon their life here as preparing them for the higher posts of business, what a change they might make in the tone of business. Just and noble sentiments might be introduced into counting-house and factory workshop' (*Memorials*, p. 173).

This should not be taken to imply that Marshall shared the widespread current hostility towards the businessman. Quite the reverse: not only was the ethos of late nineteenth-century industrialism highly congenial to him, but its entrepreneurs in particular he regarded as engaging figures, representing self-reliance, foresight, deliberation without dithering and steadfastness of purpose. In addition Marshall enthusiastically defended the businessman against charges of overcompetitiveness, dishonesty, incompetence and exploitation. But, Marshall charged, he was too much attached to the motive of financial gain. This Marshall found inexcusable. Unlike the scientist, for whom wealth was no mark of excellence, the businessman's money-earning power was the best available test of his ability. 'And so all the best businessmen want to get money ... chiefly as the most convincing proof to themselves and others that they have succeeded.'[16]

But the fact that many large incomes existed because of the desire to excel in no way altered the waste and deprivation which accompanied maldistribution of wealth.

> Now there is general agreement among thoughtful people, and especially among economists, that if society could award ... honour, position and influence by methods less blind and less wasteful; and if it could at the same time maintain all that stimulus which the free enterprise of the strongest businessmen derives from present conditions, then the resources thus set free would open out to the mass of people new possibilities of a higher life, and of larger and more varied intellectual activities.[17]

In the celebrated article in which the above passage occurs, Marshall christened this general attitude 'Economic Chivalry'. This, he said, included not only public spirit, but also 'a delight in doing noble and difficult things because they are noble and difficult ... It includes a scorn for cheap victories and a delight in succouring those who need a helping hand.[18]

Marshall's main concern was that the businessman's official task with respect to his employees stopped short of making the wage-bargain; for unless he considered aspects also of the worker's condition and character which had little direct bearing on this, he was likely to fall short even as a profit-winner, let alone as a good citizen. And with the growing complexity of commercial life, sympathy and understanding through personal contact was increasingly difficult. However, a broad training in economics would 'help him to see the drift of the complaints urged by his men, and to make concessions quickly and cordially to such as are reasonable'.[19]

In warning that growing industrial concentration at once increased and obscured the businessman's responsibilities, Marshall anticipated by a few years the demands of Durkheim, Brandeis, Tawney, Cole and others for either basic reforms or professional institutions which would create a distinctive business ethic. Durkheim's *Professional Ethics and Civic Morals* began with a particularly sharp attack on what there was of the business spirit.

> some hazy generalisations on the loyalty and devotion owed by staff and workmen to those employing them; some phrases on the moderation the employer should use in his economic dominance; some reproach for any too overtly unfair competition – that is about all there is in the moral consciousness of the various professions we are discussing. (London, 1957, p. 10)

Marshall's aversion to these facts was an ideological one. Those acquiescing in them, as Durkheim himself noted, were mainly either doctrinaire anti-interventionists who would leave the capitalist entirely alone, or socialists who saw his complete abolition as necessary and sufficient for society to organise itself in an orderly way. Marshall came between these: he saw harmony in the interests of capital and labour, but thought, first, that the market system could not make this sufficiently obvious to those concerned, and secondly, that even if it could, that would not necessarily justify its existence in its present form. This was a conventional enough opinion for its time. It was less conventional to combine it, as Marshall did, with total indifference to the attractions of any kind of nationalistic holism. Unable to see either the market or the national will as the great harmoniser, it was natural that Marshall, perhaps more than any of his colleagues, should put his trust in education.

Thus the idea of a Cambridge Economics Tripos, and the idea that it was needed for peace and progress in the world of commerce, aggregated a variety of convictions for Marshall: his social philosophy (by uniting his sense of ultimate social harmony with his sense of public duty), his identification with much but by no means all of the business ethic and his confidence in his own brand of economic theory as instructive of the right lessons. More than any other economist of his generation, he could believe that a student trained in economics would approach industrial life in a spirit both uniquely realistic and uniquely sympathetic. His militant moralism, his urge to soar into advanced analysis, his fears that the results of so soaring were not very useful, could only be welded into a constructive whole by sharing them with the businessman-to-be. So, once again, many economists turned for guidance to the man who believed most strongly what they wanted to believe.

Economics, moreover, was singular among academic disciplines in that many of its pupils later became part of the object it studied. This gave economists a unique responsibility for the professional ethics of another occupation than their own. This mission they badly needed. The late nineteenth century saw a dearth of public ends obvious and congenial to the whole consensus of liberal economics.[20] Here was such an end. The academic's task was to make the businessman more like himself, to mould him into the pre-industrial type of professionalism which still existed in the older universities and the civil service. But although in this respect there existed an 'academic view' which transcended ideologies and methodologies alike, conflict reappeared in the alternative lessons drawn from it.

The conflict, broadly, was between liberals and conservatives. For reasons discussed below (pp. 39–40), the doctrine of *laissez-faire* could by the 1880s command only a tiny extreme band of followers. With its virtual disappearance from the scene, the organic-conservative philosophy became the most popular counterweight to the suspicion that class conflict might actually be a rational activity. But its hostility to methodological individualism disposed it against an independent economics on this basis. Men like Cunningham might believe (though never as strongly as Marshall) that education could encourage co-operation between class and class, but it was moral science which they saw as the obvious apostle of self-restraint. It was not just that (in their view) economic science did insufficient justice to reality to be a didactic success: it actively omitted higher instincts as motivating forces.[21]

Thus opponents of methodological individualism, in denying to economics a special moral role, denied themselves a professional ethic *qua* economists, and arguably forfeited some of their professional status in the eyes of others. It should, however, also be noted that so far as any economist, liberal or conservative, adopted the advancement of higher entrepreneurial standards as his own professional standard, this inhibited a wholly positive analysis of capitalism, and hence worked against the adoption of ethical neutrality as a professional ethic in itself.

VI

By deriving from marginal utility theory the concepts of consumer's and producer's surplus, Marshall hoped to make economics a basis for policy without compromising scientific standards and ideological neutrality. His Cambridge inaugural lecture outlined how economics, as the science of measurable motives, could point the way to 'welfare conclusions', and, in so doing, avoid the dogmas of both extremes. In this task, his efforts were both persistent and resourceful, and his eventual disillusionment was both slow and painful, as his nephew, C. W. Guillebaud, has recalled.[22] Our present concern, however, is with the intention, not the outcome; and the degree to which it reflected a need felt by other economists.

Subtle in his tactics, habitually indecisive on political questions, lacking robustness as a polemicist and forever fearful of being misunderstood, Marshall's personal role as educator of public opinion was both intermittent and indirect. Industrial or political crisis would rouse him, sudden heresies which swept across the country, from Henry George to Chamberlain's protectionism to Sir Karl Pearson's claim that the children of alcoholics were not born disadvantaged, would temporarily engage his little-used polemical talent: but sustained campaigning for economic sense was not his forte. Less than six months after the eruption of the protection issue, he was writing to J. N. Keynes (10 October 1903), implying that as a professional claim on his time it was at an end:

So many of what I regard as the Chamberlain fallacies have been recently exposed, to the apparent conviction of even simple-minded men, that my anxiety is less than it was when I last spoke to you about it. So I feel free to lie low, at all events for the present.

And he knew the need for subtlety. As he wrote to Bishop Westcott (23 January 1901):

I think that, when the academic student takes on himself the role of preacher *he is generally less effective than when* he treats the problems of life objectively, that is when he assumes no major premises based on his own view of duty, his own ideals of social life. So I am leading up to my discussion of trade unions by studies in which the trade unionist is invited to pass judgement on problems of combination in which he has no direct interest. Then I want to imply when I come to his problems:-

De te fabula narratur.

This is one reason for abstaining now for many years from saying anything publicly on labour questions.

There were three other reasons. First, his habitual indecisiveness on political questions, his reluctance to commit himself to a single untested possibility where many others existed. Not that he raised a conservative's objections to social experimentation as such – he was too devoted to the raising of character as the only ultimate good, and too sure in himself of what constituted improved character, for that. If he consciously applied a belief that the status quo started at an advantage merely by being the status quo, he does not reveal this fact. He merely emphasises the complexity of injustice, the intellectual subtlety which must be gained before prescribing cures for it and the difficulty of choosing between alternative (and perhaps superficially similar) measures. Typical was his comment to Beatrice Potter (later Webb) after reading her first book (11 July 1891): 'You are constantly saying that there are two alternatives where there seem to me to be fifty ...'

Then there were his doubts about himself. It is hard to say how truly he felt that being outside commerce put him at a political disadvantage. He refused the presidency of the Royal Economic Society on the grounds that he was 'too unpractical and too little experienced';[23] yet, as will be shown later, he argued for academic detachment from particulars, and for the academic training needed to penetrate below the surface of events. It would seem that his personality, as much as his chosen role, held him back from controversy. His correspondence with Foxwell reveals a tendency to leave things to a more robust polemicist, notably in connection with Henry George, with Cunningham and with the admission of women to degrees at Cambridge. And his inaugural lecture of 1885 shows that it was his predecessor's personality, *not* his ministerial rank, which he envied as a public force:

His genius showed itself in his character as well as in his thought. His courage and tenderness, his self-devotion and simplicity were as great a source of strength as his marvellous force and clearness of thought. [Fawcett] was able to take a position which no other economist has held; he was able to tell the people unpalatable truths and to earn their hearty thanks for doing so. (*Present Position of Economics*, p. 152)

More important than either of these considerations was Marshall's fear of being misunderstood – a fear which, incidentally, led to most of the alterations which he made to the *Principles*. A draft preface to his memorandum on 'The Fiscal Policy of International Trade' warns that:

however clearly a professional economist may have distinguished in his own mind those aspects of the question on which his studies directly bear from those in which he has no special knowledge, the distinction is apt to be ignored by partisans on either side. And if he allows himself to be drawn *into* the heat of the fight he may himself lose sight of the distinction ... He desires to influence the public ... a full discussion of the economic bases of the problem will repel them, and be ineffective. He must lighten the discussion; he must ignore many difficulties![24]

Free trade was exceptional. Leaders on both sides had formally accepted certain economic arguments as part of the basis of their positions.

The political issues which are now chiefly before the public differ from all others of equal importance that have arisen in the country, at all events during the last two generations ...

Thus Chamberlain alone among statesmen provided Marshall with a distinctive professional function.

I know that some of the economic propositions which he has laid down as a basis of his policy are invalid. Many millions of these propositions have been circulated among people who have had no scientific training. Economists seem therefore bound to contradict these statements; and that was, so far as I know anything of the matter, the real motive of a public letter which was issued by most of the professional economists in the country in August; but which was much misunderstood.

The sporadic assault of not too obvious heresies, then, was generally the furthest Marshall let himself intervene in particular issues. But the explanation given above is incomplete. A stronger personal interest in particular social reforms might well have overcome public caution and personal diffidence. Sometimes it did. Undoubtedly the *Principles* exerted – and was meant to exert – a radical reforming influence insofar as it destroyed much self-justification among the apathetic. By making the question of poverty central and diagnosing it as avoidable, it barred the way to economics as a court of appeal for the complacent. This was especially notable among the clergy. A modern writer concludes that whereas Arnold Toynbee 'won the attention of Christian social radicals partly from motives like theirs; he had set out to offer a professional challenge to the older economics', Marshall, more systematic than Toynbee and more respectable than Henry George, was 'the liberator of the more cautious'. Thus a Wesleyan minister noted that the book was 'more humane than the general run of economic works. The Socialist and other criticisms have told on the orthodox economy.'[25]

This Marshall intended. And, theoretically, he admired an ameliorative measure which did not threaten the force of self-help only slightly less than he admired the characters of those likely to fight for it. He would have vehemently denied that his attitude to Henry George's motivation in campaigning was one of less than full sympathetic understanding. This was in tune with the trends of the time, with widespread sentiment aroused not least by George himself, but also by Christian socialists of all denominations, by urban mission houses, by the five successive Royal Commissions set up during the depressed period 1873–96, by the propaganda of the Fabian Society and by the statistical investigations of Charles Booth and others into urban poverty. To explain Marshall's detachment from the detailed message of all this activity by invoking his belief that as an economist he should only make positive statements, only pushes the question back one stage further. Moreover, it is often hard to tell when Marshall is speaking as an economist, and when he is expressing his personal opinion. Indeed, his private correspondence shows less interest in public affairs than do his published works. The real explanation is a multiple one:

(1) Having called on his colleagues to 'stand fast by science', and given his fear of leaving himself open to misinterpretation, he was

understandably reluctant to endanger his (and perhaps others') scientific role by risking the charge that he was attempting a political one. This did not prevent him speaking his mind about topics close to his feelings. But it probably exempted him from the meticulous weighing of much that he did not find immediately interesting.

(2) Marshall believed that friends of the working class should work for the day when (perhaps abruptly) it would come to maturity and take over its own affairs. Problem groups in its midst, such as the 'residual' of undeserving poor, it could already tackle sensibly. But in the main he stood out for something more general: the overall material and educational resources needed for a collective leap into rationality. This vision followed naturally from his faith that the active force of calculation, however puny to begin with, could in time push through the densest layer of custom and prejudice:

> I believe that the desire to do what is best for oneself is seldom wholly absent from human nature. Habit and prescription do indeed prevent many kinds of original individual action from being thought of at all, and they prohibit others; but there always remains a fringe of debatable ground in which a pushing character can assert itself.[26]

(3) Both the above attributes of Marshall's outlook could live undisturbed inside the general cast of his mind. His scorn for the *ad hoc* approach to economic theory, his scorn for the interim social remedy, his eschewal of controversy, even his reluctance to mention his adversaries by name, suggest a rather lofty aversion from crusading for the concrete. True, he proclaimed the need to copy the early utilitarians in welding together thought, experience and action.[27] But it is not unfair for a careful reader of the *Principles* and *Industry and Trade* to conclude that the convincing synthesis of empiricism and analytic insight, which he demanded of himself before lending support to *particular* causes, did not come to him easily.

And so vague intellectual sympathy with reform, largely uncrystallised and undifferentiated through lack of genuinely radical instincts, detachment from particulars, and the feeling that he ought to do what no one else could do equally well, combined in Marshall's mind to persuade him that a rethought scientific welfare economics was required to give broad yet applicable criteria for State intervention.

There were several reasons why any liberal economist might see this as the first priority. First, an advanced industrial economy furnished few issues which would admit of an 'economist's view', of the kind of consensus among economists which required no controversial value-judgement to be made. No one now writes of the classical theory of economic policy as a deaf lump of bigotry, monolithic and unchanging, or as a synonym for *laissez-faire*. Yet, at least until about 1850, economists found it relatively easy to agree on a broad range of topics. Where industrialisation or modern rationalism rubbed against ancient laws, the art of political economy seemed no more subjective than the science. Where distress was glaring enough, the economist was concerned to relieve it like everyone else. Yet it was still possible to believe that the extension of economic freedom and the protection of the long-term interests of the underprivileged were more complementary than competing objectives. In the 1880s, perhaps for the first time, the average middle-class liberal found it hard to answer the critics of current poverty by stressing the hope of future growth. The spreading conviction that liberty and equality could not be reconciled, but only balanced and compromised, enlarged what was expected from the State.

The rise of marginalist economics had, if anything, the opposite implication.[28] Inevitably the scientific flavour of marginal analysis advertised and dignified the limited objectives to which it could be put. By comparison, policy pronouncements which involved matters of long-term growth or distribution seemed amateurish, ideologically loaded, perched on an economic base which had somehow shrivelled. This was particularly true of distributive justice, for whereas classical and Marxian theory gave a context for discussing whether current evils were permanent or even increasing, the statics of marginal productivity theory could not frame answers as to the justice of distributive trends.

Theoretical advance, then, fatally broadened the gap between the precision of the tools and the indecision of the craftsman. And the arrival both of a more immediately rational economy and a less optimistic view of its ultimate rationality gave economics subtler and less unanimous goals, while stripping it of most of its public status as a self-conscious and irreplaceable vehicle of reason and hard sense. Thus economic theory and economic reality joined forces to supply the means, the intellectual impetus and the apparent social necessity to redefine the State's sphere of competence, and do so by aggregating microeconomic forces into welfare conclusions.

VII

Of the scientific standards Marshall envisaged, which students of economics were likely to fall short, whether by training, professional occupation or doctrinal approach?

First, there was the non-academic. Marshall's mellifluous presidential address to Section F (1890) represented the academic economist and the man of affairs as peers in the professional hierarchy, complementary forces each with equal need of the other. Quite the most interesting of Marshall's surviving unpublished manuscripts is the original version of the address. Written on the cover (apparently at a later date) is the explanation 'What follows (partly crossed out in blue) refers to the Outsider in relation to the Academic Insider in economics'; and what does follow is very different in tone from the diplomatic final version.

Marshall begins by saying that he understands that the aim of an opening address is

> that it should be addressed chiefly to those who having a real interest in the science are yet too much occupied with other affairs to be able to study it technically and at leisure. People of this kind are of more importance to economics than to any other science that is recognised by this Association: *but, to speak frankly, they are also more troublesome.*

Such people (he continues) are uniquely important for the knowledge they hold: knowledge which the economist cannot otherwise get, of 'the unpublished history of business'. With this in hand the economist could go below the surface of events and so find 'their true meaning, which is very different from their prima facie meaning'. They are troublesome *not* because they sometimes attack what the economist says and prove it wrong (though that may be annoying at the time).

> It is when they are not critical and assent readily to the arguments laid before them that they become really troublesome. For they take propositions that were intended to be limited and treat them as unlimited. They take sentences out of processes reasoning with reference to particular cases and make them into dogmas, and they run after simplicity in outward form, and become ardent disciples of those who are definite, simple and confident in their utterances.

Here the draft ends. (Note the lack of pretence that the label 'economist' ought to belong to anyone but the 'Academic Insider'.) It is reasonable to think that it represents Marshall's true feelings, but that on reflection he thought it too inflammatory to read out as president. But was it? Only a dozen years later, in pressing the case for an Economics Tripos, Marshall solicited and privately published a large number of letters from prominent businessmen, politicians and civil servants, enthusiastically acquiescing in the master–pupil relationship so far as economics was concerned.[29]

Also increasingly excluded were those who studied economics as a branch of moral science. Despite his own intellectual origins, Marshall came to regard a training in philosophy as worse than useless for the aspiring economist. As the 1890s progressed he became more impatient than ever with economics' subordinate status in the Moral Science Tripos at Cambridge. Partly responsible was Sidgwick's revision of the syllabus, as a result of which it catered less than ever for a student who wished to specialise in economics (1897). Two letters to J.N. Keynes, undated but probably referring to this reorganisation, denounce Sidgwick's plans as 'in every way bad', claiming that they gave philosophy an overwhelming hold on the third-year student's time. And on 16 August 1897, again to Keynes, he complained that, as things stood, teaching economics to 'mathematical casuals' was almost the only worthwhile aspect of his professorship. Another letter (30 January 1902) blames the philosophers for the fact that

> the crop of economists whom I got out of Oxford in a single year – Price, Harrison and Gonner – is better than those whom I have got out of the Moral Science curriculum proper in the last sixteen years. In fact McTaggart is the only first class man whom I have caught; and him I have only half caught.

It was not simply that the Moral Sciences Tripos could not train men of promise as serious economists. Equally disastrous in Marshall's view was its failure to attract the right students in the first place.

> The Mo:Sc. Tripos . . . has become in effect a post-graduate Tripos for other universities, with a few odd men thrown in, many of them more than the average age. But the fresh strong beautiful youthful minds that used to come largely to the Mo.Sc. Tripos are now scarcely ever seen there . . .[30]

And:

> The Mo.Sc. men, except the ablest, are mere parasites of textbooks; they know nothing and seem to care nothing about real life.[31]

Marshall seldom accepted as competent economists those who had studied the subject in a philosophical context. Unusual ability, remarkable industry or the opportunity and will to pursue economic studies after graduating, could produce exceptional cases. But, more typically, such training produced students like A. A. Mirza, who 'speaks too much about Logic and Metaphysics and mentions foreign economists like Marx fairly often';[32] or academics such as Jenkyn Jones; 'an able man, though slow: but of course he knows economics as a branch of philosophy i.e. he knows nothing about it!'[33]

'Historical economics', Marshall told Keynes (30 August 1891), was 'infinitely more important than philosophical economics because infinitely more real'. Even so, it was 'not economics proper. That I take to be a scientific study of existing economic facts and contemporary changes of course, not neglectful of their historical antecedents'. And while Mill's 'perception of the pliability of human motives' had taught his successors the need for a certain historical relativism, the names instanced by Marshall imply that no one school could particularly claim his mantle in this respect; 'The new temper is shown alike in Jevons' subtle analysis of utility, in Cliffe Leslie's historical inquiries and in other many-sided original work that has been done in England by Bagehot, Cairnes and other writers who are yet living' (*Principles*, 1st edn, p. 65).

To Keynes, as ever, Marshall was frank: for the economist the worst thing about history was historians. In May 1889, discussing his lecturing plans for the coming year, he wrote; 'I want however to keep my hold on the historical men: they are Kittle-Kattle; and yet important.' Then there were the 'lectures on Advanced Economic Theory, including the higher part of Statistics – I mean all that is not suitable for men of the Historical type – intelligent, more or less earnest, but not very profound ...'

Corresponding to this judgement, a section of the *Principles* (third edition onwards) implies that, as a training for analytical work, economic history is simply not challenging enough: 'Not very much analysis is essential: and most of what is needed may be supplied for himself by a man of active and inquiring mind.'[34] And Marshall's reference to Hewins, 'who is dominantly historical, but can reason straight',[35] suggests a readiness to assume any historical economist guilty of muddle-headedness until proved innocent.

'Realistic' critiques of marginalism were also likely to relegate their holders, in Marshall's eyes, to outsider status. In their connection, it is relevant to look in some detail at the exchange between Hobson and Marshall concerning the applicability of the concept of marginal product. In *The Industrial System* (1909) Hobson had written dismissively of this, claiming that the curtailment of the marginal application of a factor would so disorganise production that every other factor would work to less advantage than before: hence the loss would be more than the true marginal product of that agent. This is, of course, an empirical statement which may or may not have enough truth in it to reduce significantly the value of marginal analysis. Marshall's reply puts rather a different construction on it.

First Marshall says: 'In economics, as in physics, changes are generally continuous. Convulsive changes may indeed occur but they must be dealt with separately: and an illustration drawn from a convulsive change can throw no true light on the processes of normal steady evolution' (*Principles*, p. 409).

Marshall, then, is accusing Hobson of ignoring the difference between continuous and discontinuous variables. But it is a question-begging rejoinder. If all adjustments of factor proportions are either so gradual as to be 'continuous' or so sudden as to be 'convulsive' then indeed experience of the one does not let us theorise about the other. But even if this is judged to be so, the further judgements remain: what kind of change is more typical, and what kind of change is more important for economic theory? This, of course, depends on one's opinion of what economic theory is, and what it should try to do.

Secondly, Marshall accuses Hobson of overlooking the distinction between the first and second orders of differentiation. 'When the adjustment is such as to give the best results, a slight change in the proportions in which they are applied diminishes the efficiency of that adjustment by a quantity which is very small relatively to that change – in technical language it is of "the second order of smalls" – and it may therefore be neglected relatively to that change' (p. 409). Here the confusion is Marshall's. Rightly or wrongly, Hobson is giving his opinion that a change in factor proportions diminishes the efficiency of the entire process, not just the efficiency of the adjustment. On this assumption, the second order of differentiation does not enter the picture.

Thirdly, Marshall charges Hobson with overlooking the fact that 'there are forces constantly at work tending so to readjust the distribution of resources between their different uses that any maladjustment will be arrested before it has gone far: and the argument does not profess to apply to exceptional cases of maladjustment' (p. 409). Here Marshall is of course right to point out that minor disruptions resulting from adjustments to meet new equilibrium conditions right themselves in due course. But whether this occurs quickly enough to justify the amount of attention Marshall paid to this branch of short-term microeconomic analysis is once again a matter for individual opinion.

Altogether, it is a remarkable reply. That Hobson's judgement is speculative and ill-supported by evidence is not the point at issue. What matters is that it *is* a question of judgement, and that Marshall treats it as a question of basic understanding. In charging that Hobson ignores the built-in self-stabilising pull of short period equilibria, that he overlooks the distinction between the first and second orders of differentiation and that he ignores the contrast between continuous and discontinuous variables, Marshall is in effect indicting him for inadequate understanding both of the concept of maximisation and of its ubiquity in human behaviour; in other words, for technical incompetence.[36]

Perhaps the transcendent distinction in Marshall's mind was that between 'literary' and 'scientific' economists. This is how he discussed the forthcoming examinations of 1898 with Keynes (11 October 1897):

> I think neither you nor Sorley has specialised on the literary side of economics; while there is likely to be one candidate at least for Part II, who might be disappointed if the literary side were not represented pretty strongly. With you to examine the scientific side needs no further thought.

It hardly needs saying that Marshall was in no doubt of his own allegiance. Of Mill, he wrote to Foxwell (8 August 1883): 'I agree that he is literary and therefore full of error. But I think he and Ricardo contain the kernel of truth.'

What, then, is the significance of the literary/scientific distinction? Clearly, it is much more than a matter of style. First, there is Marshall's approval of mathematics as a trainer of 'sound instinctive habits':[37] the *Principles* (p. 85) goes further, saying that the mathematical method had 'compelled a more careful analysis of all the leading conceptions of economics, and especially of demand'. Secondly, it is presumably Mill's real cost theory of value which Marshall sees as 'full of error' and 'literary': and it is known that even before he took up economics as a full-time pursuit he translated the argument of Mill's book into mathematical symbols, in order critically to examine its assumptions and logical consistency. Thirdly, there does not seem to be any doubt that, before the Economics Tripos was started, he valued the few mathematicians he taught more than all his other pupils put together.[38] (They certainly averaged higher grades in their work for him.)[39] Thus 'literary' and 'scientific' would seem to be Marshall's way of separating the *cognoscenti* from the outsiders as regards subjective value theory, the criterion being a mathematical habit of thought. This, in Marshall's view, had little to do with the use of mathematical symbols in finished work: prose, graphics and formulae he regarded as largely interchangeable. Indeed, the sign of a truly mathematical economist was that he knew when to stop.

But, having seen Marshall side with Foxwell against the 'literary' inaccuracies of Mill, it is a little confusing, on examining his correspondence with Keynes, to find him putting Foxwell himself – at any rate as a lecturer – in the literary camp:

> I think the questions which you would naturally set would call out all that kind of knowledge and ability which I most care to foster. But I am not sure whether you (any more than I) would give as much place as would suit a man who had attended Foxwell's lectures ...[40]

But behind the apparent inconsistency is a uniformity: Marshall's idiosyncratic way of accommodating himself with his colleagues. His correspondences with Neville Keynes and with Foxwell – the two largest and most important of his life – are on the surface very different from each other. Keynes he saw as his one ally in England with the requisite combination of ability, enthusiasm and reliability to do battle with real effect for professional standards. When Keynes, in 1888, was deliberating whether to leave Cambridge for Oxford, Marshall advised him in these terms:

> You *would* be alone there. There is no one else who has given the best part of his life to mastering economic theory. On the other hand teachers of history abound there; there is a plethora of them. Putting aside all personal considerations, that seems to me (and I think it will others) to be a sufficient ground for believing that you are *the* man wanted.[41]

The position was changed in 1902.

> unless the empirical treatment of economics is completely to oust the scientific and analytical to which you and I are almost the only
> elderly
middle-aged } English economists who are perfectly loyal
> (I don't count Edgeworth because he is so extreme) ...[42]

Marshall's correspondence with Foxwell had the same note of brotherly confidentiality (until Foxwell broke it off in 1908, Marshall having opposed him as a successor to the professorship). But Foxwell he cast as an ally in the campaign to promote economics teaching and research in Cambridge,[43] a colleague whose different abilities and outlook gave him a complementary role. There was his greater tendency towards historical relativism:

As to the date at which economic history becomes modern: I agree that we do not agree ... My notion is that some questions relating to the xix and xx centuries would be wanted by you: some relating to xvi–xviii by me.[44]

But this had more general roots:

Of course our ideals in economics are different. I have noticed that when a book or a pamphlet pleases you greatly you describe it as 'scholarly': whereas I am never roused to great enthusiasm about anything which does not seem to me thoroughly 'scientific'.

I have two or three times referred to this difference when discussing our curriculum, and described it as an advantage. I think it is very important that there should be considerable diversities of temperament among the teachers of any subject, and especially of one of which the past and present are so meagre, and the future is so uncertain, as economics.[45]

Here Marshall is making the most of, rather than minimising, his distance from Foxwell: somewhat as he did with his much smaller distance from Keynes.[46] Was the (perhaps not wholly conscious) objective the same in each case: to enlist the other man's support while flattering his sense of independence? Even his insistence that Foxwell deliver the counter-attack on Cunningham, when the latter attacked the Marshallian style of economics,[47] suggests the shrewd perception that here was the one man in Cambridge guaranteed to make Foxwell look – and feel – judicious and central by comparison.

VIII

Given the Marshallian view of what the economist ought to be doing, how far could a man's political beliefs result in conceptual schemes or particular opinions which would debar him from general recognition as an economist?

Marshall himself was confident that, whatever political views economists might privately hold, a new generation of 'many-sided' economists, armed with a new spirit of scientific neutrality, was learning to transcend them. Admittedly he attributed the two extreme attitudes to capitalist enterprise to inability or unwillingness to see the world as it was, and hence associated them with economic incompetence. But within these limits, diversity was a constructive force.

> The great body of economists ... in Germany, England, America and other countries ... are bringing to the study of economic questions an unbiased desire to ascertain the truth, and a willingness to go through with the long and heavy work by which alone scientific results of value can be obtained. Varieties of mind, of temper, of training, and of opportunities lead them to work in different ways, and to give their chief attention to different parts of the problem ... This division of labour, however, implies not opposition, but harmony of purposes. (*Principles*, 1st edn, p. 93)

This is straightforward, if overoptimistic. But when we turn to Marshall's own pronouncements on controversial issues, it is often unclear whether he is speaking semi-officially for economic science or merely stating his own views. Testifying to a Royal Commission, or writing to *The Times*, he would often take pains to emphasise that he was speaking personally. But when lecturing in Cambridge or addressing the British Association, there were no such disclaimers:

> Never make the State do anything when it is possible without great violence to make the State make someone else do it. Never help the unthrifty and vicious to the extent of making them as comfortable as the thrifty and virtuous. (Lecture notes, undated, on land nationalisation.)

> Those in whom the Anglo-Saxon spirit is strongest would prefer that [monopolies], though always under public control, and sometimes even in public ownership, should wherever possible be worked and managed by private corporations. We (for I would here include myself) believe that bureaucratic management is less suitable for Anglo-Saxons than for other races ... (Presidential Address, British Association for the Advancement of Science, Section F, 1890)

We are not of course suggesting that Marshall consciously required evidence of 'Anglo-Saxon spirit' before he could respect a compatriot as a good economist. He does imply, however, that such a mentality is desirable for a realistic outlook on Anglo-Saxon problems. In practice, then, those not committed to the values of private enterprise were likely, *ceteris paribus*, to seem less skilled to Marshall than those who were. Thus in warning of the dangers of collectivism to native inventiveness, the tone of Book 6 of the *Principles* is that Marshall's attitude is the obligatory one for any practical economist, and he concludes that 'patient students of economics generally ... anticipate little good and much evil from schemes for sudden reorganisation of the economic, social and political conditions of life' (pp. 712–3).

It is beginning to sound as if Marshall's attitude to political unorthodoxy as an abstract idea was more tolerant than when he descended to particular unorthodoxies. And this we find. Apparently the decisive gulf in Marshall's mind came between 'socialistic writers [who] have been men of great scientific capacity, who have understood the economic doctrines which they have attacked',[48] and men such as Henry George. Where did this distinction lie?

Of the 'utopian socialists' of an earlier age, Owen and Spence get characteristically double-edged praise for their 'nobility'. As for Fourier, Marshall's lecture notes show inability to take him seriously at all.

> Hedges are types of the artificial hindrance to happiness caused by individualism. Common cookery etc. etc., saved unnecessary labour. Artificial family to be attained (Freedom of sexual relations). Phalanx to have about 2,000 souls. The whole world organised accordingly on paper with Constantinople as capital.[49]

Marx fares rather better, arousing Marshall's sense of duty rather than his sense of humour.

> I owe much to him. I read his book in 1870, and his excerpts from English blue-books – garbled though many of them are – were of great service to me. Now everyone knows about the state of factory labour early in the century; in 1870 few people had given their attention to it.[50]

Nonetheless the theory of surplus value is denounced as circular,[51] as a 'series of fictious principii',[52] and capital's measure of exploitation sarcastically deemed incontrovertible, 'as I can't find out what exploitation means'.[53] Marx's analysis of the laws governing economic development is nowhere mentioned.

We are obliged to rely heavily on Marshall's comments about this older generation of socialists. Obviously he was loath to make public valuations of his contemporaries either in the lecture room or in print. There are one or two straws. In the passage quoted on p. 48, one can infer a belief that radical enthusiasm was often the enemy of patient industry. This is again suggested by his comments on Hobson:

> a vigorous and suggestive writer on the realistic and social sides of economics; but, as a critic of Ricardian doctrines, he is perhaps apt to underrate the difficulty of the problems he discusses. (*Principles*, p. 409)

There is an immense deal that is most fascinating about him, and he is certainly very able. But he is in a hurry; and so he disappoints me whenever the only good work is slow work. (Letter to Professor R. Ely, 11 July 1901)

Hobson was not, in fact, a socialist when either of these comments was written. But the mixture of ardour and haste which Marshall found in him was always suggestive of socialism to the older man: in *The Present Position of Economics* for example, he asserts that the socialists' association with fervid philanthropy may perhaps cause some tendency to rapid and unscientific reasoning.[54] Even more revealing is the way he identifies 'socialists' and 'economists' as opponents on a number of issues. On poverty, his lecture notes compare 'the socialist cure' with 'the economist's remedies': better education, improved sanitary laws, inspections of mines and factories and more liberal public expenditure on behalf of the poor, to be financed by the rich.[55] On land tenure, the *Principles* (p. 48) invokes 'those master minds who have built up economic science', in order to identify the rights of property with 'solid progress'. And a rough draft of part of a projected book, dated 1912, notes that 'In the last chapter the main issues between economists and socialists should perhaps be faced.'

In short Marshall never deviated from his summary of modern socialism delivered to the British Association in 1890. The world, he said, owed much to the socialists: many a generous heart had been made more generous by reading their 'poetic aspirations'. But, before their writing could be regarded as serious contributions to economic science, 'they must make more careful analysis of competition' (*Memorials*, p. 254).

It seems, therefore, that when Marshall put to work his distinction between socialists with and without proper understanding of the principles of economics, he invariably found one of the categories empty.

IX

Given the evidence above, how has Marshall gained a reputation for trying to be all things to all men, and thus abdicating responsibility to point economics in any clear direction? The explanation is partly one of historical context.

Even in his lifetime, contemporaries revered Marshall as the great reconciler of the deductive and historical methods. Historical narrative is in no way basic to the plan of the *Principles*, but a lengthy gesture is made towards it. And while he was generally disparaging about the historical approach as practised, his comments were private. His bipartisan image rested on purely methodological pronouncements about induction and deduction:

Each study supplements the other; there is no rivalry or opposition between them; every genuine student of economics sometimes uses the inductive method and sometimes the analytical, and nearly always both of them together. There is a difference in proportion between different students; as one may eat more solid food and another may drink more fluid: but every one must both eat and drink under pain of starving or dying of thirst.[56]

That anything so blindingly obvious as this could be seen as a dynamic basis for co-operative endeavour may seem surprising. Yet the surly sterility of the German *Methodenstreit* was a threatening vision. Invective had been heard in England as well as Germany, and undoubtedly the sober methodological truisms of Marshall and J. N. Keynes prevented much fruitless debate.

This was intended. To Marshall the distinction between the professional economist and the outsider was clear; and the professionals' aim should be to discover what united them amongst themselves, not what separated them. Nor should they dissipate their energies in demonstrating the obvious; that is, their superiority over their amateur critics.

The one thing that [Henry George] says which is important, I think, is that economists are – to outward appearances at least – at loggerheads with one another. I would rather put in one brick just where it should be in the slowly rising economic edifice than plant a hundred brickbats with the utmost dexterity between the eyes of Mr. George.[57]

Undoubtedly, in the *negative* sense Marshall avoided controversy. Here his personality was important. Unassertive and anxious to please, it was hard to join battle with a man who could say, after the first publication of the *Principles*: 'I can only express briefly my thanks for the goodwill, fairness and generosity of interpretation of those who on the whole condemned the book (as well as of those who on the whole approved it).'[58]

But though in many ways a timid man, Marshall was not, one feels, a particularly modest one: and his avoidance of controversy probably stemmed just as much from a rather disdainful hauteur. On being asked to lecture on George's book he informed Foxwell

(9 February 1883) that he intended 'to avoid talking very much about George but to discuss his subject'; and (8 August) that he could not 'spare time to think of George now'. This is somewhat typical of Marshall's attitude to opponents. And there is no real evidence for the view that – even unconsciously – he actively sought peace by glossing over differences of method or anything else. He himself wrote to J. B. Clark (24 March 1908), much irritated by the suggestion 'that I try to compromise between or reconcile different schools of thought... Truth is the only thing worth having; not peace. I have never compromised on any doctrine of any kind.'

This is entirely fair. And indeed Marshall's characteristic mixture of timidity, conscientiousness, anxiety to be liked, priggishness and vanity suggest a highly introverted man who would temperamentally be more interested in resolving his own internal contradictions than the disagreements of his colleagues. This is the real key to Marshall's career. In *The Structure of Social Action* Talcott Parsons has emphasised how much of Marshall's economics hesitates between the analytical opportunities gained by a static resource framework and a dynamic theory of wants and activities.[59] But this is only one of several dualisms which together determined both the objectives which Marshall saw for himself and the obstacles which he saw in their way. Transcending the others was the dualism which had first attracted Marshall to economics: of analytical and social ends. This, we suggested, made welfare economics the only possible crown to his economic statics. But we have also seen the pursuit of the consumer surplus reconciling Marshall's general humanitarian convictions and his lack of enthusiasm for specific reforms. Economic biology attempted to synthesise scientific and moralistic preoccupations, as did the struggle for an independent economics syllabus at Cambridge.

But there was one great contradiction which Marshall did not try to reconcile. Professionalisation, a modern sociologist has pointed out, is a term which covers two opposed processes. For if some occupations become professions by developing a common intellectual framework detached from, yet basic to, particular cases, others do so by becoming more practical (industrial chemists for example). The late-Victorian economist's situation was unusual in that he aspired to both these goals at once. His dissatisfaction was twofold: that the public were coming to take from economics much less than it would like to give, but still more than it reliably could. To remedy the first problem, economics had to apply itself to more practical matters; for the second, it must put itself on a sounder theoretical and methodological basis. Unlike Jevons, Marshall saw these two objectives as fundamentally inseparable. Jevons, for instance, would never have objected to the separation of theory, history and policy in a proposed syllabus as artificial. Marshall did.[60] This attitude had grave results for economics as a whole.

It is true that, given an economic science at a particular state of development, Marshall accepted that analytical precision and social relevance might be competing objectives, and that the balance struck between them should depend on the abilities and priorities of the individual economist. In the large area where 'economic considerations are of considerable but not dominant importance', it was best for every economist to 'decide for himself how far he will extend his labours over that ground' (*Principles*, p. 770). Consideration of non-measurable motives put the economist outside the corpus of inherited expertise. His judgement must be entirely his own here, and thus should be a diffident one. But if this were kept in mind, if 'when straying far into less known and less knowable regions of social study he does his work carefully and with a full consciousness of its limitations, he will have done excellent service' (p. 770).[61]

Such words were no mere bromide, but an active force for tolerance. Marshallian economics was a vulnerable science, high in universality, low in predictive content, suspect in methodology. Inevitably, its practitioners had to fight many battles which they knew they could neither conclusively win nor lose. In this position, they could easily have tried to safeguard themselves with an absurdly narrowly based scientism, or by concerted abuse of those who saw social forces differently, or by both at once. That they did not owes much to Marshall's sensible declarations that there was useful work for all.

But this was only the immediate issue. What Marshall never admitted was that a similar choice might have to be faced in constructing improved theoretical tools for the future, even without a view to solving particular questions. Take, for example, his disbelief in the existence of a specifically mathematical economics.*

* It has been seen that Marshall valued mathematical ability very highly in an economist; and his article 'On Rent' (*Economic Journal*, March 1893) admits by implication that the concepts of marginal utility and marginal productivity could only have originated in a mathematical mind: 'These terms are used to enable ordinary readers to get the chief advantages which mathematicians derive from their

With mathematics at best only a source of inspiration, a catalyst to be translated and left behind, at worst a tempter of the naive with promises of easy certainty, he could not weigh up the relative advantages and disadvantages of concentrating on developing the mathematical method because, as an independent method in its own right, he did not think it had any advantages at all. The point is that this attitude epitomised what he did and did not see about the choices facing the economist. His own warring predilections enthroned in his mind the opposition between 'academic diversions' and 'a means towards attaining important public ends'.[62] No reader of the economic literature of the time would deny the weight of this distinction. But it seems almost to block Marshall's vision of a still larger question, which the economist could not solve simply by setting face toward duty; the opposition of theoretical and institutional, of humanly desirable relevance and humanly desirable scientific precision.

He could hardly have avoided the choice had its implications caused permanent and explicit conflict among his colleagues, had there been a general and well-publicised debate over the single issue of theory versus empiricism, disentangled from the question of economics' independence of other disciplines. But there was not, largely because the universal difficulty of applying what theory there was gave common cause to men of very different approaches. A few were prepared to do without theory altogether (whatever that means), but these stood no chance of recognition as economists. Thus the economics profession (as defined by Marshall) never sufficiently defined the issues to force him to consider, at basic level, whether his approach to economic policy was either sufficiently concrete or sufficiently short-term. Many of those who would have raised such questions he did not see as real economists. He conceded

training in the analysis of the laws of continuous growth.' But he wrote to A. L. Bowley (3 March 1901): 'A good mathematical theorem dealing with economic hypotheses will not be good economics.' He advised Bowley to:
'(1) Use mathematics as a shorthand language rather than as an engine of enquiry;
(2) Keep to them till you have done;
(3) Translate into English;
(4) Then illustrate by examples that are important in real life;
(5) Burn the mathematics;
(6) If you can't succeed in (4) burn (3).
This last I did often.'
It seems, therefore, that Marshall distinguished sharply between mathematically-minded economists and mathematical economics.

– indeed he loudly proclaimed – that the advance of economic science required a co-operative effort along different paths by men of different predilections. But he could not recognise that even in the long run analytical and social ends still had to be traded against each other, that economics could choose between different ultimate destinations, on whose relative merits reasonable men might differ; because he could not believe that any one of the many viewpoints from which the *Principles* surveyed economics – atomistic, dynamic, ethical, historical, practical, methodological, biological – was less than crucial to the safe usage of the others. That universality and accuracy might be adversaries for all time was an idea which only a superficial mind could entertain; to dispose of such dangerous talk, all he had to do was utter his favourite phrase 'The Many In One, the One in Many.' With this motto in mind, Marshall could largely forget the need to choose between economics the pure science and economics the profession with humanity its client.

APPENDIX

Letters to Marshall Supporting his Plea for the Creation of a Curriculum in Economics and Associated Branches of Political Science (1902)

Sir Thomas Sutherland, Chairman of P. & O.:

Most men whose sons were intended to follow this life would, I think, be only too happy to enter them for a curriculum such as that indicated in your paper. I should certainly embrace the opportunity myself.

Rt. Hon. A. J. Balfour, Prime Minister:

I am entirely at one with you in thinking that there is a pressing need for promoting economic research. The conditions of industry, national and international, are now widely different from those which prevailed when our classic works on political economy were written. There is much to be done in the direction of submitting these new phenomena to scientific treatment; and I most earnestly hope that if any change in our curriculum is required to enable Cambridge to take its full share in these investigations, that change will be adopted.

Sir T. H. Elliot, Secretary to the Board of Agriculture:

My own point of view is of course mainly that of the Civil Service, in which I have lived and worked for more than thirty years, and of Local Authorities of all grades ... In both cases the advantages of training in Economics and the associated branches of Political Science can scarcely be overestimated, in the interests alike of the individuals themselves and of those they serve ... There is a constant demand for the services of men who have been taught and accustomed themselves to grapple with intricate social and financial problems ... A well-trained Economist has been taught to be accurate and comprehensive in the collection of facts, to distinguish between the real and the apparent, and to follow a chain of abstract reasoning without being entangled in its links.

3

John Neville Keynes, a reluctant lieutenant

Economics becomes a profession when 'who chooses economics?' becomes a less important question that 'who does economics choose?' Until a group of specialists begins to decide how many recruits it needs, what kind of recruits it needs and how to select from competing applicants to join its own ranks, it can hardly call itself a profession. And the question of who chose whom not only pervades the Marshall era, but underlines its transitional nature. On the one hand Marshall had strong ideas as to who was wanted unconditionally, who was wanted if he came trailing his own reins, who could be more or less tolerated, who should be sent away to colonise the empiricist outlands and who should be sent away with a just-sufficient reference and a sigh of relief. On the other hand, it took him fifteen years to find a single graduate of acceptable calibre who was also willing to specialise in economics. And when he tried to make full use of Pigou he promptly antagonised his most senior colleague.*

Nor is there any evidence that Marshall tried to recruit economists for Cambridge from outside. On the contrary, the dearth of good (i.e. theoretically competent) economists outside Cambridge was such that he felt duty bound to be a net exporter. Marshall's attempts to persuade Neville Keynes – his most valued ally in Cambridge – to move to Oxford will be reviewed below.

Even as late as 1900, then, Cambridge economics was largely shaped by the independent decisions of established dons to specialise or to dabble or to leave alone. It is the last category which is the

* 'But it is not the case that I only get beginners at my general lectures: and I much prefer a salting of the better class of men: but I almost fancy Marshall does not like them to come to me; for we have a great many differences on these matters: culminating in his having engaged Pigou to deliver an elementary course: a man, of all I have known, least qualified to deal with a general class, as he is such a prig!' (Foxwell to J. N. Keynes, 6 October 1900, Keynes Papers, Marshall Library.)

troublesome one. The character of the discipline was determined as much by those who decided to stay away as by those who decided to become involved. Unfortunately this leaves us obliged to try to answer the difficult, indeed limitless, question: who could have become an economist but chose not to? The only inviting aspect of this question is that at least it is easier than its inevitable successor: what kind of economics would these people have taught and written if they had taken it up?

One possible line of investigation would be to look at academics who are known to have considered specialising in economics but in the end decided not to. Bertrand Russell for one was considering an economist's life in 1894–5. He canvassed the idea in Cambridge, and was discouraged by C. P. Sanger, who could not understand how anyone capable of studying the nature of space would want to study the nature of utility and the demand for tobacco; by James Ward, who said there was nothing philosophical to be done in economics; and by his fellow Apostles. Despite all this Russell decided to set to work on economics at once, telling his fiancée:

> Sanger is working at statistics, and explained several hideous difficulties in the theory, important for practice too, since the whole question of Bimetallism and many others turn on them. I had never suspected such difficulties before, and they inspired me with keen intellectual delight from the thought of obstacles to be overcome.[1]

He spent the first three months of 1895 'chiefly' studying economics at the University of Berlin. Then he apparently abandoned it: nor does his autobiography say why. And, writing in the 1950s, Russell claimed that he did not know enough about economics to be able to evaluate the importance of (Maynard) Keynes.

It is at this point that the career of John Neville Keynes becomes important. Keynes, of course, did study, teach and write about economics – but as an example of someone who nearly did not, he throws light on the probable characteristics of those who did not but nearly did. That is the first reason for this chapter. The second reason is the major role, indeed collection of roles, Keynes was expected to play in reconstructing the economic 'engine of analysis', recruiting and training those equipped to use and extend it and diffusing Marshallian technique and Marshallian attitudes to the outside world. The final reason for this chapter is to ask why Marshall chose such an unenthusiastic lieutenant.

Keynes went up to Pembroke College to read mathematics in

1872. Within a term he was determined to change to the Moral Sciences Tripos. The arguments placed in his way explain much about Marshall's inability, thirty years later, to obtain satisfactory students.

First, Keynes was assailed by Henry Fawcett, a neighbour of the Keynes family at their home near Salisbury. Fawcett, despite his own chair within the Faculty of Moral Sciences, strongly urged Keynes to continue with mathematics, telling him that the Master of Peterhouse expected him to be 'at least among the first twenty Wranglers'.[2] Keynes himself reflected in his diary a few weeks later that 'I suppose all chance of my getting a fellowship is at an end now that I have definitely decided on giving up mathematics.'[3] Besant, Keynes' tutor in Pembroke, actually told him that he was too logical to be a logician;[4] while Stephen of Corpus told him that if he stuck to mathematics, he would obtain 'a higher degree than the Moral Science Tripos is capable of conferring'.[5]

If able students were discouraged from the Moral Sciences Tripos in this way, being told, in effect, that the twentieth wrangler was a better man, with a better future, than any mere logician could ever be, it is not surprising that Marshall claimed in 1902 that 'mathematical casuals' were the only students worth teaching he ever had. There must surely have been other mathematicians, both before and after Keynes, whose interest in logic might have led them into moral sciences and thence perhaps into political economy, but who showed less determination than Keynes in the face of a chorus of donnish disapproval. It is hard to resist the conclusion that the Mathematical Tripos, not the Moral Sciences Tripos, was the real dam which cut off the supply of good economists. And those mathematicians who did change to moral sciences may have found themselves without the mathematical habits of thought which, to Marshall, infallibly and indispensably represented economic worth. It is something of a shock to find even Keynes noting in his diary (15 April 1884): 'I have been working at Cournot on Monopoly, but now I am come to a dead stop, until I can confer with some mathematical friend.'

II

For over thirty years Marshall thought of Keynes as a very scarce resource to be used in a wholly economic way. Even before his departure for Bristol, he was planning Keynes' future with reference to the needs of economics in Cambridge. In 1875 James Ward told Keynes, 'Marshall thinks you ought to lay yourself out for Economic History, a subject that wants teaching thoroughly both for the moral and the History Men, and there is nobody to do it.'[6] But it was only after Marshall's return to Cambridge in 1884 that his long campaign got under way – a campaign to persuade Keynes to combine ability with portability. Marshall had by now appointed himself to the dual task of professionalising Cambridge economics and professionalising British economics as a whole. His repeated attempts to persuade Keynes to go elsewhere, his repeated declarations that only on personal grounds would he prefer Keynes to stay, demonstrated that when these two objectives clashed, it was the narrower one that gave way.

Marshall's first attempt to move Keynes was occasioned by his own move to Cambridge, and his relentless badgering of his colleague on this occasion shows something of the gap between his enthusiasm and his available resources. On 18 December 1884, Marshall and his wife called on Keynes to suggest that he take over Marshall's vacated post at Oxford. Keynes was away in Reading so Mrs Keynes wrote to tell him that 'The Master of Balliol, who has a good deal of influence in the matter, has been questioning Mr. Marshall about possible candidates and he told him that yours was the finest economic mind he knew – or something to that effect.' On 20 December, Marshall followed this up with a telegram urging Keynes to stand. On 26 December Keynes declined. On 29 December Marshall sent another telegram urging Keynes to stand. Keynes wired back another refusal. Marshall promptly wired back a refusal to accept the refusal. Keynes decided to try and explain in a letter. It crossed in the post with a letter from Marshall, urging Keynes to stand. Before Keynes could reply, another letter from Marshall arrived (31 December), urging him at least to take the Oxford work temporarily. After this there was a truce until 11 January. That afternoon Mrs Marshall called: 'She and her husband had evidently set their hearts on my going to Oxford.' The next day there was another telegram from Marshall, '... if still least doubt, telegraph and I return tomorrow'. Keynes telegraphed back that his mind was made up. But Marshall was still not defeated. On 31 January, he called on Keynes, who recorded, 'He wants me to go to Oxford one day a week.' Keynes went.[7]

In 1887, Marshall for the first time 'pressed' Keynes 'very strongly' to take the editorship of the projected *Economic Journal*.[8] Then, in 1888, the Oxford professorship fell vacant with the death of Bonamy Price. Marshall lost no time in congratulating Keynes on his candidature:

Marshall writes – 'I was very glad for ye sake of To π y [*sic*] to hear that you intend to be a candidate for the Oxford professorship; though sorry on personal and patriotic grounds.' This is the first I have heard of my having made up my mind on the subject. The thing is perhaps just worth considering.[9]

Keynes did stand, but Thorold Rogers was elected. In April his diary recorded that 'Marshall is on at me again about editing the economic journal; but I have told him that it would worry me beyond measure.' But by now Marshall was perhaps beginning to realise what Keynes would and would not do. He does not seem to have pressed him to stand for the Oxford chair when Rogers died in 1890. And eventually he turned his attention to the next generation. On 26 November 1905, Keynes wrote in his diary that Maynard 'does a good deal of work for Marshall who describes some of his answers as brilliant. I am afraid Marshall is endeavouring to persuade him to give up everything for Economics.' And on 3 December: 'Marshall writes, "Your son is doing excellent work in Economics. I have told him that I should be greatly delighted if he should decide on the career of a professional economist. But of course I must not press him."'

Explicit irony is unnecessary in diaries.

III

Why did Marshall value Keynes so much more highly than any other Cambridge economist? His enthusiasm had reached full strength well before he saw the proofs of Keynes' *Scope and Method of Political Economy*. There is no record that he ever attended any of Keynes' lectures. One might try to explain Marshall's sentiments in terms of his belief, recorded in the previous chapter, that analytical sophistication, whatever its current outlet, was the one quality without which all others could have little value to economics. Keynes' *Logic* may thus have qualified him, in Marshall's eyes, as a reputable economist before he had written a word of economics.

But just as important to Marshall was Keynes' stance on the issue of theory versus empiricism. As has been seen, he congratulated

Keynes in 1902 as being the only other economist in England wholly loyal to the analytical, rather than the empirical, conception of economics,[10] Keynes certainly shared Marshall's assessments of who was, and who was not, a reputable economist. 'Foxwell ... personally agrees with me in not estimating Cunningham particularly highly. We cannot think him in any way thorough.' Cunningham's article of 1892 'A Plea for Pure Theory' is dismissed as 'ridiculous'. As an *economic historian* Ashley was 'good (I fancy better than Cunningham) except when he goes out of his way to attack orthodox political economy'. Bonamy Price, old and long uncontaminated by analytic activity, was Keynes' co-examiner for several years at London University. 'If possible I feel more strongly how ludicrous and scandalous is Bonamy Price's appointment as examiner.' Palgrave was limited to his own practical field. 'He is silly except when he talks on banking.' Later Keynes began to have doubts even about the banking. 'At breakfast Palgrave talked great bosh on currency questions – sometimes he does not seem to understand the most elementary principles.'[11] Such comments must have delighted Marshall.

Another of Keynes' recommendations must have been his exceptional lack of interest in public affairs. His diaries (until 1914) show an uninterrupted indifference to events outside Cambridge. His very occasional references (about one every three or four years) to economic events would lead no one to guess that an economist, or former economist, was writing. The only indirect reference to the agricultural depression of the 1880s is that his aunt's farm is losing money; the only indirect reference to Lloyd George's fiscal policies concerns his own tax position; Stock Exchange fluctuations are occasionally mentioned, but mostly in connection with Keynes' own investments; and Tariff Reform is mentioned only in connection with the free trade 'manifesto' which appeared in *The Times* above the signature of fourteen economists. Keynes considered the manifesto 'unwise and likely to injure the authority of professional economists'.[12] For years he did not take a daily newspaper, until he started buying *The Times* while on holiday and decided he liked it. Later he gave it up again. And the peak of political commitment in forty years of thorough diary entries is the following:

The Lords have thrown out the budget and there is to be a General Election in January. Florence and I feel rather strongly on the general situation and find some of the speeches very interesting.[13]

Indifference is the safest form of neutrality; and Marshall must also have known that he had a colleague who would oppose pleas for 'relevance' before the foundations of economics had been made strong.

IV

Unfortunately, by 1900, Keynes' indifference had extended to strenuous intellectual activity in general, to economics, to the future of Cambridge economics, to economics students and above all to the professor of economics. A keen, hard-working and popular administrator, first as Domestic Bursar of Pembroke and then as University Registrary, he was in any case left with less and less time for research. But the diaries show a general slackening of intellectual impetus after 1890 or thereabouts. Logic gives way to administration, chess to Kriegspiel (losing chess, very much easier) and Hegel to Mrs Henry Wood. And economics found itself with a falling share of a declining whole. It is true that as late as 8 January 1895 Keynes could write to Professor Laughlin of Chicago (who had offered him a post there) as follows:

> It would for many reasons be a great satisfaction to me to be able to devote myself exclusively or almost exclusively to Economics, and to enrol myself – however unworthy – amongst the very able and energetic band of Economists who are doing so much to advance ~~the science of Political Economy~~ in the
> United States. our science

But even here there is the tell-tale correction in the last line. An enthusiast would have written either 'the science of political economy' or 'our science': only a man summoning up an enthusiasm he did not spontaneously feel would alter 'the' to 'our' as an afterthought.

When the time came for the foundation of the Economics Tripos, Keynes was no longer able to see it other than as a time-consuming bore. During the academic year 1902–3, the Economics Syndicate, responsible for designing the tripos, met on Wednesday afternoons. It seems to have been the only part of Keynes' administrative duties which he ever really disliked. On 22 October 1902, he noted with relief that 'We have appointed a large sub-syndicate, who are likely to take some little time over their Report. That will give the rest of us a holiday.' On 5 March, the report was signed: 'I am glad that this business is practically at an end.' For 7 May 1903, Keynes records:

'2.15 Economics Discussion, I left at 4. It went on till 5.15.' It is abundantly clear, both from what Keynes says about himself, and from what he records others as saying about him, that he was willing, dedicated to administrative propriety and conscientious to a fault. Leaving early from a committee meeting suggests his unique impatience with the subject in hand.

With the tripos under way, Keynes got down to recording his opinion of it and of its students. In 1905, he merely noted that there had been little difficulty in deciding how to place the candidates. In 1906 he was not an examiner. But in 1907 much of the work in Part I was 'poor in the extreme ... quite extraordinarily bad'. This may have contributed to Keynes' growing desire to sever his links with the tripos. On 6 November 1907 he wrote 'I am glad that I shall not have to examine for the Economics Tripos next year.' But on 3 June 1908, immediately after Pigou's election to succeed Marshall as professor, Keynes consented to be chairman of the Economics Board for the following year 'though it is much against my own inclination'. Keynes' reluctance had been strengthened by the circumstances of Pigou's election on 30 May. The diaries refer to Marshall's 'manoeuvring ... I certainly do not think Marshall has come out of the whole thing well'. Foxwell, Keynes noted, had already begun to write his inaugural lecture. 'He is very bitter against Marshall, and at this I do not wonder.'

No careful reader of Keynes' diaries can fail to conclude that he disliked Marshall as much as Marshall liked him. Irritation with Marshall's behaviour on committees is a constant theme; examples could be quoted almost endlessly. Narrow and egotistical, a dreaded prospect as head of faculty, a dreadful bore, exceedingly irrelevant, 'the most exasperating talker I know', as ridiculous as usual[14] ... this is no more than a short-list. It is, of course, possible for an exasperating colleague also to be regarded as a pleasant acquaintance. But the complete absence of friendly references, the scarcity even of neutral ones, in Keynes' diaries, rules this idea out. The Keyneses entertained extensively: the diaries record every guest list for more than thirty years. Not once does Marshall's name appear.[15]

V

Keynes' diaries are revealing. Throughout their length Marshall, the Economics Tripos and the economics students cannot muster a single favourable mention between them. In the light of this, Marshall's insistence that Keynes was his principal ally can only be seen as the wishful thinking of an isolated and disappointed man. His talent for generating antagonism among his contemporaries is remarkable. Keynes, Cannan, Nicholson and (latterly) Foxwell – four economists all of whom to varying degrees aligned themselves with Marshall's conception of what economics was, and should do – adopt, respectively, notes of boredom, hostility, condescension and bitterness towards Marshall the man. Yet Marshall was the unpopular apostle of an ambition which few economists could resist. Economists equipped by nature and training to work within, and upon, the neoclassical idea almost without exception did so. This book will argue that few of the dissenters had much choice in the matter. This is not intended as an authoritative value-judgement that Marshall's disciples were better economists than their opponents (though this writer believes that on the whole they were); still less is it an assertion (which would be a ludicrous one indeed) that opposition to Marshall was mainly a matter of sour grapes. Rather it can be argued that the automatic adherence to the neoclassical paradigm of anyone who could handle it is the most disquieting aspect of the professionalisation of economics.

Part 2

MARSHALL'S PEERS?

The economists featured in this part of the book have been chosen to represent both different degrees of orthodoxy and different degrees of theoretical sophistication. (How far the two are correlated is one of our most fundamental questions.) If we locate Marshall at the centre of the new orthodoxy in economics – and after about 1885 no British economist, whatever he thought about Marshall's objectives and his ways of pursuing them, denied this – then we can reconstruct the emerging profession in a series of concentric circles. Part 2, therefore, travels outward, through middle-distance sceptics (Cannan and Nicholson), and through Marshall's historicist adversaries (the word is not too strong in the case of Cunningham, the man we have chosen to carry the banner for the most persistent and entrenched group of Marshall's critics.) Next, orthodoxies being definable in terms of those whom they exclude, the little-remembered figures of Henry Dunning Macleod and John Beattie Crozier are chosen to stand for two different kinds of 'economic outsider'. Finally the critique of marginalism by J. A. Hobson, because it is so closely bound up with his welfare economics, provides a bridge into part 3.

4

Cannan and Nicholson

Let us now leave Cambridge for the time being. This chapter begins a journey – to be continued in chapters 5 and 6 – from the professionalising core to the outermost fringe of economics, taking in what we hope are some representative and interesting planets (and comets) on the way. Still on the margins of marginalism are Edwin Cannan and Joseph Shield Nicholson, the two subjects of the present chapter. Though eleven years divided them in age, they have much in common. Both combined a basically orthodox approach to economics with a dislike of what they saw as Marshallian regimentation. Both were men of strong convictions who wrote forcefully for audiences of plain men like themselves. Both celebrated their early radicalism with socially concerned entries for the Cobden Essay Prize (Nicholson won, Cannan did not) but set off in a conservative direction immediately afterwards, ending up well to the right of centre. Both did something to counteract the rather bored attitude of the neoclassicals to monetary questions. Both could write scholarly and engaging economic history, but neither saw himself as primarily an historian (still less a historicist). Both were stimulating and dedicated teachers.

In fact Cannan and Nicholson have enough in common to make two full-length portraits a superfluity in the present context. But both were interesting and influential men who deserve more than thumbnail sketches. This book has therefore picked out Nicholson – the more important and also the more neglected of the two – for the more rounded assessment, and deals with Cannan mainly in his role as a critic of theoretical oversophistication, illegitimate uses of neoclassical theory, and the man he promised to 'show up before I've done' – Marshall. Let us take Cannan first.

II

To present Cannan primarily as a critic is not, in fact, to do him an injustice. He used to tell his students that 'the greatest part of an economist's duty will always be upsetting false theories' and he also saw this as the rationale for studying the history of economic thought. In *Theories of Production and Distribution*, which appeared in 1893, Cannan kicked Smith, Ricardo and Mill off their pedestals with an agility and relish that shocked some of his contemporaries. By the time he came to inveigh against some of the more rarefied aspects of neoclassicism, the florid abusiveness of *Theories of Production and Distribution* was left behind and he had arrived at the tough, humorous style of debate which characterised the books, lectures and journalism of his maturity. His article 'The Division of Income' (1905)[1] has a conscientious young man, appalled at the extremes of wealth and poverty he sees around him, going to a series of lectures on distribution theory given by an eminent professor.

> Putting together a number of rectangles of equal breadth, but gradually diminishing height, he will tell his class that each rectangle represents the return to an equal unit or 'dose' (the class laughs politely) of capital and labour, the taller rectangles being the return on the earlier, and the smaller the return on the later units of capital. Taking his chalk in hand, he then draws a horizontal line from the top of the shortest rectangle to the outside of the tallest, and concludes triumphantly 'The amount above that line constitutes rent.' (*Economic Outlook*, p. 219)

The student feels no wiser than before. He has come to find out whether rent is increasing or decreasing its share of the national income, and why some people have so much rent and others none at all. 'He even wanted to know whether he ought to vote for candidates who promised to abolish rent altogether . . . He wanted bread, and the professor has given him a stone.' The dialogue between teacher and student is not helped by the fact that many of the latter's questions are far too simple for the professor to take in without sustained effort.

> Buttonholing the Professor after the lecture, he places his difficulties before him. The Professor has some difficulty before he can understand, and then he says 'Ah! I see. But those are historical and statistical questions with which I have nothing to do.' (p. 221)

In his own lectures at the London School of Economics, Cannan explicitly eschewed not only the professorial behaviour lampooned above, but also anything purporting to penetrate to the 'essence' of rent, interest or wages. 'If anyone asks what determines the rate of interest, I should take as a good answer one which simply explained and classified the causes of rise and fall.'[2] And Cannan's first-year lectures at the L.S.E. formed the basis of his book *Wealth*, which appeared in 1914. In it Cannan skated over much which received detailed analysis from Marshall, Wicksteed and Pigou. It is of course illegitimate to make a straight comparison between a short introductory textbook and, say, Marshall's *Principles*. Nevertheless, to pick just one of a possible multitude of examples, it is hard to imagine Marshall being satisfied with telling students that 'where increased production lowers the cost of the commodity per unit, the "increase in demand" will not be checked by a rise in price but will be "stimulated by a fall in price".'[3] Yet this is the only reference in *Wealth* to the possibility of a falling supply curve.

At the same time, however, Cannan included much that Marshall's *Principles* left out. Following on from the parable of the complacent professor, *Wealth* made an explicit effort to tackle the issue of the distribution of income between property-owners and workers. Cannan scarcely came to startling conclusions, saying, in effect, little more than that the share of wages in national income is positively related to the demand for labour but could be either positively or negatively related to the supply. But he was surely justified in complaining of a post-Jevonian neglect of distributive shares. *Wealth* also discussed why women were worse paid than men, mentioning the occupations which were conventionally barred to women, sexual prejudice, the fact that women were generally worse trained and even the fact that they were worse fed. Again Cannan was saying nothing very original, even for 1914, but he was making another creditable attempt to widen the agenda of economic debate.

Wealth has some perverse touches, as when Cannan 'refutes' the labour theory of value by arguing that labour *destroys* value rather than creating it: 'Every minute of labour given to the production of anything tends to reduce the value of such things by increasing their quantity' (p. 190). It also has much pleasant historical and anecdotal information – Cannan tells us that it was once common for ambitious fathers to give their sons handkerchiefs 'on which the career of the industrious apprentice to the loftiest commercial position was depicted in lurid prints' (p. 189).

One feels that Cannan himself would have been only too happy to see his own economic apprentices blowing their noses on embroidered Alfred Marshalls. His correspondence with C. R. Fay on the subject enabled the latter to pen an entertaining, gossipy obituary of Cannan very different from the dutiful and distant solemnities with which Cannan himself had publicly dispatched Marshall. Cannan told Fay 'I'll show up Marshall before I've done';[4] told him to keep up his golf club subscription because good health would help him assist 'the disappearance of the Marshall tradition'; helpfully suggested 'Alfred' as a name for Fay's second son; and told Fay, after the latter had had some minor difference of opinion with Marshall, to get himself a food taster as soon as possible.[5] Nonetheless, as Fay's obituary said, Cannan lectured on Marshall 'more faithfully and fully than any other'.[6] Cannan in fact had, in 1891–2, taken the trouble to travel 160 miles a week to attend Marshall's lectures; and, when he came to give his own professorial lectures, chose Marshall's *Principles* as the theme. In these lectures Cannan described Marshall as 'the greatest English writer'[7] of economics, and said that his influence would be even greater than it was already 'if he could get a populariser such as Fawcett was to Mill'.[8] Cannan's lecture notes contain many specific criticisms of Marshall's *Principles*; but they still make it clear that the course was meant as exposition, not demolition.

Cannan's extensive correspondence with Fay is perhaps the definitive guide to his attitude to, and understanding of, neoclassical theory. His discomfort with mathematics comes across very clearly:

> I don't quite see why something a year for ever isn't infinite in amount. Obviously it isn't. Ten pounds per year, for example, is a horribly finite amount. And if we save up £100, we certainly don't regard ourselves as having got an infinite amount either for ourselves or our descendants: £1000 would bring in ten times as much and you can't have ten times infinity can you? Damn mathematics: but thank God we are not like Bickerdike! (30 December 1908)

And the general picture is of an economist who avoided the main neoclassical preoccupations because his grasp of Marshall's engine of analysis was a student's, not a potential contributor's, grasp. A long exchange of letters on consumer surplus has Cannan in a terrible muddle. He begins by confessing that

> I can't understand Macgregor in this E.J. It's a pity none of us can understand each other except Edgeworth Bickerdike and Pigou Marshall. You Cambridge people will never be intelligible till you stop gibbering about

consumer surplus. I was horrified to hear you do it the other day. (17 December 1908)

In the correspondence which follows, we go from buying tea with money to buying tea with hours of labour and then to whether, and how, Fay would derive consumer's surplus if Cannan made him an allowance of two shillings a day on condition that Fay put sixpence into a hospital moneybox every time he went to the lavatory – 'you will, according to Marshallesque computation, as far as I can make out, have more "satisfactions" than at present' – and then back to tea, where a man is buying successive pounds against a background of falling prices in 1713–14 and drinking each pound quicker than the last . . .[9] The correspondence, however, seems to have done some good. Cannan's lectures of 1907–8 had some confusion as to the nature of marginal utility. He had taken up Marshall's claim (*Principles*, 5th edn., p. 125) that if a man is willing to buy a pound of tea at 20/- and 2 lb at 14/- each, then that proves the man would rather buy 2 lb for 34/- in all than buy none at all. Cannan's comment had been

Alone one pound will, according to the information given, be worth [20/-], but in conjunction with another pound it may be worth anything down to 14/-.[10]

It was Fay who showed Cannan why this criticism was invalid;[11] and in his lectures of 1909–10 Cannan changed tack and sought to show that Marshallian consumer surplus analysis was not illogical but platitudinous.

All that is alleged is that he gets more from his expenditure on the commodity than he would from the same expenditure if he were not allowed to have any of it at all and so was driven to *increase* his expenditure on other things. This seems to be true enough: it would inconvenience any of us to be suddenly prevented from buying something which we are in the habit of buying although we should of course then have the money to spend on something else.[12]

It might seem unfair to Cannan to spend so much proportionate time dissecting a single episode in which he showed limited understanding. If this were a rounded biographical portrait of Cannan, it *would* be unfair; but, as already said, Cannan is being used as representative of the kinds of criticism the Marshallian orthodoxy received from middle-distance opponents. It is the case that when these opponents challenged marginalist logic they invariably lost the argument; and this must have done as much as any single factor to create a distinction between professionals, borderline cases and outsiders. In fact, why *did* Cannan attack Marshall's theory on logical as opposed to realistic grounds? It may be that he wanted to show that he was as good a theorist as Marshall – why else, after all, give students a minute account of the *Principles* as a lecture course? Cannan, we know, was in general an entertaining lecturer, but a page-by-page dissection of the *Principles*, no matter in whose hands, must have been desperately dull.

But when rank amateurs attacked Marshall, Cannan rallied to his professional colleague:

> Can't somebody be put up to slaughter J. A. Smith for writing such bosh in the Economic Review? I can't do it because I slaughtered A. J. Carlyle too short a time ago – the knife still reeks. Carlyle has said very little ever since. It's quite true that the part of Marshall that Smith attacks is very bad, but that's no reason for not making an example of another of these outsiders.[13]

And, to the suggestion that Pigou might be asked to execute the unfortunate Smith, Cannan retorted 'You can't expect the Astronomer Royal to answer every crank who says the earth is flat.'[14]

III

Cannan's simplicity and force earned him a wide readership. *Wealth*, greeted by the *Cambridge Magazine* as the work of 'one of the very few living economists in England who can place his learning at the service of the general public',[15] even got a review in *The Grocer's Assistant*, which told readers that 'Professor Cannan is widely regarded as the foremost of our living economists'.[16] In his last years, he was best known for his series of articles in *The Observer* in which he argued against additional government spending to counteract the great slump. Politically, Cannan had by then come a long way. His unpublished *Communism in Relation to Production* (1887) was conceived in opposition to the belief that political economy was 'the science which proves communism to be impossible', and those who propagated such a belief came in for the full weight of Cannan's ire.

> 'But' . . . it is objected . . . 'you must admit that communism would remove all present restraints and checks to the growth of population.' Yes: communism would probably remove the checks to which we are accustomed. Infants would probably cease to be starved or poisoned with 'Godfrey'[17] owing to the poverty of their parents, and cease to be murdered for the sake of the

insurance which our negligent legislature allows to be effected on their lives. (p. 85)

Shortly after this Sidney Webb wrote to Cannan that 'I am very glad to hear you are a Communist as regards ideal, and I don't suppose that we really differ at all.'[18] But by 1921, Cannan had reached the stage of telling Taussig 'Tawney is living in a world that is past: government management is hopelessly discredited for this generation at least.' And by 1931 he was in the slender and eccentric ranks of those who thought the government should do nothing about unemployment.

IV

Nicholson had died four years earlier, most of the obituaries hailing him as a great economist. Today he is neglected by historians of economic thought. Even Schumpeter's *History of Economic Analysis* relegates Nicholson to three scattered footnotes, saying that his major work, the *Principles of Political Economy* is 'entirely unoriginal and dwarfed by Marshall's performance' but is nonetheless 'a creditable achievement'.[19]

The *Principles* is indeed a creditable achievement; and whether it has any 'originality' depends on how one defines that ambiguous word. In one respect, at least, the *Principles* is a rare feat; it is one of only two full-length general treatises on economics to come from Britain between Mill and the present day (Wicksteed's *Common Sense* is the other). What is a 'general treatise', of course, is even more open to debate than what is original. But it is this writer's opinion that Sidgwick is too short and Macleod too selective to qualify, while Marshall's *Principles*, a self-proclaimed 'Volume I' until its fifth edition, is a non-starter. Nicholson's *Principles* was eleven years in the writing – eleven years during which Nicholson, a fluent and prolific author, found time to publish no other book. It is reasonable to guess that when he started it, he was not fully aware what he was letting himself in for.

Neville Keynes' (contemporary) judgement of Nicholson's *Principles* is consistent with Schumpeter's.

I have today finished Nicholson's proof sheets. He is interesting throughout, though not profound. I think he really intends to write for the practical man, and for this end his work is admirable. He avoids the refinements and subtleties of Marshall and Sidgwick, and it is these refinements and subleties that the practical man hates.[20]

Nicholson's concern that economics should be understood by the practical man had already been expressed in 'Political Economy and Journalism', a paper he had read to the British Economic Association in 1894. It is typical of Nicholson's pugnacious character that, rather than indulge in any tedious breast-beating that economists had failed the public, he invited the public to make a proper effort to master the economists.

The journalist who has been trained in economic studies will have a readiness and variety of resource that his untrained rival will envy. Instead of being able to abuse the Government, he can abuse the budget itself, clause by clause. And it will not be that common sort of abuse that is equally available to the man in the street.[21]

Nicholson then went on to claim that if journalists knew more economics, questions which were 'really of an economic character' would be taken, to a much greater extent, out of party politics.

But in spite of his general view that journalistic ignorance of economics was for journalists to remedy, Nicholson admitted that economists were partly to blame. They had suffered too passively 'the persistent misrepresentation by popular writers of the teaching of eminent economists'.

Carlyle in a severe attack of dyspepsia, physical and mental, applied the term dismal to the men and the thing, forgetting or ignorant of the high eulogium passed on Adam Smith by Robert Burns. Mr. Ruskin tortured his imagination and the English language to express his loathing for what nobody ever was or ever wrote – the economist to his view as a one-eyed flat fish with the side on which there was an eye always in the mud. (*Strikes and Social Problems*, p. 155)

To make things worse, Nicholson continued, Mill had been succeeded by men who could not or would not 'master the work already done': a step without which 'originality is only another name for ignorance'. This shaft, it is immediately revealed, is intended for Jevons, whose 'ignorance' is linked to his excessive partiality for 'our friend on the margin of cultivation'. In Jevons's hands:

Our old friend, like other patriarchs, has begotten an innumerable progeny of marginal increments. It is possible that the new developments and the new language may ultimately lead to greater scientific precision, but, if so, it will only be attained at the cost of popularity. (p. 161)

And an unpopular political economy left a dangerous political gap; a conviction which grew still stronger on Nicholson in his later years. Writing to Cannan in 1918, he inveighed against 'the Marshallians and the Pigouese' whose attempts to make 'the great truths of political economy' mathematical had merely made them 'unintelligible or vapid'.

The ordinary teaching of Political Economy has been boycotted and sneered at – hence the revival of the old fallacies of inflation, extravagance and the weightlessness of national debts. As regards yourself and I shall add myself and a few others – perhaps more than we think – who have not bowed the knee to the new mathematical socialism – we cannot reproach ourselves for not being plain.[22]

Indeed not.

However, Nicholson's doubts as to the value of marginal analysis did not just concern its wide intelligibility. He did not have a high opinion of its logical *applicability*, even at an avowedly theoretical level, as he told J. N. Keynes shortly before the publication of volume 1 of the *Principles*.

I may tell you – privately of course – that I think even more highly of Mill than I did. I am inclined to suspect that the recent developments of 'utility' are more formal than real – e.g. I think 'total utility' is as unmeaning as absolute rest.[23]

We can take the 'privately of course', with its delightful hint of a neoclassical thought police operating from Balliol Croft,[24] as humorously meant. But the joke, perhaps, would not have occurred to Nicholson without some serious concern that a new orthodoxy was consolidating its reign and threatening to relegate the likes of him.

And when volume 1 finally appeared, it provoked a major controversy with Edgeworth over the merits of marginal utility theory and consumer's surplus analysis. The dispute began with courtesies all round. Nicholson introduced his criticisms of neoclassicism with the thought that 'The idea of measuring such an intangible variable as utility by such a concrete reality as price is certainly very fascinating.'[25] Edgeworth said he was going to discuss the one passage in Nicholson's 'splendid' book which did not command his 'admiration and assent'. Since each made two contributions,[26] and there were three issues in dispute, we have resorted to heavy paraphrase and a dramatic form of dialogue.

First Issue. *Nicholson*: You cannot make interpersonal comparisons of utility unless you make the absurd assumption that all buyers have the same incomes and tastes. Marshall's *Principles* only avoided admitting this by sleight of hand, inviting its readers to 'neglect' the difficulties 'for the moment' and then, far from reintroducing them, going on to contend that tax changes have the same effects on different income groups.
Edgeworth: Marshall is making interpersonal comparisons, not between different classes but between, say a thousand people living in Leeds and a thousand living in Sheffield. So long as the two towns have the same pattern of incomes, and their inhabitants have the same pattern of temperaments, the law of averages makes comparison legitimate.
Nicholson: The similarity between Leeds and Sheffield 'is only postulated and the conclusion is formal'.
Edgeworth: Nothing.

(It is uncertain exactly what Nicholson means by 'the conclusion is formal': but how legitimate it is to postulate similarities between two groups of people remains contentious to this day: in fact Edgeworth's and Nicholson's armed stalemate has lasted ninety years without much change in the basic arguments.)

Second Issue. *Nicholson*: Even for the individual, and at the margin, money does not measure utility. Just as a thermometer measures the heat of the body but not the corresponding feeling, so price measures exchange value but not the corresponding subjective satisfaction.
Edgeworth: Of course a penny does not measure utility as a yard measures length; but the analogy of the thermometer is favourable to my case, and not yours. Thermometers advise us how to promote the comfort of both individuals and groups – thus in the British Museum reading-room the temperature is maintained at a steady 65°. Your argument implies that such an adjustment is futile.
Nicholson: I was talking about a clinical thermometer: and the temperature of the blood has little or no connection with how warm or cold a patient feels, in or out of the British Museum.
Edgeworth: Nothing.

(This uninspiring exchange comes about only because Edgeworth cannot resort to the concept of ordinal utility: and he cannot resort to the concept of ordinal utility because he has just been defending interpersonal comparisons.)

Third Issue. *Nicholson*: Marshall admits that the total utility of necessities cannot be measured because the utility of anything needed to sustain life is infinite: he also admits that the marginal utility of income varies. He should therefore admit that the idea of measuring 'consumer surplus' is both illogical and impractical. Anyone who tries it ends up saying things like 'The utility of an income of £100 a year is worth £1000 a year.' What is the point of statements like this?

Edgeworth: Consumer surplus analysis should be applied only to economic changes modest enough to make both the measurement of total utility and the consideration of changing marginal utility of income unnecessary. Thus the statement that X's £100 a year gives him a utility of £1000 will never need to be made. All consumer surplus analysis tries to do is compare the *changes* in consumer's rent resulting from alternative proposals.
Nicholson: Even if you restrict the application of consumer surplus analysis so that necessaries are not involved (which is a pretty drastic restriction) you will still not have restricted it enough to allow you to dispense with the variation in the marginal utility of income. A theory which neglects this variation is an unreal theory. 'It is only applicable to a few careless millionaires.'
Edgeworth: We differ as to whether, in the process of abstraction, the elements rejected are more important than the elements retained. 'A difference of opinion on this question is not likely to be removed by the prolongation of the controversy.'

In the debate as a whole, Nicholson has at least held his own; particularly as he is right, and Edgeworth wrong, as to whether Marshall sanctioned interpersonal comparisons of utility between different income groups. Marshall did!

But let us now consider why Nicholson has done so much better against Marshall on consumer surplus than Cannan did. It is because he has attacked, not the logic of Marshall's arguments, but their realism. It is *unrealistic*, says Nicholson, to assume that Leeds and Sheffield have the same likes and dislikes, or that there is a large class of economic adjustments over which variations in the marginal utility of incomes are insignificant. Unlike Cannan's unsuccessful logical attack on consumer surplus, unlike the unsuccessful logical attack by Hobson on the psychological foundations of marginalism which we shall see in chapter 7, unlike even the realistic Hobsonian critique of marginal productivity theory which Marshall twisted into a matter of incompetent logic, the Nicholson–Edgeworth dispute must surely have been seen by neoclassical sympathisers as a case where their champion had been held to a draw. That, after all, seems to have been Edgeworth's own impression.

As the reader will now expect, there is no use of the marginal principle anywhere in Nicholson's *magnum opus* – and the kind of truncated vagueness which often results is typified by his treatment of monopoly pricing.

under ordinary conditions the monopoly price will exceed the competition price. The former tends to be fixed above the cost of production price, whilst the latter tends to equality with it. (vol. 2, p. 63)

And, on the effects of changes in demand:

The monopolist, in the face of a fall in demand, may, indeed, maintain his minimum price, but in most cases he will no longer obtain the maximum return possible, and in some cases the maintenance of the price might involve an actual loss. (p. 66)

As introductory remarks to the theory of monopoly pricing, these statements would have been unexceptionable; but, introducing nothing but themselves, they are decidedly primitive for 1897.

V

That it was Marshall who stood for the moderate, eclectic wing of neoclassical economics seems to have been a consistent conviction of Nicholson's. In the *Principles* he emphasises that much of his dispute with Marshall is terminological;[27] something he clearly does not feel about his differences from Jevons.[28] In private correspondence, however, he was much more critical of Marshall than in print. In July 1890 he sent Neville Keynes a copy of his review, for *The Scotsman*, of Marshall's *Principles*

there can be no question that it is the most important and valuable contribution to the general theory of political economy, whether in this country or abroad, since the publication of J. S. Mill's *Principles*.

But the letter which accompanied the cutting is very different in tone:

His history is vague, old-fashioned and excessively weak; his examples are mainly of the old a priori kind or at best curious rather than important; the repetition is so great that the plan must be faulty; and if he is to cover the whole ground of what I understand by Political Economy he will at the same rate take 6 volumes.[29]

Why did Nicholson, normally the most outspoken of men, conceal these criticisms from the public? It may have been from a desire to spare Marshall's feelings; but a later letter to Neville Keynes suggests that Nicholson did not greatly care for Marshall as a man.[30] Nicholson's own explanation to Keynes of his inconsistency was that he had written the review after reading Marshall's book once, and realised its weaknesses only after he had read it twice. Perhaps this should be taken at face value, but it is also possible that Nicholson, like Marshall, suffered from professional *esprit de corps*. Whatever the explanation, the last sentence of Nicholson's letter is the most significant. 'I shall accordingly wait no longer but at once put to work my notes in the form of a complete proportioned text book of about the size of Mill in the extreme.' Nicholson, then, was waiting to make sure he would *not* be 'dwarfed by Marshall' before embarking on his own major work.

Despite his coolness towards the idea of marginal utility, and despite his unflattering assessment of Marshall's powers as an historian, Nicholson must be termed an 'orthodox' economist. He had little time for evolutionism, at any rate as a counsel for economists. 'No manipulation of biological ideas and phrases', says the *Principles*, 'can bring us in sight of economic problems, such as the rate of interest, the incidence of taxation and the level of prices. (vol. 1, p. 12). Historicists are given an occasional 'pat on the head' in public; but letters to J. N. Keynes – who seems, whether he liked it or not, to have been everybody's confidential banker in backbiting – include an attack on Ingram, who 'has failed to throw any light on the connection between economic theory and economic history ... for the simple reason that he does not understand the theory and has never read the history';[31] and a pardonable explosion of boredom with the whole methodological question. 'I told Nicholson of my proposed book on Method. He scoffs, and says anyone could write such a book as that. He says he is sick of disquisitions on method, and that what we want is useful *applications* of the right method.'[32]

VI

Downright in his opinions and uncomplicated in his basic ideology Nicholson may have been, but in policy matters he was no inflexible doctrinaire. Indeed his ability to present with equal pungency, if not necessarily equal conviction, both sides of a question make *The Effect of Machinery on Wages* (1879), the *Essays on Present Monetary Problems* (1888), *The Tariff Question* (1903) and the policy-oriented sections of the *Principles* among the most worthwhile writing on economic policy of the whole period. Only the late *Inflation* (1919) lapses into the empty rhetoric which disfigures much of his directly political writing. For the most part he is a conciliatory bimetallist, a moderate underconsumptionist, a pragmatic free-trader, and a subtle defender of the quantity theory of money.

The Effect of Machinery on Wages, in its original form, won in 1876 the first-ever Cobden Essay Prize. In 1879 Nicholson published a slightly extended version. It is one of his best books. Nicholson attacked his subject with relish, claiming with justification that 'writers of repute' had almost without exception overrated the good and underrated the evil which mechanisation had done to the working class. Certainly, Nicholson said, for fifty years after the technical innovations which marked the beginning of the machine era 'the working classes instead of benefit . . . received injury'.[33] Even in the 1870s, though many advances towards stability had been made, 'the severe fluctuations in trade, the strikes and the lock-outs, the recognised defects in the sanitary conditions of work, all point to inadequate adjustments'. This was partly due to 'the absurd extremes to which the doctrine of *laissez-faire* has been carried'. An attack on *laissez-faire* in general, and Herbert Spencer in particular, then followed.

What were Nicholson's remedies? How were workers to benefit from labour-saving machinery instead of being thrown out of work by it? Nicholson began by calling for better general and technical education. His second proposal was for 'radical changes in international policy' (p. 138). Nicholson then declined to say what these changes should be! 'What direction legislation in these matters should take, it would be presumptuous to discuss in a superficial way at the conclusion of an essay on a special subject.' But he hinted at some form of protection when he complained that Britain permitted its industries to 'depend on the passions of other nations, and with no security that a quarrel which it does nothing to originate may not lead to the destruction of its commerce and the misery of its inhabitants' (p. 140). Finally Nicholson, asserting that 'morality has advanced undoubtedly, and this development must be fostered now more than ever', appealed to the philanthropy of industrialists.

Better education, unspecified changes in trade policy, and nicer capitalists – it is a fairly platitudinous conclusion. But, as Nicholson himself says, the suggested remedies are only to be seen as a brief epilogue tacked on to the main body of the essay. The essay itself is a well-written piece of economic historiography: and Nicholson confirms at the outset that he is going to be primarily inductive, even blaming the deductive method for 'the doctrine of the Wages Fund' (p. 5). This historicist tendency was soon to pass away in Nicholson's work; so were the vaguely protectionist noises.

Perhaps the most interesting passage in *The Effect of Machinery on Wages* concerns the possibility of a general glut. Mill's denial that general overproduction could occur, Nicholson says, 'can never appear other than paradoxical [to] men of affairs. In the language of theoretical economists the disturbing causes are of greater importance than the original hypothesis' (pp. 68–9). Nicholson then considers, and rejects, the possibility that Mill only meant the 'no glut' theory to apply to an ideal world of frictionless economic motion. He states adamantly that Mill's contention was intended, and therefore should be treated, as a 'practical doctrine'. And here, says Nicholson, 'we have one of the most striking examples of the dangers of the deductive method', for Mill's argument does in fact only work in an unreal world where capital and labour are both perfectly mobile (p. 69).

Nicholson, then, ranged himself behind Sismondi and Malthus. And though he did not, to my knowledge, ever reiterate this position, he did not retract it either. It is noticeable that although his last book, *The Revival of Marxism*, tries to pin on to Marx almost every conceivable economic fallacy that Nicholson can dredge up, it does *not* rebuke Marx for being an underconsumptionist. Can we perhaps then assume that the belief in the possibility of a general glut stayed with Nicholson to the end of his life? If so, it seems at first to square badly with the tenacious economic liberalism of his middle and later years. But the 'paradox' disappears when we realise what kind of economic liberal Nicholson was. He was not a proto-Mises or Hayek, with a strong positive belief in the blind wisdom of the market; rather he was a late representative of the type of classical liberal who has unbounded belief in the potential for incompetence of the State.

VII

Nicholson's adoption of an aggressive economic liberalism was self-conscious and well publicised. Like countless other rightward pilgrims before and since, he said it was the world, not he, that had changed. The opening chapter of his *Principles* (1893) warns that 'We [are] rapidly adopting the presumption that individuals, if left to themselves, are capable of everything bad, and that government management is capable of everything good.'[34] An address of the same year to the Edinburgh Chamber of Commerce ends with Nicholson insisting that, if he looks like an anti-union curmudgeon now, he was unfashionably pro-union in his youth.

I have been abused, in the most extreme language the rules of polite society admit of, for defending Trade Unions, and now I shall, no doubt, be equally abused for attacking them ... It is not pleasant for a man at my time of life to be accused of being reactionary, old-fashioned and fossilised. But a public teacher has first of all and last of all to look at the truth ... Let the Unions be warned in time – the attempt to keep wages up at the expense of the consumer, or to force capital to work without profit, is a suicidal policy. If we only lose our markets no amount of strikes will restore them.[35]

Nicholson disliked monopolies, whether on the side of capital or of labour; and, as he grew older, saw himself increasingly as the champion of the unfashionable cause of competition. In 'Labour Combinations and Competition', a public lecture given at Edinburgh University in 1894, Nicholson said that 'It is so long since anyone had a good word to say for perfect competition that a display of its excellencies ought to be as interesting as removing the dirt from an old picture.'[36] If perfect competition could be realised, Nicholson continued, 'there would be realised, but in a far nobler form, the dream of the idealists of the great French Revolution – liberty, equality and fraternity. I say in a nobler form, because, instead of equality being determined by heads, it would be determined by brains.'[37] Nicholson even allowed himself some wishful thinking that increasing concentration might be reversed, saying for example that as electricity replaced steam as a motive power there might be a revival of hand-loom weaving (*Principles*, vol. 1, p. 130).

Nicholson's distrust of monopoly was at the root of his dislike of socialism. He made the curious claim that even socialists admitted that, so far as production was concerned, the system of free competition was the most effective.[38] (Which socialists he had in mind, he did not say.) But, he said, what socialists did not sufficiently appreciate was the State's inability to perform the tasks they proposed to lay upon it. 'People know a great deal better than Governments can tell them the best way to manage their own business so as to get the best return.'[39] Socialists, say the *Principles* (vol. 1, p. 248)

have a child-like faith in the omnipotence of a duly reformed Parliament, in the altruism of the common man, and in the value of obedience. On these points, however, I have to confess myself a disciple of Adam Smith, who believed very little in senates, and less in those who profess to trade for the public good and who, in his praise of liberty, has had the singular honour of furnishing mottoes and texts to the literature of the Russian anarchists.

Although Nicholson always involved Adam Smith before any other economist in his attacks on socialism, he did claim, as did several of his contemporaries (explicitly or by implication), that economic science as a whole condemned socialistic experiments. In his inaugural lecture at Edinburgh (1881) he said that 'those who imagine they could easily provide an industrial order superior to the present one' were people who 'knew nothing of political economy'.[40] And in a paper read to Section F in 1894 Nicholson joined Marshall in distinguishing between 'economists' and 'socialists'.[41]

Nevertheless, Nicholson made clear distinction between economists who had manned the defences against socialism and those who had, perhaps unwittingly, weakened them. Heading the first category was Smith; and Nicholson valued the political conservative in Smith as much as the economic liberal. *A Project of Empire* (1909) is, among other things, a determined effort to rescue the conservative (and patriotic) aspects of Smith's thought; the mutual admiration between Smith and Burke is documented, and a particularly Burkean passage from the *Wealth of Nations* quoted with approval.[42] And it was Smith the conservative who was invoked in Nicholson's Presidential Address to Section F in 1893, as a warning to the piecemeal reformer who thought every issue should be taken separately on its own merits.

> Let him read a chapter of Adam Smith – in the original and not in the stale pemmican of popular dogmatism. And if he still thinks that every law must be considered in isolation on its own merits, that it is a temporary remedy for a passing emergency, then let him resign his seat in Parliament; he has mistaken his vocation; in the name of common sense and the happiness of the greatest number let him cease to be a legislator and become a policeman.[43]

Smith, Nicholson continued, had upheld economic liberalism not just as a desirable system but as the only workable system. Here he was to be contrasted with Mill, whose teaching about the optional nature of income distribution led in a very different direction. If, says Nicholson, the distribution of wealth 'depends entirely on the options of mankind', and these opinions are 'indefinitely pliable', then no scheme of distribution can be called impracticable, 'and we arrive at the conclusion of the whole matter. And practically that conclusion is nothing less than State socialism ... nothing could be more opposed to the traditional English political economy.'[44] Luckily, says the *Principles*, Mill was wrong: the distribution of wealth engendered must be consonant with 'prevalent commonsense morality'. It follows that it 'can only be gradually altered within narrow limits' (vol. 1, p. 225).

'Historical Progress and Ideal Socialism', read to the British Association in 1894 and then printed separately, was Nicholson's most sustained attack on socialism. If audiences get the conference papers they deserve, then Nicholson's choleric splutterings on this occasion are hardly a compliment to Section F. His bloodcurdling visions of forced labour and income tax at twenty shillings in the pound (average rate) were, incredibly, described as 'a brilliant discourse' by F.C. Montague in the *Economic Journal*.[45] More accurate was Sidney Ball's summary in the *Economic Review*: 'His method is indeed, simple to a degree: collect from whatever source you can all the ideas which may seem fatal to progress, put them into the most extravagant form they can bear, and call the whole the Socialistic Movement.'[46] *The Revival of Marxism*, Nicholson's last book, is in parts just as bad. Nevertheless, the book does contain several valid criticisms of Marx, is not a whit too unkind to Lenin and is certainly much less silly overall than Edgeworth's review of it, which begins 'We have much sympathy with those who hold that the theories of Marx are beneath the notice of a scientific writer',[47] and continues in similar vein throughout.

Nicholson's defence of capitalism was, on the whole, much more interesting than his attacks on socialism. Some of it was unfashionable in the context of its time. He defended egoism against public spirit, taking issue with Marshall's claim that evolution favoured societies where the individual was most willing to sacrifice himself for the benefit of the mass, and quoting Sir James Steuart: '"Were public spirit instead of private utility to become the spring of action in the individuals of a well-governed state, I apprehend it would spoil all"' (*Principles*, vol. 1, p. 85). And, *contra* Jevons, Nicholson defended the classical presumption against State interventionism. 'A Plea for Industrial Liberty' argues that on this issue pragmatism cannot be neutral: he who does not take a general stand against the State will drift into a general stand for it.

Once you ... profess to decide every case on its own merits, you are certain to think the merits [of State intervention] overcome the demerits, for the simple reason that the former are particular, concrete and obvious; while the latter are general, indirect, and below the surface ... the question on which the presumption lies is by no means purely abstract; on the contrary, it has most important practical bearings.[48]

Nicholson reinforced this point by contending that once the State began to implement its own (or anyone else's) ideas of social justice, it would soon be imitating the amateur carpenter who, unable to equalise the lengths of his table legs, sawed and sawed away until he was left with a flat board. There is a large grain of gruth in this; but the modern reader's sympathies are not engaged when Nicholson proceeds to use it against the provision of old age pensions.

Where would be the justice of giving to a man of the physique of Mr. Gladstone a pension of 5s. a week at sixty-five, whilst a worn-out steel grinder, with his lungs ruined with steel-dust, is left to die unassisted before he is sixty? If you adopt this scheme of Mr. Booth's the natural sense of justice will make it grow rapidly, and every growth will mean more taxation. ('A Plea', p. 144)

'A Plea for Industrial Liberty' ends by raising the argument above considerations of mere economic efficiency. Too many laws, Nicholson says, make a society lawless; undue restraint increases, and may even glamorise, crime. He quotes Smith's contention that it was the absurdly high tariffs of the eighteenth century which made the smuggler a popular romantic figure; this despite the fact that 'the cruelties practised by armed gangs of smugglers on those who were even suspected of being informers were incredibly brutal'. Nicholson accepts that 'the system of liberty does not tend to equality', and that it must be curtailed where, for example, the interests of children are concerned. But he does argue that, so far as the existing distribution of wealth falls short of 'natural justice',[49] the remedy is generally 'not more authority, but fuller liberty'.

Take the case of those who strive to gain a living from land that is too poor in quality and insufficient in quantity ... The only real remedy in such a case is to break down the prejudices that bind him like a serf to the soil, and make him feel that he is a free man with the world before him where to choose. (p. 149)

In a few cases, Nicholson admits, government regulation may secure advantages to individuals which their own efforts cannot bring about. But here Nicholson shifts tack, and makes a plea for 'liberty, independence, self-reliance' to be followed as moral ends in themselves. Marshall would not have disagreed. Nonetheless Marshall's reaction to socialistic assumptions of moral superiority was often defensive and conciliatory. Nicholson consistently goes into the attack. A liberal economic system, he claims, fosters a Christian generosity which puts to shame, but is also endangered by, the compulsory redistributive exactions of the State. This emphasis on the fragility of the charitable impulse is a reflection of Nicholson's general belief that man's goodness is easily lost and hard won. And his first book uses a mundane discussion of urban housing to advance the Christian message that, the more effort it takes to avoid evil, the better and stronger the resulting way of life will be.[50]

VIII

No assessment of Nicholson would be complete without a mention of his three novels, all published anonymously. First, they show there was a side to Nicholson's nature which could not be satisfied by writing about economics; secondly, they give useful information about his outlook on a range of subjects; thirdly, they are an excellent read! *Thoth* (1888) is set in ancient Greece and in a mythical kingdom to the East. It is a light book, carried along by Nicholson's powerful, even grotesque imagination – though in the fall of Thoth's kingdom we can certainly see the moral, if we wish, that a society where men do not respect women may not survive and does not deserve to. It also shows that Nicholson was in some things far from conservative – he writes with evident approval of the heroine's wish to be the right sort of mistress rather than the wrong sort of wife:

> Daphne had determined ... to enter into no forced marriage, but to form a fitting connection with some man whom she loved and honoured, if chance willed it, in marriage, but if not, even as Aspasia with Pericles. (*Thoth*, p. 23)

It would be going too far, on the strength of one remark about one woman safely away in classical Athens, to dub Nicholson the first protagonist of capitalism and the permissive society. But his sympathy for, and tolerance of, the 'weakness' of his heroines is also marked in *Toxar* (1890), whose main character is a kind of satanic factotum, forever humbly protesting that he is no more than a 'man of means' who advises successive masters how to achieve their desired ends. Each master in turn meets a horrible fate, but it would certainly be pretentious to read a sermon about the inseparability of means and ends into a book which is even more obviously meant as entertainment than *Thoth*.

Between *Thoth* and *Toxar*, however, comes *A Dreamer of Dreams* (1889), which for its first hundred pages seemed destined for higher things. But when Nicholson brings in the Devil as a major character – something which only a very great artist or an unpretentious story-teller ought to do – the novel slips down a notch, from a fine book to a splendid tale. The Devil appears as Mr Smith, a wealthy London solicitor (hardly any disguise at all, the hero's clergyman friend is made to comment), and his tempting and tormenting of Newman, the hero, constitute most of the rest of the book. But *A Dreamer of Dreams* has a serious theme – that freedom is valueless without purpose, yet purpose must severely constrain freedom – and some of Nicholson's writing has an almost poetic quality absent from *Toxar* and *Thoth*.

> The air was pervaded through and through, with the stagnation of the fens, and the people, man and woman, boy and girl, dotard and infant, were thick, stolid and inert – of the fens, fenny – of the mud, muddy. They spoke to one another, when they spoke at all, as if they were miles apart and their voices would only just carry the distance. They jerked out the words in high and shrill tones, and yet in some mysterious manner their effect was deadened, and they failed to penetrate the dull ears into which they were thrown. No one was startled by this human noise; it was only part of the monotonous cackling and barking and other voices of the farmyard. (p. 100)

Newman's meanderings round the world reveal that Nicholson shares Marshall's peculiar illusion that the further north you go the more racial character improves; Nicholson even seems to associate Arctic latitude with marital fidelity. One can hardly imagine Marshall, however, writing a novel in which the hero 'bursts into shouts of laughter' after he and his boat are deliberately capsized by a little girl trying on the part of Die Lorelei! Indeed the humour of *A Dreamer of Dreams* is one of its pleasantest features; often innocent, but sometimes ironic and occasionally savage:

> The family lawyer discovered, after nearly a year's search, that Stephen had died in a colonial prison, and that, to leave no doubt on the matter, he had been dissected by the prison doctor by way of practice.[51]

IX

If bias there has to be, it should be open and not secret; so this book will confess a strong liking both for Nicholson the man and for his approach to economics. Nicholson's own likes and dislikes were never anything but transparent. A clear mind, a warm temperament and a forceful style make him the most readable of the economists of his day. Even his devotion to Adam Smith is attractive, loyal but not uncritical, admiring but not unctuous. When Nicholson died, *The Times* wrote that 'he knew his "Wealth of Nations" as the Scottish peasant knows his Bible, and believed in it almost as thoroughly'.[52] And there is a very strong case for saying that Nicholson, though certainly not the greatest, is the truest of all the disciples of Adam Smith.

5

Cunningham and historicism

There is a recurring difference between those who think of the greatest happiness of the greatest number and those who resent the sacrifice of individual lives for distant impersonal advantages.

Cunningham, *Christianity and Social Questions* (1910)

No one can have a greater dislike of the minute study of medieval history than I.

Marshall to Foxwell, 1902.

William Cunningham's crowded life – Cambridge lecturer, Chaplain of Trinity, Vicar of Great St Mary's, Archdeacon of Ely, Professor of Statistics at Kings College, London, campaigner against free trade, and author of over thirty books – was not, on the whole, the life he would have chosen for himself. Unable to find a teaching post in philosophy, he 'drifted' – the word is his daughter's – 'into spending much of his life on a subject which did not especially attract him'.[1] His incumbency of Great St Mary's seems to have been shouldered reluctantly and out of a sense of duty. And the two appointments which Cunningham prized most – his fellowship at Trinity and the archdeaconship – were neither planned nor expected.

Even Cunningham's migration south from his native Scotland, at the age of nineteen, had nothing to do with the commonplace motive of personal ambition. On the contrary, he felt he could have risen furthest in the Church of his native land, and believed himself to be sacrificing career to conscience, after a period of introspection had convinced him that ordination into the Church of England alone was consistent with his deepest theological beliefs.

There was, nonetheless, much more of Dr Grantly than of Mr Harding in Cunningham. A worldly man – he once preached a sermon at the Jockey Club – with a dominating personality, he had the faults as well as the virtues characteristic of the Church's

Plumstead Tendency. There were few lengths to which he would not go to win an argument, pushing professional and political disputes to an *ad hominem* stage with a minimum of delay. Whatever view one takes of conscientious objectors, it is hard not to be offended by parts of *Christianity and Politics* (1916); while one of Cunningham's wartime sermons on the subject enraged a group of pacifists into almost abandoning their principles in King's Parade, directly after matins.

Yet most people who knew Cunningham seem to have liked and admired him. F. R. Salter, who was an undergraduate and then a Fellow of Trinity in Cunningham's later years, gives a picture of a conscientious and kindly man. 'Slow and deliberate of gait, slow and deliberate of speech with pauses between the words and a slightly booming voice, he seemed to us the embodiment of dignity, sincerity and wisdom, a wisdom that was sure of itself and had no doubts, being based on extensive reading, incisive thinking, and a wide experience of practical affairs.' Clapham's correspondence of the 1920s contains more than one affectionate tribute to 'Archdeacon Bill'. The most effusive expression of personal regard, however, would certainly not have compensated Cunningham for Clapham's contention that, even as an economic historian, Archdeacon Bill was Marshall's inferior. For Cunningham, more than anyone else, embodied the historical school's claim to supply ingredients to economic thought that were beyond Marshall's power. Cliffe Leslie's attacks on orthodoxy may have been more radical, Ashley's writing may have been more thorough and scholarly, but no one combined the critic's and contributor's roles as forcefully, doggedly and protractedly as Cunningham. It can be presumed that no one dared remind Marshall, on his retirement in 1908, that to date Cunningham had written more works of political economy than all other Cambridge dons, living and dead, put together.

Cunningham's academic mission was to establish economic history as an independent discipline. His ideological mission, in his daughter's words, was to rescue English thought and English politics from 'the a-moral and a-national prejudices of Liberal economics and Whig history'.[2] In particular, as the quotation at the head of this chapter implies, Cunningham's work is suffused with a deep dislike of utilitarianism and of everything he associated with it.

I

Some of the English marginalists identified themselves with utilitarianism; others opposed it. But all saw modern economic theory as freed from its methodological limits and (Edgeworth alone disagreeing) from its ideological grip. Cunningham accepted neither claim and, by arguing from alternative assumptions to very different conclusions, proved his point in nearly everything he wrote. His profound antagonism to utilitarianism in its broadest sense, by making marginal utility theory and Marshallian welfare economics unacceptable to him, explains much of his isolation from the Cambridge stream; by giving him his terminological tastes and aversions, and a focus for his rhetoric, it emphasised the rest of it.

Cunningham felt a double dislike for utilitarianism as logically tied to self-interest and historically associated with *laissez-faire*. Discussing the 'Utilitarian State' he seems to associate it with self-interest not just as a methodological fiction but also as a social desideratum. Blaming utilitarianism's appeal on the Manchester School, he continues:

> But it was only plausible, because these writers assumed that self-interest was more or less enlightened. In so far as any man prefers to be comfortable in the present at all hazards, whether he has to beg, borrow, or steal, or even to live on his wife's earnings – he cannot be allowed to carry out his own view of what he likes without detriment to the community. The indulgence of the personal desire for immediate enjoyment is apt to distract from a consideration of the well-being of the community. As the individual lives are shorter than the life of the community the aggregate of personal interest, at any one time, can never be identical with that of the community as a whole.[3]

Elsewhere the position is a little more complicated. At one point Cunningham refuses to be drawn into the debate whether or not all ostensibly altruistic motives are in fact selfish. In 'Nationalism and Cosmopolitanism in Economics' the implication is that even if they are, economics still needs the qualitative dimension of utility developed by Mill and thrown away by Jevons:

> It is far less important to measure the force of self-interest than to distinguish the cases where self-interest coincides with family welfare and national prosperity, and those where it does not. Here, if anywhere, it is essential that we should keep abreast of the times, and recognise the importance of qualitative as well as quantitative distinctions in discussing the motives which influence men in their moral concerns. But some recent economists seem satisfied that a defective analysis is good enough for them; the crude

method which Bentham suggested has been adopted by Jevons; the quantitative analysis of individual motives is spoken of as if it were the principal work of an economist; writers still discuss quanta of pleasure and pain, of utility and disutility; and the individual, as Bentham analysed him, is still a fundamental conception in current economic treatises. 'Put a penny in the slot and the machine will work'.[4]

Cunningham is not here demanding the moral evaluation of motives for its own sake; if he were, he would have condemned Mill's ethics too. He is speaking from his life-long belief that the economist's most important function is to guide the State. But it is only by evaluating the *motives* of men when they are left to themselves that we can predict the ultimate effect on human nature of a particular State intervention. Thus (and this theme will appear again) subjective value theory prevents the marginal school from discharging their responsibilities.

Cunningham also attacked marginalism in more specific ways. *The Wisdom of the Wise* (1906) objects that economics has become 'an individualistic rather than a social science ... Personal utility or disutility may explain why a man joins a trade union, but does not directly account for the action of the union as a body.' *Modern Civilisation in Some of Its Economic Aspects* (1896) spells out the limits of money as a yardstick of measurement of utility: '[It] is not applicable to things that are not the subject of property, or to property which cannot be exchanged. Health and Honesty, Genius and Self-Sacrifice are important elements in well-being.'[5] *Christianity and Social Questions* (1910) shows that Cunningham was equally unenthusiastic about the marginal productivity theory of distribution. He attacked it for what he imagined to be its ethical implications, arguing that marginal productivity seldom corresponded to just desert. Allied to this was a call for a more historical approach, which, however, Cunningham also demanded in order to see how closely factor contributions conformed in reality to their ideal forms under the theory. But in the main Cunningham was characteristically urging that the human aspect be kept in sight. To treat men as factors of production was to obscure the fact that 'The mutual relations of human beings to one another are being constantly readjusted, and there are, under diverse conditions, different opportunities for a man to develop his personality and improve intelligence and character.'[6]

But Cunningham's strongest assault on marginalism appropriately comes in his address to the Scottish Society of Economists, 'Back to Adam Smith' (1904). Even the classical economists, he said, had latterly been basing ever wider pretensions and predictions on an ever narrower view of man. But the neoclassical cure had been worse than the disease; by making the idea of utility the very basis of economic analysis, by ignoring the process of bargaining, let alone the variety of types of bargainer, the marginalists had done no less than abolish the very idea of exchange value.

Value-in-Exchange assumes the existence of two bargainers; it gives us a basis for examining their relations. Value-in-Use has to do with the individual and his estimate of utility and dis-utility. We can derive no help from it in co-ordinating observed fact – it is all in a different plane. We cannot but regard it as a grave misfortune that Jevons and his school should have spent their energies so much in analysing the phenomena of value-in-use, which the author of the *Wealth of Nations* had rightly discarded. The ingenious fabric of reasoning that has been built up is curiously alien to Adam Smith's habit of mind. ('Back to Adam Smith', p. 11)

Did Cunningham have a value theory of his own to put in marginalism's place? Although it would appear that value theory as such held little interest for him, and although his discussion of costs was confined to making moral distinctions between different forms of cost-cutting, he did nonetheless make two substantial excursions, ten years apart, into the theory of price determination.[7] On each occasion two facts stand out immediately: Cunningham's concentration on the seller rather than the buyer, and his focus on exchange rather than production.

By making the seller displaying his goods the key figure in the economic process, Cunningham believed that he – or someone else – could make an empirical study of the determination of price in different classes of transaction, which would yet take full account of what was good in the orthodox theory. To attend exclusively to the seller as a living man was not to neglect the buyer as an economic force, since the seller's calculations included the operation of the demand-function as he saw it. 'If we study one side, that of the seller, thoroughly, we shall have taken sufficient account of the buyer, indirectly' (*Modern Civilisation*, p. 57).

Asymmetry of emphasis may remain theoretically sound, but what are its positive advantages? Why does a parametric demand-schedule suffice to describe the consumer's behaviour? This question has answers at two levels.

I. Cunningham gives two explicit reasons.

(1) The seller may make up his mind beforehand and set a price at which he is willing to sell (i.e. the supply price is communicated to the buyer, but not the demand price to the seller) (p. 57).

(2) 'As the owner, he has the last word in closing the bargain; it rests with him to accept an offer or not and to decide at what price he will agree to sell' (p. 57).

II. These statements need no comment: graphic use of supply and demand curves would have prevented Cunningham from making them. But another reason for Cunningham's choice runs through his price theory as a common thread and, unlike the above, is more than a matter of elementary misunderstanding. This is the fact that Cunningham believed the various types of seller both could and should be classified more precisely than the various types of buyer. In the first place the economist had to allow for the fact that 'some competitors have more knowledge, more judgement, more business capacity, more enterprise than others', for it was 'through the action of these qualities' that a price was 'made'.[8] Secondly, Cunningham said, sellers should be classified according to their degree of monopoly (monopsony was apparently outside his view). Thirdly, since the entrepreneur set his price with reference to his 'business connection' (the nature and extent of the area from which purchasers could be expected), it was up to the economist to classify different types of business connection too.[9]

Lying behind all other explanations of Cunningham's lop-sided price theory is the psychological one: Cunningham's sympathetic interest in the fortunes of the individual seller. As early as 1879 he was regretting 'the terrible anxieties of men of business, the harassing struggles against increasing competition, the feverish excitement of speculative dealings'.[10] These people, he felt, were being standardised, and their individualities discredited, by contemporary microeconomics; whereas the consumers, less appealing figures, could legitimately be aggregated into an impersonal 'demand'.

Whatever the reasons why Cunningham set himself the priority of classifying different types of exchange – and doubtless it also reflected a deeper disinclination to penetrate very far into price analysis – it committed him to writing discursive prologues to empirical work which lack of time or lack of confidence in its genuine value prevented him from carrying out.

II

In the pursuit of popularity with honour, the conflict over tactics was exacerbated by different conceptions of the working-class audience. For Marshall, it was to be instructed with special tact and everyday language in its own journals, or to be helped indirectly by a syllabus that would turn out imaginative and sympathetic businessmen. Cunningham's introduction to the *Report of the Industrial Remuneration Conference* of 1885 showed that in his mind the working class played a less passive part, deserving respectful attention for the aims it demanded of political economy, for its criticism of current techniques and for the dignity of its self-portrait.

Cunningham began by endorsing working-class distrust of quantitative economics. The conference, he said, had featured a clear division along class lines insofar as statistical investigations about wage levels 'which appeared to most middle-class intellects to be completely established, have failed to make much impression on the minds of working men'.[11] The working men were right, he went on; the kind of statistics which middle-class delegates had been quoting and praising were crude and misleading, invariably omitting the fact that shorter hours might be accompanied by increased intensity of labour, and the fact that higher wages might coincide with greater irregularity of unemployment. But there was also a deeper objection – that the premiss implied by making such inquiries at all was irrelevant to 'the issue which working-men are debating; the writers discuss the condition of the working-man as an eating, drinking and clothes-wearing animal, while some members of the conference desired to see him as a member of a civilised society'.[12]

Cunningham's introduction to the conference report exemplifies his life-long desire to make economics more effectual by making it less unpopular. And though he accepted that the working class was misunderstanding as well as misunderstood, he believed that ignorance might be easier to conquer than well-deserved prejudice against political economy. Economics, in fact, had a dual task: to reduce exaggerated popular ideas of what it could do (for which it was itself largely to blame) and to enhance its real authority. Cunningham returned to this theme six years later, in his inaugural lecture as Tooke Professor at King's College, London.

If there is one thing from which political economy has suffered more than another it is from the fact that the public have formed an undue estimate of what it could really do and have then been disappointed because it has failed to come up to their expectations. I have thought that in beginning my work as Professor, nothing can be more important than that I should not come under false pretences ...[13]

And, later in the inaugural, Cunningham addressed himself to the related question of the desirable moral influence, if any, of political economy. He began with a passage which, taken in isolation, sounds like a strong plea for the reunification of economics with ethics.

The economic calculus ... only tells what tends to happen; it only explains how bargains are adjusted. Whether these bargains are wise or foolish, whether they are tending on the whole to the good of human beings or natural power, are matters on which individual economists may offer excellent opinions, but these are things on which the science in its most recent form has nothing to say as science. ('Relativity of Economic Doctrines', pp. 11–12)

But Cunningham then went on to say that political economy 'certainly cannot set forth positive rules of duty. All it can do, as a practical doctrine, is to prescribe means to a given end ... It cannot lay down any criterion as to the end which ought to be pursued' (p. 15).

Thus Cunningham's criticism of 'the science in its most recent form' cannot be taken to mean that he thought his economist contemporaries should, in their role as economists, be making ethical judgements. It can only be interpreted as a criticism of what he saw as their inadequate powers of guidance even when social ends were given. This was a constant claim by Cunningham, who further believed that, while some of the exponents of marginal utility theory might caution against the dogmatic application of so partial a view of human motivation, its authoritativeness was bound to be exaggerated by others and taken for granted by much of the intelligent public. The neoclassical economist thus must either neglect his advisory function, allowing its misuse by others, or else misuse it himself.

III

Just as important as Cunningham's challenges to orthodoxy over theory – and much better publicised – were his challenges over method. Methodologically speaking, his criticisms of Marshallianism traced a rough parabola, rising from the conciliatory *Politics and Economics* (1885) to a peak of provocative scorn during the public dispute with Marshall (1892), and then subsiding through the years into the valedictory amiability of *Christianity and Economic Science* (1914). And between 1885 and 1895 Cunningham's methodological path was so intimately interwined with the course of his personal and professional antagonism to Marshall that the two stories can only be told together.

Marshall's election to the professorship of political economy at Cambridge in 1884 was a blow to Cunningham for reasons beside the obvious one that he had been a candidate himself. Fawcett's death and Cunningham's candidature had briefly opened for economic history the unexpectedly early prospect of controlling the Cambridge chair. Instead, Marshall's election delivered the prize to a style of economics which Cunningham saw as positively anti-historical, and, worse still, condemned him personally to help to implement it. Fawcett had left his colleagues free to teach as they chose, and Cunningham had chosen to lecture on economic history, introducing theoretical questions as they arose in concrete form. Marshall had other ideas. His aspirations for a 'scientific' economics made him intervene from the start in his colleagues' work where it fell short of what he desired. Cunningham's antagonism to Marshall dates from the latter's ruling, confirmed by the Faculty Board, that Cunningham must lecture on formal political economy for at least one term in each year.

There was also the matter of Marshall's inaugural lecture, 'The Present Position of Economic Science'. This contained a magnanimous tribute to the historical challenge to orthodox economics, couched, however, in a decidedly obituary tone, and followed by a much less friendly passage which Cunningham interpreted as representing Marshall's real feelings. (The praise was in the perfect tense, the criticisms in the present.) Marshall even turned the historicist charge that deductive economics was biased economics back on the historicists, arguing that to reason from one event to another, without a prior perspective on what was important and what was not, led to a far more dangerously selective approach to evidence than did a measure of unabashed deductivism.[14] He then predicted that 'economic science' would soon be even more successful than it was already in 'break[ing] up and explain[ing] what are called economic customs, very much as the telescope breaks up a nebula'. To say any arrangement was due to custom, Marshall went on, was little more than a confession of ignorance of its true causes. It was for economic analysis to shed light where ignorance had previously reigned: to demonstrate, for example, that 'rents seldom diverge much for a long time from their Ricardian level in the East'.

Cunningham saw this lecture as a personal and public affront. 'I am afraid you must think me very fidgety', he wrote to Neville Keynes on 27 April 1885, after what had evidently been an awkward conversation the previous day. 'But I have felt greatly annoyed at Marshall's lecture . . . The appearance to the Cambridge public is that the line of study with which I am identified has been severely handled, and that there is nothing to be said in reply.'[15] This last impression, Cunningham said, existed only because he did not want to risk his present relations with Marshall by publicly criticising his lecture.

Marshall's inaugural was delivered while Cunningham's *Politics and Economics* was in the press. What must have especially stung Cunningham was the fact that he had just opened his new book with remarks not just conciliatory to deductive economics, but actively taking its side against the historical school:

> the deductive school have followed out the consequences wrought by the desire of wealth and the action of individual competition, with more or less notice of the influence of custom or other forms of friction: while the so-called historical school seem to regard the interaction of causes as so complicated that they content themselves with chronicling the course of events, and seem to deny the possibility of arriving at principles at all.[16]

Yet when Neville Keynes tried to discuss the book with Cunningham after its publication, Cunningham apparently adopted this latter position himself.

> Last night I dined with Cunningham at Trinity. I attacked him for the way in which in his last book he talks about Economic Principles. His reply is practically a denial of the possibility of an Economic Theory.[17]

What could have prompted this change of outlook but Marshall's inaugural? And could there be a clearer demonstration that Cunningham's methodological pronouncements were the result, as much as the cause, of his growing rift with Marshall?

IV

Cunningham regained his pedagogic freedom in 1888. Appointed a college lecturer at Trinity, he immediately resigned his university post. But he remained dissatisfied, believing that his position was seen by Marshall as 'a privilege granted to a man of eccentric views and not an established principle'.[18] And he was still looking for a chance to reply to Marshall from a suitably authoritative standpoint – such as the Drummond Professorship of Political Economy at Oxford.

This morning walk and talk with Cunningham. He is keen on being elected, and also sanguine. He is anxious to have in his inaugural lecture an opportunity of delivering a manifesto from the historical point of view in opposition to Marshall and Sidgwick. (Keynes diaries, 15 March 1888)

But, disappointed at Oxford, Cunningham had to make do with a paper the following year at the British Association for the Advancement of Science. Here at last he opened hostilities; and the fact that it took three years and five published attacks to provoke Marshall into full public self-defence did nothing to diminish his resentment.

'Professor Marshall', Cunningham told his 1889 audience, 'instead of accepting the description of mediaeval or Indian economic forms as they actually occur, sets himself to show that the accounts of them can be so arranged and stated as to afford illustrations of Ricardo's law of rent.'[19] Marshall, however, took exception to this interpretation of his views, and when the lecture came to be published it contained a footnote in which Cunningham, 'sorry to learn that Professor Marshall considered himself aggrieved', 'gladly' appended his disclaimer. He then gave himself the last word, briefly noting how Marshall had now thrown 'a little fresh light' on his views, before switching the attack to Marshall's 'disparagement' of the historical school of economists in his inaugural lecture of 1885.[20]

In February 1890 Cunningham again attacked Marshall's claim that Ricardo's theory could supply 'a solvent which will explain much that is unintelligible in mediaeval history'.[21] But perhaps Marshall's effort was just a pedant's attempt at joviality: 'it is not always easy to tell when the Professor of the dismal science is making a joke'.[22]

The last sarcasm was delivered in September 1891 to the British Association, Cunningham speaking this time as Section F's President. 'Nationalism and Cosmopolitanism in Economics' made lengthy comparisons between Oxford and Cambridge, very much to the disadvantage of the latter, and by no means confined to political economy. There was a *general* tendency in Cambridge, Cunningham said, to be 'so engrossed in the study of things that we have no time to spare for trying to know ourselves. If we ever do give our thoughts to man, we like to think of him as if he were a kind of thing, so that we may apply the same methods which we are wont to use in the study of physical phenomena.' Thus Cambridge historians classified constitutions and called the result political science; Cambridge classicists saw their texts not as literature or philosophy but as philology and phonology; while Cambridge economists 'treat the individual as if he were a mere mechanism; and busy ourselves in measuring the force of the motives that may be brought to bear on him'[23] – an obvious dig at Marshall's 'science of measurable motives'.

'A Plea for Pure Theory', published in January 1892, represents the high point of Cunningham's methodological campaign against orthodox economics (though the fiercest direct criticism of Marshall was yet to come). Far from being a plea for pure theory, it was a peremptory demand for the demise of economic theory, and the partition of political economy into economic history on the one hand and economic lexicography on the other. Such a programme, if carried out, would have resulted in the complete subordination of economics to economic history; Cunningham was not even prepared to allow the 'pure theorists' to study the causal relations between the concepts they would be classifying. 'The attempt to treat economics as a science of causation has been most unfortunate and has introduced hopeless confusion.'[24]

'A Plea for Pure Theory' pleased no one. Neville Keynes, fresh from his own book on method, dismissed it as 'ridiculous';[25] but more significant for Cunningham was the opposition of his historically-minded colleagues. Their views were represented by D. G. Ritchie, who argued in reply to Cunningham that it was impossible either to define a concept like 'rent' without investigating why it existed, or to write economic history without some systematic theoretical knowledge.[26]

But by now Cunningham had a massive new target – Marshall's *Principles*. This began with two provocative chapters purporting to show the ubiquity of the calculating, maximising spirit in economic life, and representing the economic history of the second millennium as the gradual victory of this higher rationalism over the institutionalised oppression of custom and tradition. In September 1892 the *Economic Journal* published Cunningham's rejoinder, 'The Perversion of Economic History'. Marshall, he declared, assumed that 'the same motives have been at work in all ages, and have produced similar results, and that, therefore, it is possible to formulate economic laws which describe the action of economic causes at all times and in all places' (p. 493). This disqualified Marshall as an economic historian: when a scholar entered the past already sure of the key human motives involved, the neglect of most of the facts and the misinterpretation of many of the rest of them, must follow. Cunningham cited excerpts from the *Principles*, some of which were fair, whereas others involved wilful – and because so transparent, curiously pointless – intellectual dishonesty.* And he thereby finally succeeded in goading Marshall into breaking his rule of not replying to criticism.

The real meaning of his *Principles*, said Marshall, was the opposite of that ascribed by Cunningham. It was that 'similar causes acting on people under dissimilar conditions produce more or less divergent effects'.[27] He had proposed no universalist dogma, merely the suggestions that the forces of supply and demand operated slowly and subtly enough to penetrate even the most hidebound economy, and that only with some universal *tools* of analysis could the economist dig far enough down through the crust of habit and tradition to observe his brother in calculation, the maximising peasant, pushing his way up.

Cunningham's overstatement of his case gave Marshall the best of the debate. On rent, at least, he deserved it. But it would be remarkable if Cunningham's attack had not brought home to Marshall how vague and unsatisfactory was his excursion into medieval history, with its facile equation of political freedom with economic individualism, and its recurring metaphor of 'economic causes pressed below the surface', without attempting to gauge their precise nature, strength and depth. Cunningham could have made more of this, although not in the *Economic Journal*, which denied him a reply. But, reduced to the letters column of the *Pall Mall Gazette*,[28] he did little beyond repeating his previous words; and on 2 January 1893, Marshall's old mentor, Benjamin Jowett, wrote to Mrs Marshall well pleased with the news that 'notwithstanding such

* They can be classified as: one genuine difference of judgement (about the amount of free enterprise in ancient Rome), one correction of a factual mistake, two misinterpretations of Marshall's meaning invited by the extreme compression of his account, one misinterpretation arising from a misprint, one manipulation of Marshall's meaning by quoting his words out of context and one infiltration of a rogue word into a plausible generalisation so as to turn it into an absurd one.

insects and wasps as Dr. Cunningham, Alfred looks back on his last year with such satisfaction'.

V

Whatever Marshall was feeling, the clash of 1892 left Cunningham in a decidedly sullen mood. An article written in 1894 complained that

> Those who choose to refuse to conform to the reigning fashion in the community in which they live must expect to be ostracised . . . Anyone who has refused to follow the economic fashion in recent years in England must have been greatly hampered in his efforts to pursue his own studies or guide those of others; boards of studies would exercise a galling control, and editors and publishers would view his writing with suspicion. That is the natural fate of those who do not swim with the stream.[29]

One of Cunningham's most important engagements with the 'reigning fashion' was to come in 1903, when, in a fly-sheet designed to persuade the Cambridge Senate to reject the proposed Economics Tripos,[30] he produced a remarkably concentrated summary of everything Marshall regarded as regressive and obstructive of competent economic science. Cunningham did not want an Economics Tripos for exactly the reason why Marshall did want one: the fact that an independent degree course would free the subject from philosophical control and historical influence. A subsidiary concern of Cunningham's was that, since the Economics Tripos would appeal to two different types of student – tomorrow's businessmen and tomorrow's academics – this would make it undesirable, if not impossible, to construct a single basic syllabus appropriate to everyone. Marshall agreed – with enthusiasm – that the tripos would be seen as a preparation both for business and for academic life, but he rejected the implication that two distinct syllabuses were needed. To Marshall there was only one way to master economics, whoever you were.

Cunningham's opposition to the tripos resulted in the Economics Faculty Board opposing his appointment as Director of Studies in Economics at Trinity in 1905. The Board 'ventured most respectfully to submit' that Cunningham had 'publicly declared himself to be out of sympathy with the study of Economics as it is pursued under the direction of the Board', and that if students at Cambridge's largest college were to be placed under Cunningham's direction 'the prospects of the Tripos may be seriously prejudiced'.[31] Trinity took no notice. It is quite possible that Cunningham took no notice either, for he was now in the thick of his exertions on behalf of Imperial Preference. These, his duties as Vicar of Great St Mary's and his historical writings kept him more than fully occupied for the next few years. In 1908, however, he took time off to castigate Pigou's inaugural lecture in familiar terms.

> Professor Pigou in his inaugural lecture insisted on the practical aspects of Economic Science, though he reserved the right to speak authoritatively to the chosen few who can conjure with the mysteries of statistics. He does not disclaim the power of giving positive guidance: he seems to think the scientific economist really could do it if only he had time enough. Unfortunately the age is in a hurry, and wants to act, while academic economists are temporising and weaving a web of pretentious words.[32]

But a more conciliatory note was about to creep in. It is already palpable in *Christianity and Social Questions* (1910); and *Christianity and Economic Science* (1914) resounds with the unfamiliar swish of a massive olive branch vigorously waved.

> a new school of economists has arisen, both in Austria, France and England, who are inclined to revert to the mediaeval standpoint, and to put consumption in the forefront. There is much to be said for the proposal to recast Economic Science along these lines ... in human needs there is something that is common to all mankind, and this opens up the prospect of formulating a science with laws and maxims of universal validity for all times and places.[33]

VI

At the basic epistemological level, nothing had ever divided Cunningham and Marshall. They agreed that the laws of behaviour must be established inductively, but that they might then be used to isolate particular classes of phenomena for causal analysis.[34] Generalisations, then, were searchlights to increase knowledge by pointing impartially at both anomalous and confirming facts. Cunningham's charge was that Marshall had instead squeezed and bruised the facts into whatever 'laws' would maximise the apparent area of applicability of his own brand of economics. In this attempt to turn economics into a universal science, he had instead theorised himself out of the capacity to offer opinions on the issues of the day other than as a private layman. Economics, as Cunningham saw it, was there to criticise particular legislation, and any principles developed for this end must be 'consonant with the particular needs and aims and ambitions of the nation, in which the legislation is carried out'.[35]

A nationalistic, and nationally relativistic, theory of economic policy was the aim of *Politics and Economics* (1885), in which Cunningham introduced his alternative to orthodox welfare economics – National Husbandry. Its four main distinguishing factors were as follows:

1 The claims of the present and the claims of posterity might conflict. 'We cannot be satisfied with economic principles which are almost wholly concerned with the greatest production of useful things in the present, but we require principles that shall help us to husband the strength and resources of the nation to the best of our wisdom' (*Politics and Economics*, p. 119).
2 The interests of the nation ranked above those of an individual.
3 The interests of the nation ranked above those of a single class.
4 Publicly controlled monopolies were generally preferable to privately controlled ones.

Most economists of the day would have agreed with these four tenets. Nevertheless, the individualist basis of orthodox economics had hostile implications for all but the fourth. In the case of (1) and (2) this is obvious. (3) seems equivocal – surely individualism diverts the attention from class interests as much as from national ones? But Cunningham saw the question differently. He was convinced, as we have seen, that methodological individualism emphasised and even glorified egoism; he also saw class loyalty as a 'lower' form of altruism and patriotism as a 'higher'; and he thought that the encouragement of altruism in general would also encourage its higher, patriotic, variety at the expense of its lower, sectional one. In Cunningham's logic, therefore, methodological individualism helped to promote class strife.[36]

Having defined National Husbandry in broad terms, the rest of *Politics and Economics* discusses topical social problems in its light. Book 2, chapter 2, deals with 'Enactments Directly Economic'; chapter 3 analyses recent examples of 'Social Legislation – and its Economic Bearings'. Of fourteen enacted laws chosen for study, Cunningham condemns but two: the Merchant Shipping Act of 1876 and the Irish Land Act of 1881. Both of these mistakes were made, the final chapter concludes, not because of exclusive reliance on economic criteria, but rather because the heated spirit in which the two issues were discussed ensured that economic arguments were largely omitted.

> Agitation in these days is most likely to be formidable when it is directed by men such as Mr. Plimsoll or Mr. George, who take their stand on some great moral principle, but abstract moral principles cannot serve as safe guides for practical legislation ... the miserable condition of Ireland now is a standing warning against legislating for social and political purposes without taking the economic considerations into full account. (pp. 271–2)

There is no evidence that National Husbandry was consciously set up as a collectivist alternative to conventional welfare economics. But this is what it objectively was. Its ideological basis, its method of procedure and its topical presentation implicitly contested the validity and applicability of Edgeworth's box, consumer's surplus, Pareto-optimality and the like. It is unlikely that it lost them many adherents in doing so: its appeal rested on attitudes of mind already hostile to such ideas. But Cunningham may have limited National Husbandry's attractions by failing to endow it with any understanding of the trade-off between production and distribution in the policy-making field. Rhetorical attacks on egalitarianism were no substitute. It is doubtless true that absolutely equal opportunity requires the building of 'enough orphanages to house all the nation's children';[37] and that it is 'impossible to be always introducing such readjustments that each individual shall regularly be treated exactly like everyone else'.[38] But such truisms will not do in place of detailed discussion of redistributive measures and their likely effects on production.

Politics and Economics is stamped with convinced nationalism, relativism and holism from start to finish. It begins with the assertion, repeated incessantly through the book, that an increase in national wealth must not be identified with the aggregate of increases in individual wealth. It ends with the exhortation that 'the duty we owe to posterity' is 'to make the future of our nation as great and noble as lies within our power'.[39] In the meantime Cunningham has kept his readers' eyes firmly on the fact that policy recommendations are as historically relative as economic principles, even suggesting at one point that the fact that a measure has worked well in very different circumstances is a consideration *against* proposing it here and now.[40]

National Husbandry was the product of broad ideological beliefs which stayed with Cunningham all his life. On the theory of economic policy his position was less static. Audrey Cunningham has chronicled her father's gradual approach, in the years following the publication of *Politics and Economics* in 1885, towards the opinion that political economy was 'not to be trusted in practical matters'.[41] And on actual policy issues *Politics and Economics* was succeeded by some years' silence. Addressing Section F in 1891, Cunningham explained why.

For the last thirteen years I have given such time as I could spare from clerical duty and the routine of teaching to the study of English industry and commerce in the past, and I have made no pretence of keeping myself fully informed about the burning questions of the present day. To me the burning controversies of two or three centuries ago are much more fascinating, because we generally know how they ended, and we can hope to decide with some approximation to the truth who was in the right and who was in the wrong, or how far both were in the wrong. ('Nationalism and Cosmopolitanism', p. 725)

These sentiments of detachment notwithstanding, Cunningham continued his address with a eulogy of free trade. Protection in England, he said, had been effectively killed in 1846; the free traders had demonstrated 'that the world as a whole will be better provided with material goods if each nation specialises in those kinds of protection for which it is particularly adapted' (*ibid.*, pp. 726–7).

Cunningham's next address to the British Association on the subject of free trade came in 1903, in the aftermath of Chamberlain's conversion to tariff reform and the notorious letter to *The Times* by fourteen free-trading economists. 'The Failure of Free Traders to Attain Their Ideals', as Cunningham called his paper, upheld universal free trade as 'the ultimate aim' but rebuked the signatories of the *Times*' letter (they included Marshall) for, first, 'tak[ing] for granted that an economic principle which is framed on the assumption that all political considerations are neglected also holds good in all political considerations alike';[42] and, secondly, for making an unjustified claim to authority in the practical sphere.

These two criticisms were of course closely related to one another. They were also of long standing. Throughout his career Cunningham had been quick to emphasise the limited practical authority of the political economist given that the solution to many ostensibly economic problems must to a large extent be non-economic in character. Over the years, however, he did accommodate his changing sentiments by enlarging this set of topics. Free trade itself is the clearest example. In 1885, the explicit equation of national wealth with national power had enabled *Politics and Economics* to claim that the tariff issue divided not into economic and political arguments, but into nationalist-economic and cosmopolitan-economic ones. Compare the approach of *Modern Civilisation* (1896), which instances the free trade doctrine as a paradigm of classical political economy, concedes the theoretical case for it, yet continues:

> The argument is the basis of our free trade policy, and so far as it goes it is impregnable, there is no flaw in the reasoning, but yet, as we know by experience, it is not convincing. It is merely an economic argument and does not touch the political and social issues which weigh with statesmen and with nations. (p. 98)

The political risk to Britain was starvation in a wartime blockade. The logic of free trade for Australia was 'a country given up to stations and squatters' but

> the inhabitants may deliberately prefer protection, as a means of introducing and maintaining the varied industrial and commercial life of a civilised community even though they realise that it is costly. In some cases the cost may be temporary, and by developing skill and opening up resources, they may succeed in rivalling and even underselling the older lands. (p. 99)

By the time he came to write *Christianity and Social Questions* (1910) Cunningham's conversion to protectionism was complete. It had run alongside, and interacted with, a waxing conviction that there were drastic limits to the relevance of economic theory, *any* economic theory, in policy questions. But his special contempt for the Marshallian approach remained unaltered. His right to hold it was slender; it is hard not to conclude that he simply observed colleagues with more advanced techniques but less deeply felt political attitudes than himself and drew the wrong lesson.

VII

So far we have discussed Cunningham almost without reference to what he undoubtedly regarded as the most important influence on his economic and social thought – his religion. It would have been possible in the preceding pages to have brought out, more explicitly than we have done, the expressly Christian presuppositions underlying Cunningham's work. It would have been possible; but it is not necessary. For Cunningham himself, towards the end of his life, published a trilogy which performs this very task – *Christianity and Social Questions* (1910), *Christianity and Economic Science* (1914) and *Christianity and Politics* (1916).

In these books Cunningham makes no attempt to advance the specific claims of Anglicanism – indeed *Christianity and Politics* singles out 'Roman writers' (to the implied comparative detriment of the Anglicans) for their 'sane and judicial tone' amid 'the chaos of opinions which are expressed by different authors in the name of Christianity'; for 'never allow[ing] themselves to forget that the work of the Church is essentially spiritual'; and for declining 'to fall into false abstractions, and to look on society as merely mechanical' (pp. 28–9). The Church of England, by contrast, is at one point subjected to a verbal assault hardly to be expected from a Conservative archdeacon writing in 1914:

> since the early part of the nineteenth century, there has been occasion to point out the crying evils which have arisen in connection with the capitalist organisation of industry, and the ruthless disregard for human life which it has exhibited from time to time, when uncontrolled. Religion has had to bear the blame of this inhumanity on the part of the forces of progress to which it has given its sanction; and it is plausible to say that for the last two hundred years religion has been on the side of the rich, and has done little to protect the poor, who have never seemed to gain anything in the course of progress, and have often incidentally lost much. The increasing jealousy of the power of the capitalists and the growing suspicions as to the manner in which this power may be used, help to account for the widely diffused indifference to religion in progressive countries. (*Christianity and Economic Science*, pp. 70–1)

The trilogy contains restatements of most of Cunningham's economic and political beliefs, not necessarily in an explicitly Christian context. National loyalty is exalted above vague cosmopolitan sentiments ('I cannot set much store by a man's interest in the well-being of strangers who is indifferent about the land of his fathers'),[43] while in *Christianity and Economic Science* Cunningham warns, as he has before, that 'it is misleading to take individual happiness as a unit from which the good of mankind can be built up . . . the individual finds his personal welfare by sharing in the life of a well-ordered community' (pp. 92–3). A well-ordered community, to Cunningham, is one which places a high value on personal liberty, provided it is 'the liberty of self-disciplined men'. This, Cunningham says, is the goal of all 'those societies which have the most inherent vitality'.[44] Here Cunningham is at his most optimistic, seeing liberty and self-discipline as allies which, once harnessed to one another, will protect one another. Improved character permits greater liberty; liberty further improves character:

> the morality of those who merely conform to the environment in which they live is somewhat shallow. There is more depth in the character of the man whose habits and conduct are the outcome of his own experience and his own determination; in modern times we desire that the individual should have free play to realise the best that is in him.[45]

Christianity and Social Questions is, more than anything else, an attempt to argue the superior strength of Christian over secular morality. The latter, Cunningham says, is purely negative, no more than a series of externally imposed prohibitions, whereas 'the gospel aims at influencing the inner life and character ... not by mere prohibition, but by holding up an ideal' (p. 183). Consequently, 'Christianity goes far deeper than any social morality, and brings more effective influence to bear upon the personal life.' Thus, for instance, a Christian employer was

> called upon to give his thought and care to ameliorate the conditions and raise the character of the lives of those who are dependent on him – not out of any mere humanitarian sentiment of brotherhood but because this is the duty enjoined by his Master on all who administer any part of His household. (p. 189)

Cunningham's target was precisely those Christians who, in his view, were reducing their religion to a 'mere humanitarian sentiment of brotherhood'; *Christianity and Social Questions* ends with the following warning to 'Avowedly Christian Socialists':

> The methods of social reform which are most in vogue in the present day are non-Christian in character; they do not rely on the effect of holding up a high ideal and on the attraction it exercises on men personally; they aim instead at compelling men to do at least a minimum of duty, and at trying to stamp out evil or hindering men from falling into it. These may be very right and wise things for the State to attempt, and for philanthropists to try and carry out, but they are not specifically Christian ... and though they may be pursued like other secular duties from Christian motives and a Christian spirit, there is, nevertheless, a danger of their being advocated in an unchristian spirit. (pp. 211–12)

Cunningham, then, is asserting the independence of Christian practice and institutionalised social reform from one another; an assertion which is repeated in *Christianity and Politics*: 'The difficulty about Christian principles vanishes if they are regarded not as principles for the organisation of society, but as the basis of personal duty in society; they may furnish us, each and all, with conceptions of what our personal conduct ought to be' (p. 24). The gap between 'personal conduct' and the 'organisation of society' is bridged, however, by Cunningham's belief that, although Christian principles could not be authoritatively invoked in support of specific social reforms, such reforms still could, and should, be approached in a 'Christian spirit'. In fact Cunningham believed that the secular utilitarian reformer, whether the general direction of his proposals was to reduce or to increase the role of the State, was apt to unite the worst respective features of individualism and collectivism. On the one hand, he had to fall back on secular, 'rational' grounds in order to be able to feel, and persuade others to feel, a sense of duty to the community; and Cunningham believed insufficient grounds existed once 'the religious element' was eliminated from politics. On the other hand, it was precisely the lack of a sense of duty to the community which led to the oppression of the individual by the mass. An excessively individualistic society was a selfish society, whose attitudes would even taint its reformers, who would be 'ready to insist with Mr. Birrell,[46] that minorities must suffer, but they will be at pains to see that someone else does the suffering, and that they are not called upon to suffer themselves' (p. 127).

Cunningham, then, used a religious standpoint to attack old and new liberals indiscriminately. On the whole he was far less unsympathetic to socialism (Christian socialism excepted), and he would exert himself to point out matters on which socialists and non-socialists could unite. Thus an article of 1895 hoped that

> avowed socialists will welcome attempts to develop personal responsibility, and thus to strengthen society on that side on which their own system has least to offer; while they may regard the development of private monopolies as a step towards the realisation of their hope of introducing monopoly by the state.[47]

Cunningham, like Ashley in his later years, was in fact a Christian conservative of the 'anything but liberalism' variety. The breed is far from extinct today. But Cunningham and Ashley were the last of the breed to possess a pervasive belief in the possibility and desirability of human progress. Cunningham, unlike many conservatives, invariably uses 'progressive' as a term of approbation.[48]

VIII

In some respects Cunningham was unrepresentative of the historicist challenge to orthodox political economy. On a methodological level, as we have seen, 'A Plea for Pure Theory' placed him in an isolated position within the historical camp. But not too much should be made of this. 'A Plea' is best seen as a methodological aberration. Nothing in Cunningham's previous work leads up to it; and – perhaps because of the criticisms of Ritchie and Hewins – nothing in his subsequent work leads on from it. It is quite true that both before and after 'A Plea', Cunningham engaged in the classificatory overhaul of economic terms which 'A Plea' defined as 'pure theory'. But the results were invariably presented as rather overdue spadework; not as a revolution in economic analysis.

A second respect in which Cunningham stood out from most of his co-historicists was in his lack of enthusiasm for, indeed (at one stage) downright opposition to, the Comtist conception of history. Whereas Ashley claimed that 'the historical school' must 'attempt to discover the laws of social development',[49] Cunningham eschewed the idea of general historical laws and defended 'economic science' against Comtist challenges. Again, however, the distinction between Cunningham and the rest of the historical school was blunted in practice. The latter, to a man, were unwilling to claim that the 'laws of history' could teach any very specific lessons about anything, with the result that Comtist conceptions tended to be wheeled out at irregular intervals to provide pseudo-scientific adornment to a style of historiography little different from Cunningham's.

But Cunningham also distinguished himself from the field by the fierceness and – where Marshall was involved – personal animosity in which his methodological pronouncements were often couched. Whatever historically minded economists in general may have thought of Marshall's inaugural of 1885, most of them seem to have regarded the opening chapters of the *Principles* as a peace offering, not, as Cunningham did, a provocation. Thus Ashley, in his own inaugural at Harvard, said that

> Professor Marshall so clearly realises that the understanding of modern conditions is assisted by a consideration of their genesis that he introduces his work by two chapters on 'The Growth of Free Industry and Enterprise', and by another chapter on 'The Growth of Economic Science.'[50]

And, referring to the previous year's clash between Marshall and Cunningham:

to most of us the recent exchange of hostilities between two distinguished English economists has seemed almost an anachronism.[51]

Indeed the publication, in 1890, of both Marshall's *Principles* and Keynes' *Scope and Method*, was followed by a newly conciliatory spirit on all sides. Edgeworth and Keynes corresponded about the desirability of keeping controversial articles on method out of the *Economic Journal*, while L. L. Price spoke of old quarrels giving way to 'a hearty desire to recognise good work wherever it is to be found, and to an honest endeavour to seek for grounds of agreement rather than reasons for difference'.[52]

For the 'moderates' on his own side Cunningham had words almost as harsh as those he bestowed on Marshall:

in the freer atmosphere of the New World [Ashley] can even allow himself the luxury of bestowing good advice on fellow workers who are forced to engage in controversies on method . . . So long as practical influences exclude those who devote themselves to political economy as an empirical science from taking any part in teaching or writing on modern affairs, the controversy about method is likely to continue.[53]

Cunningham also stood out to some extent for his political views. Almost alone among the heterodox economists of the nineteenth century he was a strong conservative, and one of a peculiarly romantic and anti-rationalistic disposition.[54] Distaste for much of the modern world is sounded more often, and more heartily, than in the works of almost any other economist of the time.

Despite its discomforts and limitations, life in the Middle Ages was so far satisfying that few would have thought it possible or desirable to get away from it altogether; but there are very few in our day who profess to find the conditions of modern life satisfying in any sense at all. (*Christianity and Economic Science*, p. 83)

Cunningham's conservatism was a handicap to his efforts at countering the Marshallian orthodoxy: the most compelling way to oppose the idea of economics as a discipline comparable to the natural sciences was to present it as an adjunct to social reform. And Cunningham's ideology gave a further twist to his contempt for Marshall's methods of writing economic history. The historically intended chapter of the *Principles* caused no offence to those economic historians who surveyed the scene from Marshall's own standpoint of rationalist liberalism. His assertion that the calculating spirit might eventually overcome any weight of habit, prejudice and custom was shared by men such as Thorold Rogers, and indeed Cunningham's attack on Marshall in 'The Perversion of Economic History' was followed by a less personally aggressive, but equally intellectually radical, attack on Rogers.

Yet the ways in which Cunningham typified the historicist challenge are more important than the ways in which he was unrepresentative. In the first place, he sums up and illuminates, better than anyone else, the common elements in the historicist attitude to neoclassical theory. None of the opponents of marginalism had a sufficiently thorough understanding of the nature and significance of the paradigm they attacked. In many cases this was not due to any intellectual inferiority, but simply because they did not value the potential results of marginalism highly enough to acquire a thorough training in it – and a thorough training was the prerequisite for a thorough counter-attack. In Cunningham's case, his unfamiliarity with marginalism led him to underestimate its central role in orthodox economics, and this in turn prevented him from challenging it convincingly. Unlike some of his contemporaries, Cunningham was not particularly late in recognising that marginalism existed, and that 'the final degree of utility' – as he reluctantly called it when he felt he had to be technical – was the cornerstone of a body of theory. But not one of his numerous attacks on what he called 'the new economics' can be interpreted as identifying marginal analysis as its dominant feature. Even his most sustained assault on neoclassicism, contained in the public address he provocatively entitled 'Back to Adam Smith', is immediately followed by the assertion that the 1870s saw 'a still more startling departure' in the theory of economic policy, while elsewhere the decadence of the new economics is largely blamed on – of all people – Cairnes.[55] Cunningham's underestimation of the dominance of marginalism was helped along by the Marshallian custom of translating mathematical insights (many of which could not have originated other than mathematically), into traditional-sounding prose. Even Edgeworth seldom permitted an integral sign above the footnotes. Consequently Cunningham thought himself less alien to the Cambridge tradition than he actually was; and his attempts to channel his opposition to the marginal school into detailed criticisms from a scientific standpoint became patently fumbling. Such criticisms demanded either quite exceptional economic gifts or the assimilation of Marshallian economics as an intimate part of one's own experience. On this depended what A. W. Coats has called in another context 'the analyst's skill both in distinguishing relevant from irrelevant variables and in knowing how far to pursue the implications of a given problem'.

Cunningham's complaints about the ascendancy of a-historical and 'cosmopolitan' economic theorising were also representative of the feelings of the entire historical 'school' – though, again, his aggressive mode of expression often singled him out from his colleagues. Very different was the manner – though not the matter – of Ashley's inaugural lecture as professor of economic history at Harvard in 1893, which contained a long passage giving advice to an imaginary student who wanted to study economics. The study of theory, Ashley told this abstract figure, 'will supply you with points of view which you will afterwards find convenient, and it will introduce you to an interesting chapter of modern thought.'[56] But, summing up, Ashley confessed that he had given this advice 'chiefly from a sense of justice to the man himself in the present state of opinion. Theoretic political economy is still so strong in the support of most teachers in England and America that it would be hardly fair to set a man against the current – especially if his professional prospects as a teacher were at all involved – unless he were in a position to judge for himself.'[57]

Cunningham's differences from other historicists, moreover, emphasise the looseness of the historical grouping among economists – it was, in fact, typical to be untypical. Britain lacked a consciously united historical school with its own articles of faith. At a secondary methodological level, that is in terms of the *proportions* in which they thought the economist should combine induction with deduction, they were divided among themselves. And at the level at which they *were* united – that of basic epistemology – they were also united with the Marshallians. The calm methodological common sense of Mill, and later of Neville Keynes, meant that those with historicist tendencies were denied a dogma distinctive enough to act as a common badge of membership. Nor had they (unlike their German counterparts) a common political platform on which to unite. The strict positivism of Senior and Mill helped British economists to see more clearly than the Germans that different policy decisions do not stem from different methodologies but rather from different value-judgements.

But though a consciously united historical school was lacking, there remained a diversified yet fundamentally homogeneous historicist challenge to Marshallian orthodoxy. It is true that how we perceive it depends rather greatly on which individual economist we are examining at the time. In the hands of Bonamy Price, historicism appears as little more than a last empirical refuge for untheoretically minded individuals left behind by the marginal revolution. Ashley, to whom the terms 'historical economics' and 'economic history' were interchangeable, gave it the responsibility of a pioneering stage in a new academic subject. Cliffe Leslie used it trenchantly as a sharp corrective to what he saw as a tendency to build mountains of analysis on pinpoints of behavioural generalisation and Cunningham, when he was not being purely polemical – and sometimes when he was – used it as the basis of a new theory of economic policy. Yet all had a common emphasis on historical relativism, on factual and statistical thoroughness, on entering unfamiliar territory with an open mind and doing painstaking research before allowing the first tentative inductive generalisations about the human nature of the situation. Their failure to create an orthodoxy to rival Marshall's was to a certain extent due to their lack of a sense of community. But they failed to weaken the Marshallian position even from outsiders' standpoints, and this was because of the thinness of their actual contribution to economics. Little empirical work materialised.

If historicism had had its own Marshall, the story might have been different. But it did not. Few of the historicists desired to create a historical economics even to rival, let alone to supersede, the orthodox version. Most saw themselves, first, as critics of deductive excess and guardians of an empirical tradition which had never quite died out in political economy, and, secondly, as contributors to the emerging discipline of economic history. Ashley's position, however, was rather more complicated than this – as his inaugural lecture at Harvard showed. On the one hand he congratulated the 'historical movement' on having affected 'the character of the teaching of economic theory', and on 'settling down into a channel of its own ... the actual investigation of economic history itself'[58] and suggested that economic theory and economic history should for the next twenty years 'leave one another severely alone and see what will come of it'.[59] On the other hand, he also claimed that Cliffe Leslie and Ingram had failed to achieve their desired transformation of economic science because they had not been radical enough.

> [They] were still so far under the spell of the old discipline as to conceive of economics under the forms made familiar by the manuals. They still had before their eyes the customary rubrics of Production, Distribution and Exchange; they still handled the sacred terms Value, Supply, Demand, Capital, Rent, and the rest – terms which, to use Oliver Wendell Holmes's phrase, were just as much in need of *depolarization* as the terms of theology; they still looked forward to framing 'laws' similar in character, however different in content, to the 'laws' in possession of the field. Aiming, as they unconsciously did, at the construction of a body of general propositions dealing with just the same relations between individuals as the older school had given its attention to, it was natural that they should fall back on the use of that deductive method which is certainly of service for the analysis of modern competitive conditions, although they had begun by unnecessarily rejecting it. And thus the 'methodological' arguments of the orthodox may seem to have gained an easy victory.[60]

Ashley, moreover – in direct contrast to Cunningham – became more, not less, publicly critical of orthodox economics as he grew older. In 'The Present Position of Political Economy', his Presidential Address of 1907 to Section F, he criticised marginal utility theory as superficial and unable to provide answers to the 'things we really want to know'; used Marshall's excursions into 'economic biology' to disparage the static parts of his analysis; expressed regret that 'the criticisms of the historical school have not led, so far, to the creation of a new political economy on historical lines';[61] and abrogated, six years early, the twenty-year separation he had proposed between economic theory and economic history with the warning that 'There is an inclination to regard each as a specialisation unconcerned with the other, and represented by a different expert; or, if sometimes combined in one person, kept in separate compartments of the brain.'[62]

Ashley himself, however, did very little to act on the vision of a historical economics. Cunningham did rather more, despite the fact that in his case the vision was both more intermittent and less precisely formulated. But Cunningham had no real wish to define a movement to change the course of economics, still less a new economic orthodoxy to replace Marshall's, around himself. He had too many other intellectual interests. As an isolate and a polymath, he readily acted the wide-ranging maverick without aspirations to prophetic and diplomatic responsibilities. No obligation to write his own equivalent of the *Principles* troubled him. Instead, he ranged unsystematically through economics, writing and lecturing about whatever interested him at the time. Above all, he was left free to be as polemical as he liked.

Certainly Cunningham's public attack on Marshall should be seen as motivated by a desire to defend the specialised study of economic history rather than a desire to destroy deductive economic theory. His tactical skill cannot altogether be commended: Marshall could hardly acquiesce in the interdisciplinary treaty envisaged in 'A Plea for Pure Theory'. But, prudent or not, Cunningham's tactics were entirely characteristic of the man. Attack was always the best form of defence to the priest who once told his congregation at Great St Mary's that the joys of heaven would be incomplete if they did not include the joy of conflict.

6

Two economic outsiders: Macleod and Crozier

It would not be hard to guess that Henry Dunning Macleod was a barrister. As Smith, Ricardo and Mill go through the witness-box and, under ruthless cross-examination, tie themselves up in self-contradiction, anyone who is meeting them for the first time must surely wonder how they ever came to be taken seriously. By comparison with Macleod, even Cannan's *Theories of Production and Distribution* sounds almost unctuous. And when Macleod is not terrifying the classical economists, he likes nothing better than a monumentally slow dissection with the help of a cloud of friendly witnesses (preferably culled from antiquity) of the precise meaning of various economic terms.

It is, however, Macleod the polemicist who makes the first impact. A barrage of uninterrupted invective beats down upon the reader, page after page; all sensations being relative, we feel the sweetness of respite when, occasionally, overbearing rudeness is throttled back to mere stridency. The hectoring, at first entertaining, soon becomes as wearisome as the hair-splitting. Macleod, taken more than a few pages at a time, is not a very readable writer.

This is a pity. For Macleod has distinctive virtues as well as vices. He introduced a subjective theory of value (though without the key idea of diminishing marginal utility) to England well before Jevons. His analysis of the inconsistencies of classical economists, if erratic, does reveal that he has thought long and hard to arrive at a conception of the scope and nature of economics which is clear, unified, distinctive and at least leads him into less serious inconsistencies than those he exposes. Macleod, at least on occasion, manages to sound like an ideologue convincingly belabouring pragmatists – no small achievement when Ricardo is his victim. But if a conception of the nature of economics were the same thing as a body of analysis, everyone mentioned in this book would rank as a theorist. Macleod's reconstruction of the science of political economy is there, virtually complete, in his first book, *The Theory and Practice of Banking* (1855). In his last book, *The History of Economics* (1896), as in all the intervening ones, the basis for a new science is brought out yet again, still almost in its original state of nature. Why did Macleod encumber it with so little real analysis? Was his conception of the *purpose* of economic writing too legalistic and insufficiently analytical? Or did he merely build a machine which proved impossible to start? Among other things, this chapter will try to give an answer.

Macleod's main strength, however, is as a writer on money and banking. Even here, in fact especially here, the staged definitional clashes between upright classical philosophers and decadent classical economists go on far too long. But his judgements on monetary policy are always sound, while on monetary theory he is both more original and more modern than Marshall. But, just as a school of economic thought gets more critical justice in the end than the individual economist does, so does an economist get more justice overall than his separate works do. Macleod's fate was to be ignored as a monetary economist because of his other limitations. More original than Bagehot, Goschen or Palgrave, he was less highly regarded, and then more quickly forgotten, largely because unlike the above he committed the (by 1870) unforgivable sin of writing outside his range.

He was born in 1821 at Invergordon Castle, Ross and Cromarty; and, after Eton, went up to Trinity College, Cambridge, where he graduated as tenth Senior Optime in 1843. But the previous year he had visited Manchester: the same town, the same year, as Engels made his visit. His impressions of the suffering there were no weaker than Engels': but the remedy he proposed was not communism but free trade.[1] For this cause his enthusiasm never abated, but for ten years it remained the single economic track of his many-tracked mind. Managing the family estate, reorganising pauper relief in Easter Ross, studying to qualify as a barrister, were the tasks of his twenties and early thirties. But in 1854 he was invited to join the directorate of a joint-stock bank. This, he relates, compelled him to go thoroughly into the whole subject of economics. The bank he joined was involved in a lengthy controversy with the Board of Trade. Macleod argued the bank's case to the law officers of the crown, who decided in his favour: 'It was this case which was the origin of the modern science of Economics.'[2] The case, Macleod relates, raised points which were 'perfectly novel', and he thought that existing economists might shed some light on them. So, for the first time, he studied Smith, Ricardo and Mill.

> they were in flat contradiction to themselves and to each other on every single point. In fact, they were in no sense a science, but the butchery of a science. I saw that the greatest opportunity that had come to any man since the days of Galileo had come to me.[3]

Macleod embraced this opportunity with two distinct series of books: general economic treatises and specialised works on money and banking. Since all the former treat monetary economics at some length, and all the latter (except for the brief *Bimetallism*) begin with substantial general economic introductions, the distinction matters less than it might have. In addition, however, Macleod published in 1863 the first volume of an intended dictionary of political economy. Entirely written by Macleod, and published at his own expense, it was, he says, received 'with the warmest approval by the most distinguished foreign economists ... but, of course, the devotees of John Stuart Mill utterly ignored it ... it scarcely paid its expenses, and I did not think it advisable to continue such thankless work'.[4]

So the dictionary only reaches letter C. It does, however, halt more gracefully than the *Elements of Economics*,[5] which actually ends in the middle of a sentence. One can only assume that a three-volume work was planned, and the publishers, with more than two-thirds of the text in hand, put typographical considerations first, thus turning Macleod into a kind of unlyrical economic Schubert.

II

Other economists may have had doubts about the standing of their subject. Macleod had none. 'The Queen of all sciences'[6] was also 'the profoundest and most complicated branch of human knowledge'.[7] The 'noblest and grandest creation of the human intellect'[8] was 'in itself a complete liberal education'.[9] Macleod nowhere says that such eulogies must be limited to the tradition in which he places himself. But his strictures on all alternatives leave this conclusion in little doubt.

Macleod's extravagant praise is based on two root assertions. The first is that economics alone is both a physical and moral science, being 'the only Moral science which is capable of being raised to the rank of an exact science'.[10] Although writing in 1881, Macleod delivers his reasons for this judgement without any hint that he might have heard the historicist controversy:

the same general laws of exchange hold good among all nations, among the rudest and the most civilised in all ages and countries. We find that the same causes are invariably followed by the same effects: and that is the reason why Economics may be raised to the rank of an exact science: a permanent and universal science of the same nature as the physical ones: because it is based upon principles of human nature which are found to be as permanent and universal as those of the physical substances on which the physical sciences are based.[11]

This passage implies that Macleod is ignorant of the historicists, not that he is ignoring them. As will be seen later Macleod, even for an 'outsider', was surprisingly out of touch with developments in and around economics after 1870. Nor were tacit dismissals, however lofty, in Macleod's style.

Macleod's other claim on behalf of economics was that it encompassed a wider range of knowledge than any other subject. His two applications, in 1863 and 1884, for the chair of political economy at Cambridge suggest that he chose its 'necessary' range of knowledge to coincide with his own. Thus, in 1884, Macleod's *Address to the Electors* said:

To reform or advance Economics at the present day it is indispensable to have given many years to the study of the Principles of Natural Philosophy and Mathematics – many years to the study of Law and especially Mercantile Law – many years to the acquisition of practical knowledge in business both agricultural and mercantile – and many years to the diligent and close study of preceding writers, to ascertain how much of their works are true and how much to be rejected – as I have done during the space of thirty years.[12]

While, back in 1863, Macleod the all-rounder had warned off his narrower rivals in a specially written pamphlet:

If any candidate therefore be conscious that he does not possess the knowledge necessary to fulfil the contract which he enters into before the world with the University, and for which he is to receive wages – if he be conscious that he is wholly ignorant of Commercial Law – if he be conscious that he is not thoroughly familiar with the previous history of the science – he should at once retire. Economics is the great rising science of the age, and this Professorship is the grandest scientific prize of the day. Let every man, therefore, reflect deeply and sincerely before he puts out his hand to grasp it ...[13]

The need to be a competent classicist is not mentioned on either occasion. Macleod, however, did tell the electors of 1884 that there was not a single principle in the Pandects of Justinian that was not in his article on credit in his dictionary; this despite the fact that he had written the latter before he had read the former! And knowledge of, and harmony with, the ancients' definitions of economic categories is, to Macleod, a touchstone of economic competence. Whately, rebuked for not realising that *oikos* is Greek not only for a house but for all kinds of property,[14] is then immediately praised for agreeing exactly with 'the unanimous doctrine of the ancients that *exchangeability* is the sole essence and principle of wealth'.[15]

III

Adam Smith is let off relatively lightly by Macleod. Ricardo, however, was 'totally inadequate' for the tasks he set himself in his *Principles of Political Economy*, knowing no classics, no mercantile law and nothing of the organisation of banking. He also made the 'fatal error' of never applying himself properly to mathematics, despite having 'surprising quickness of figures and calculation, somewhat of the genius of the calculating boy, like Mr. Goschen'.[16] But even Ricardo fares better than Mill.

> Every page of [Mill's] work is full of the most glaring ignorance and blunders; and there is scarcely a single point in which he does not contradict himself. Now, in sober seriousness, we must ask how is this more consistent with scientific morality than cheating at cards, or forgery, or issuing base coin.[17]

And when he turns to specific classical doctrines, Macleod's attitude is equally hostile. He denies Adam Smith's contention that the division of labour is stultifying: on the contrary, he claims, simple specialised work is the friend of mental cultivation; instead of confining the mind to the process in hand, it liberates it.[18] The classical distinction between productive and unproductive labour receives ten pages of mockery and caricature.[19] Against the 'iron law of wages' Macleod contends that 'it is not the price of food which regulates wages, but the wages received which indicate the most expensive food the labourer can afford to buy'.[20]

Ricardo's theory of rent is a major target. Macleod says:

> it is *not* the cost of cultivating the worst lands which determines price, but the precise reverse ... it is the average value or price of corn which

determines the worst quality, and most ill-situated land that can be cultivated with a profit, and also decides whether there can be any Rent for it.[21]

Considering that Macleod has spent much of the first volume of the *Elements* stressing the simultaneous determination, by the interaction of cost and utility functions, of output and price, it is surprising that he does not apply his own teaching here. Even more puzzling is his belief that the issue between himself and Ricardo is not logical but empirical. His own assertion that price determines the location of the margin, not the other way round, derives, he says, 'from an intimate knowledge of the action of prices in an agricultural district, and the views of farmers in taking farms'.[22] Then how would the farmers have had to behave, we may ask, for *Ricardo* to have been right? Immediately after all this comes the claim that Ricardo was unaware of the existence of scarcity rent. Macleod seems to be in some confusion.

But his most basic quarrel with the classical economists was over their definition of wealth. Wealth, to Macleod, was anything exchangeable: it thus comprised material things, labour and all exchangeable rights. In ancient Greece and Rome men had been able to see this; not so the Physiocrats who had limited wealth to material things. The classical economists had switched backwards and forwards between right and wrong, sometimes living up to the broad vision of what was wealth, but more often sunk back in the narrow one. Not only was this dual definition of economics' central concept 'totally repugnant to the fundamental principles of Natural Philosophy',[23] but it was the root of most of the other classical inconsistencies. In the realm of value theory, it caused Mill's basic, but false, distinction between values governed by the law of supply and demand and values governed by cost of production. Astronomy might as well say: 'In this class of case the Ptolemaic theory fails us, and we must adopt the other, or Copernican Theory, to supply the Vacancy', commented Macleod.[24] And it was the self-contradictory core of classical economics which had forced its exponents to give up the whole subject of banking 'in hopeless despair'.[25] Let us move on to Macleod's own value and monetary theories.

IV

The Physiocrats, to Macleod, were the 'First School of Economics'. Smith, Ricardo, Say and Mill were the principal members of the

Second School. The Third School, founded by Condillac, included Bastiat – 'the brightest genius who ever adorned the science of Economics'[26] – Whately, Arthur Latham Perry and Macleod himself. Its distinguishing characteristic was the doctrine that 'Demand is the sole Origin, Source and Cause of Value'.[27]

This theory of value, Macleod asserts, prevents mistakes about the nature of wealth. If demand is the only source of value, then whether or not a thing is wealth must also depend on demand. Hence, since things are *exchangeable* when and only when there is a demand for them, the subjective theory of value and the ancients' definition of wealth as exchangeability are logically implied by one another.

Macleod endorses Whately's attack on the labour theory of value, quoting with approval the older economist's contention that men dive for pearls because pearls fetch a high price, not the other way round (*History*, p. 110). That value is subjective, says Macleod, can be seen by the following example:

> A tureen full of train oil would be a great delicacy and highly prized among the Eskimos, but it would probably not have the same value at the Lord Mayor's dinner. (*Elements*, vol. 1, p. 250)

However, when Macleod moves on to the actual determination of particular prices, an exceptionally cumbersome pair of Marshallian scissors is brought out.

> Lord Lauderdale, in a work quoted by Ricardo, says that of two Quantities which may each vary, if we suppose the variation to take place in one of them first, the other remaining the same, its value would be influenced by *four* Causes.
>
> It would Increase in Value –
>
> 1. From a Diminution in Quantity.
> 2. From an Increase in Demand.
>
> It would Diminish in Value –
>
> 1. From an Increase in Quantity.
> 2. From a Diminution in Demand.
>
> Now, as the variation of the other Quantity will be influenced by the very same *four* causes, it is quite clear that the Variations in both Quantities will be influenced by Eight independent causes; and if these be connected in the form of an Algebraical Equation, that will manifestly be the true General Law of Value: or the true General Equation of Economics. This General Equation must manifestly contain the whole science: and as it is in the form of a fraction containing no less than Eight Independent Variables, it at once shows the extremely complicated nature of the science. (*Elements*, vol. 1, p. 257)

This can hardly be described as a handy tool for the logical investigation; and Macleod's apparent lack of interest in sharpening or streamlining it suggests that economic analysis, to him, meant primarily analysis of the meaning of terms.

Macleod's attitude to Jevons and the marginal school is both eccentric and revealing. Macleod stands out as the only living British economist who might have been *passively* swung into fashion by the marginal revolution. He was acutely conscious of his outsider status, and of its relation to his intemperate attacks on Ricardo and Mill. One would expect him to advertise the fact that his conception of value, little more than a deviant curiosity when he began his career, was in line with an authoritative orthodoxy when he ended it. Instead, the *History of Economics* (1896), after introducing Jevons with the words 'We must now notice a writer whose work has attracted considerable attention', treats him as someone too uneducated to be fully appreciative of real originality.

> Jevons says: 'I may here remark that all the writing of Mr Henry Dunning Macleod exhibits a strong tendency to mathematical treatment ... It is not my business to criticise his ingenious views, or to determine how far he has really created a mathematical system.' Jevons' hesitancy to accept my system only arose from his want of knowledge of Jurisprudence and practical business. (p. 156)[28]

Macleod then disposes of Jevons' *Theory of Political Economy* by denying that value depends on utility. This, coming from Macleod, seems a surprising statement until we read on and find that he retains a 'classical' non-subjective meaning for 'utility'. Utility, says Macleod, is 'a quality of an object', value is 'an affection of the mind' (p. 158). Thus, when he attacks Jevons for identifying value with utility, he is attacking him for *not* having a subjective theory of value! That Macleod could publish a statement like this in 1896 is strange, but no more strange than his omission (on this and all other occasions) of any reference to the marginal principle. Whether Macleod actually failed to notice marginalism, or merely ignored it, the implication is much the same. The marginal concept was the cutting-edge of Jevons' subjective value theory. Macleod, alone among the economists of his generation, could have put it to work without having to recant anything. His neglect of it is further testimony to his static and definitional conception of economics. So is his portrayal of Jevons as just another deficient lexicographer who had never worked in a bank.

V

Macleod believed that the principles of monetary theory were matters of pure geometrical demonstration, no more matters of opinion than were 'the proofs of Euclid'.[29] The starting-point was a correct understanding of the nature of debt, and this required a grasp of what Macleod called the 'Theory of Positive and Negative Signs'. A debt, Macleod contended, *was* a negative quantity, but not in the sense that orthodox economists had said it was.

Macleod, here as on other occasions, singled out J. B. Say for especial attack. Say had denied that credit could add anything to the world's resources, asserting that anyone who thought it could must imagine that the same thing could be in two places at the same time. This 'silly sarcasm', said Macleod, had been repeated by 'careless and indolent readers' until it had attained the status of a dogma.[30] But Say was mistaken. The creditor's right to receive was not neutralised by the debtor's duty to pay.

> the whole of the money remains the Debtor's property, which he can sell or exchange as he pleases; and also there is the Property, or Right, in the person of the Creditor, which he can also sell or exchange as he pleases: and which may be sold or exchanged any number of times, till it is paid off and extinguished. Hence in this case there are two Economic Quantities in existence, which may circulate in commerce at the same time. (*Elements*, vol. 1, p. 293)

Hence, said Macleod, the right to receive a future payment should be included in the present wealth of the creditor, but the duty to pay should not be substracted from the present wealth of the debtor. Someone with £500, who has accepted a bill for £50 payable in three months time, has not £450 but £500 coupled with the duty to pay £50 in the future.

This analysis of the nature of debt naturally leads to a denial of any important distinction between money and credit.

> Credit is the Right to demand something from a particular person, and ... Money is a general Right to demand anything from the commercial community. Hence it is clear that Money and Credit are homogeneous quantities, and that Money is the highest and most general form of Credit.[31]

The spectrum of credit, with money at one end, encompassed at the other 'the Purchasing Power of Character'. For 'a man may use his personal Character, Skills, Abilities, Energy and Probity ... for the purpose of purchasing goods, materials etc. by giving a promise to pay in future instead of actual payment in Money, and selling these goods again with a profit ...'[32] Elsewhere, Macleod claims that all credit is capital and all capital is wealth. Indeed, he comes close to stating that all wealth is credit, saying that the possession of a consumer good is a right to consume not essentially different from the right held by the possessor of an I.O.U.

Given Macleod's emphasis on credit, it is unsurprising that he denies any close connection between the price level and the quantity of coins and banknotes.

> the Quantity of Credit which is used in commerce may be approximately estimated at about 50 times the quantity of metallic coin. Hence ... it is the excessive creation of Credit which produces more changes in the price of commodities at the present time than anything else. (*Elements*, vol. 1, p. 192)

Macleod's writing on monetary policy centres on (i) preventing excessive credit creation and (ii) dealing with the consequences if excess credit has nonetheless been created. Although *Theory and Practice of Banking* takes world monetary history as far back as it can go, the effective starting-point for Macleod's analysis is the Bullion Committee of 1810. This committee he praises as having shown two of the three causes of a drain of bullion from the country: national indebtedness and overissue of paper. *Theory and Practice of Banking*, however, adds a third: a rate of discount between any two places which differs by more than the cost of transmitting bullion from one place to another. The importance and originality of this principle, originally put forward in the book's first edition (1856), is emphasised in Macleod's short primer *Elements of Banking* (1876):

> however it might be known among commercial men, [it] had never yet, that we have seen, found its way into any commercial book whatever, and most certainly had never been brought prominently before the public in currency discussions, as a cause of an adverse Exchange wholly irrespective of any indebtedness of the country, or of the state of the paper currency. (p. 215)

And, Macleod continues, once the directors of the Bank of England had grasped the point, the Bank Charter Act of 1844 became redundant. For the Act (which restricted the bank's power of issuing notes to the amount of its bullion reserves plus £14 million) had been but a legislative 'strait waistcoat' necessitated by the directors' persistent failure to prevent the drain of bullion.

Without the strait waistcoat, Macleod said, the bank was free to choose between expanding and restricting credit when there was a commercial crisis. Which policy was right depended on the crisis' cause. Where a drain of gold was caused by an unfavourable exchange rate, retrenchment was the answer. But where it was caused by the demand for gold for domestic purposes, reflecting a temporary failure of confidence, it was right to expand note issues, and wrong to have any regulations to check such an expansion. Indeed such regulations, if they existed, were likely to be abandoned in such a crisis – as had happened in 1847, 1857 and 1867.

VI

Radical critics of 'bourgeois' economics have not yet discovered Macleod. Scenes reminiscent of the California gold rush can be expected when they do. For Macleod was a votary of 'economic man' at his narrowest; a proponent of timeless unchangeable economic laws; a critic of attempts to drag the sphere of production into what was a pure science of exchange; and an intemperate critic of socialism who believed no adequate economist could be anything else. And Macleod's unsparing ridicule of the right to work, and J. B. Clark's hard-working remark about marginal productivity theory can be sent into well-earned retirement. Macleod was almost everything the neoclassical school has ever been accused of being.

Economics, said Macleod, was the study of quantities which possessed the quality of wealth. 'Was', note, not 'should be' – recommendation was not in Macleod's nature. And economics took no notice of any other qualities which these quantities possessed. Above all the economist had no business to go behind or beyond supply and demand curves.

> An Economist, qua Economist, has no more to do with the causes which produce Demand, than an Astronomer, qua Astronomer, has to do with the cause of Gravity. So also an Economist, qua Economist, *has nothing to do with the process of agriculture and manufactures*, any more than the Astronomer, qua Astronomer, has to do with the methods by which the heavenly bodies were formed.[33]

Having thus established that 'economists' who actually looked at how wealth was produced were unprofessional busybodies, it was an easy step for Macleod to dismiss all historical relativism. This he did in a sentence.

The laws of commerce are identically the same today as they were when commerce sprang into being, and they will remain the same to the end of time.[34]

But how does one make sense of the contrast between economics the pinnacle of intellectual endeavour and economics the study of price determination? Did Macleod really think that the study of price determination should be proclaimed sovereign of all mental activities (with his own inauguration at Cambridge as the coronation)? One can only conclude that he did. Yet, as we have seen, he apparently lacked the ambition (and therefore the means) to push this investigation very far. Suppose he had become professor at Cambridge in 1863, with over thirty years' active mental life ahead of him. How would he have filled his time?

Some of it he would have filled by being assertive politically. Not on free trade – the infant economics had already destroyed protection 'like Hercules strangling the serpent in his cradle'.[35] But protection's 'twin' was socialism:

The system of Protection is the right to have remunerative Profits provided for the producer by law out of the means of society – it is the Socialism of Capitalists ... In fact, Protection and Socialism are incompatible with the rights of Property.[36]

And socialism had not yet been strangled, though Macleod, like Marshall, saw economists and socialists, not as overlapping categories, but as heavily unequal combatants.

all Economists have assumed it as a matter of course that the right of private property exists ... Hence we see at once the fundamental distinction between a Socialistic and an Economic State of society.[37]

As had the French socialists in 1848:

[They] knew instinctively that true Economics was their deadly enemy, so they abolished all the chairs of Economics in France.[38]

Macleod, however, admitted that the enemy was within the gates; he denounced the labour theory of value both as 'the foundation of socialism' and as 'the canker and the ruin of English Economics'.[39] Indeed, the doctrine that the working man was the creator of all wealth was 'suicidal'.

Where would working men be without rich men? ... A Capitalist is a man whose business it is to rack his brains to provide work for the working men: and to give them their reward before he gets any for himself: and often, indeed, he gives them their reward and gets none for himself. (*Elements*, p. 214)

Among the notions which socialism had encouraged was the one that the State should provide work for the unemployed. Macleod sneered.

Every man who chooses to adopt the Law as a profession should have a certain number of ten-guinea briefs deposited by the State upon his breakfast-table every morning: every painter should be commissioned to paint endless Madonnas: every sculptor should be employed to produce perpetual Apollos: every author should have a certain number of copies of his work ordered by the State, which criminals might be sentenced to read: every editor should have a certain number of copies of his paper ordered by the State: though it might be somewhat difficult for the State to provide patients for medical men and surgeons at will. (*Elements*, p. 212)

VII

Macleod was always conscious of being an economic outsider. His inability to refrain from quoting anything complimentary said about him – men with far less status as economists than Macleod found their private remarks about him printed in his next book – is an indication of this. His *Address to the Electors*, on the occasion of his second application for the Cambridge chair, said that both he and the electors were aware that there was 'a vast amount of prejudice' against him: prejudice caused by his opposition to economic orthodoxy. On this occasion (though not on any other) Macleod declared himself strictly in accordance with Adam Smith and Ricardo. He was to be set against only Mill: and here 'many persons of distinguished eminence as Professors, and others with the sense of high official responsibility' together with 'the majority of independent thinkers throughout the world', in fact, 'an overwhelming weight of authority', had come down on Macleod's side. Macleod did not repeat his action of 1863, when he had submitted four testimonials relating to his part in the formation of the Easter Ross Poorhouse Union. But neither did he submit a single testimonial from a recognised economist. Instead, there was the assurance (from Macleod) that 'Professor Birks, who was Second Wrangler' thought Macleod was superior to Smith or Mill, and the claim that Clerk Maxwell had 'pointed out several coincidences of thought between his work and mine, and perfectly acknowledged the application of algebraical signs to book-keeping'.

Given Macleod's whole-hearted and inclusive abuse of orthodox economists, it is not surprising that this is the best he could do. Perhaps more surprising are the 'authorities' enlisted on his side in his books. The final word on Ricardo's theory of rent is given to 'the learned Judge, Mr. Justice Byles',[40] The final (and very extended) word refuting the wage-fund theory comes from 'Sir Rupert Kettle, County Court Judge of Worcestershire, a gentleman of great experience and success in adjusting disputes between masters and men'.[41] The implication that, as late as 1886, no one more authoritative than Sir Rupert Kettle could be found to criticise the wage-fund theory indicates either that Macleod would go to considerable lengths to avoid publicly agreeing with any 'established' economist, or that he was strangely out of touch with doctrines not his own. The latter would seem to be the true explanation, given Macleod's attack on Jevons for lacking a subjective theory of value, his failure to signify even once in all his work that he was aware the historical school existed – even his assurance to his readers that 'there is not a single Economist who has seen that a Profit of 5% made in a day is a different Rate of Profit from a Profit of 5% made in a Week, a Month or a Year'.[42] How did he manage to be quite so out of touch? And what is the significance, for our main theme, of the fact that he was? Before answering these questions, let us take in our other 'economic outsiders'.

VIII

John Beattie Crozier came to economics late in life – indeed he only came to it when his publishers, Longmans, suggested he wrote a book about it. Crozier's autobiography tells us that, during the year he spent writing *The Wheel of Wealth*, he read ninety books on political economy. These, Crozier says, might for practical purposes be thinned down to not more than a dozen or so. 'The rest, for any good they were ever likely to do anyone, might have been allowed to sleep on their dusty shelves.' However, Crozier's approved economists are eclectic: 'Smith, Ricardo, Mill, Jevons, Ruskin, Marx, Henry George, Bohm-Bawerk, Gunton, Hobson and Mummery, and Mallock'.[43]

The Wheel of Wealth – and the circumstances under which it was written – shows how far the professionalisation of economics had still to go in 1907. Twenty-two years after Marshall's inauguration as professor at Cambridge, a major publisher seeking a new economic treatise could still approach an elderly doctor who as yet knew no economics at all. For their pains they received an outspoken and eccentric book whose mistakes and misunderstandings can only have tarnished the reputation of the forward-looking ideas it did contain.

In economics Crozier was an amateur who attacked specialists; in medicine he was a specialist who attacked amateurs. He saw no inconsistency in this. Medicine, he said, was the physical science of man, with the principle of evolution unifying it and infusing its every branch. Economics, by contrast, was only *part* of a social science of man, a science of civilisation which had yet to be created, and whose unifying Principle had yet to be discovered. 'Until enough material had been dug out to construct a general science of civilisation', Crozier said, the labours of economic specialists had been 'entirely beneficial, because necessary'.[44] And, once a science was actually founded, economists might return to their specialism, their labours now 'co-ordinated and reduced to harmony'[45] with those of historians, theologians, political scientists, philosophers, psychologists and sociologists. But, currently, when a general science of civilisation was possible but not actual, the specialist economist was comparable to a doctor trying to derive general principles of physiology by pretending a body was all ear or all kidney. 'The Economists ... ignoring alike Morality, History and Sociology, continue to hug all the more closely their pasteboard "economic man"' (*Wheel of Wealth*, p. 18).

These sentiments have a Comtean ring. But in fact Comte, too, was dismissed as a specialist looking for a science of man narrow enough to fit his own restricted concerns. The same went for Hegel, Buckle and Spencer. Thus, said Crozier, it fell to him to dismantle political economy down to its foundations and reconstruct it 'from the point of view of Civilisation as a whole, or General Sociology' (p. 24).

In the meantime, however,

> the old Economy still lives and flourishes in academic haunts, perpetuating itself there from generation to generation, and by its subtle interfusion of politics and political power at every point, infecting the mind of each generation in turn with its fallacies and illusions, like old Theology, so that they neither really believe in it, not yet dare altogether repudiate it. (p. 65)

But outside these academic haunts the story was different. Henry George had 'demolished once and for all' the wage-fund theory and this 'like the removal of a linch-pin or key-stone' had 'heralded the downfall of the orthodox political economy which since his time has so quickly ensued' (p. 52). Orthodox economics was now 'contemptuously rejected by the thoughtful general public as a species of perpetual-motion scheming, useless or utopian' (p. 29).

To Crozier, orthodox economics was characterised by pointless abstractions, useless mathematics and the dressing up of trivial truths in ponderous jargon. This last was Marshall's main contribution to economics; he excelled in

> giving names to super-subtle distinctions which the ordinary businessman takes for granted as truisms and matters of course – such impressive looking abstractions for example as 'Marginal Utility', 'Producers Rent', 'Consumer Rent', 'Composite Supply', 'Quasi-Rent' and the like, most of which ideas I had to use in this volume without giving them these high-sounding names, and so boring the reader by elevating into importance platitudes he already knows. (p. 467)

And mathematical abstraction was consciously used as a 'shield' to protect academic economics from 'the taunts of the vulgar', and to lend it a spurious air of scientific precision (p. 472).

The one charge Crozier does not make against orthodox economics is that of being too circumscribed. On the contrary, he argues that goods produced under conditions of monopoly should be excluded from value theory (p. 404), that the distribution of income is determined by 'extraneous influences which have nothing to do with the Science of Political Economy' (p. 112), even that money 'belongs as much to the province of sociology as it does to that of Political Economy'. Why? Because money is provisional and transitional 'lying as it does between the age of barter, when it was not used, and the millennial state when it will be superseded and no longer wanted' (p. 69).

The anti-historicist implications of the last statement are as extreme as anything in Macleod. The idea that a means of exchange over two thousand years old should be donated to sociology as too transitory to be used by economics is, in a sense, the antipode of Macleod's assertions that very little in economics is historically or geographically relative. But both men end up with an economics from which relativism has been banished. In his emphasis on the indispensability of theory, too, Crozier distanced himself from the historicists, although his explicit target was Carlyle, who did not confront 'a single doctrine of the orthodox Economy with a parallel but opposite one of his own', with the result that 'his diatribes had not the slightest effect'.[46] There follows a long and impassioned account of the book Carlyle could have written, and would have written had he sat down and thought. It sounds identical to Crozier's own.

IX

Much of Crozier's critique of orthodox economics has itself become the ruling orthodoxy today. Every first-year economics student is told that neoclassical economics deals in statics not dynamics, and that its atomistic premisses prevent it from questioning either the social determination of preferences or the distribution of economic power. In 1907, however, to emphasise such points was to be genuinely radical. And Crozier emphasised them at length and with relish.

> these later academic economists . . . propose . . . to shear off at a stroke all the dynamical elements in the problems of a science which is itself purely dynamical and when they have in this way taken the life out of them, to reduce them to their purely statical elements, as in a body after it is dead; the excluded dynamical elements being afterwards allowed for under the innocent looking phrase 'other things being equal'. Now this is to kill your subject first, and add the life afterwards – a hopeless procedure. (*Wheel of Wealth*, p. 441)

And in laying atomistic foundations to economics, the marginalists are to be compared to a man who has ground a brick into dust and then tried to build with it. 'Better by far leave it as a simple brick, and not be too curious as to the nature or composition of its ultimate constituents.' Such an approach has prevented academic economists writing about power: 'The power of landlord over tenant, of capitalist over workman, of the money-lender over the money-borrower – all of which, like loaded dice, give their possessors an advantage in every, the smallest, individual transaction and bargain' (p. 387).

So far Crozier's metaphors are sufficiently under control to help illuminate his meaning. But when he descends to assault particular neoclassical doctrines his imagery soars off, perversely, in the opposite direction, into an airy realm of pure fantasy. Marginal utility theory, with its 'array of mathematical formulae, curves and diagrams' is 'like the apothecary's shop in Romeo and Juliet with its old dried fish-skins, empty boxes, bladders and stuffed alligators "thinly scattered to make up a show"'.[47] Jevons is likened to 'a man with a candle groping about the miscellaneous contents of a cellar';[48] while Carlyle, if as well as being Carlyle he had also been a theorist, would not have been permitted

> any tail-end or 'marginal' pieces of useless No-Rent land, any 'marginal' machines or wage-earners 'eating their heads off' and earning no profits, to make their way into the data of the science, but would have cut them off ruthlessly to start with, as butchers do bits of head and useless carcass, and so have done with them once and for all ...[49]

And, when refuting neoclassical economics is the order of the day, the content can be as remarkable as the language. Crozier on capital: If, as orthodox economists say, the working man is fed, kept and paid out of circulating capital, he cannot be capital himself, for that would be double counting. But if he is not capital and uses capital up, he must be a deduction from the nation's capital: in which case a pestilence or natural calamity would increase the nation's capital (pp. 58–60). On the alleged tendency of rates of profit to equality in all industries: this is refuted in agriculture by differential rent of land, and in industry by the fact that profits '[roll] themselves up like snowballs as the capital increases' (p. 441). On Marx: an economist of some ability, who, however, neglected economic dynamics (p. 491).

Crozier, then, was a magnificently bad economist. Taking style and content together, it is not going too far to call him the William McGonogall of economics. So far, however, we have only considered him as a critic of other men's ideas. What were his own? What was the 'Wheel of Wealth'?

Crozier was an underconsumptionist, and a wheel was the analogy which he used to emphasise the interdependence of production and consumption. (Crozier claimed this was more than an analogy: presumably his definition of 'analogy', like so much else, was idiosyncratic.) Producers threw goods onto the wheel; consumers, standing on the other side, took them off. Check the wheel on either side, Crozier said, and, obviously, the whole mechanism will slow down. Orthodox economists could not see this because they could not see the wheel; instead, they saw 'a rod or stick of wealth, whose increase will depend on as little as possible being cut off its end for consumption at each remove'. This was why they mistook the nature and functions of saving. Savings, said Crozier, did not come out of production. 'They come, like the sparks thrown off a grindstone, from a continuously revolving double-sided wheel of production *and* consumption, where what is produced must be consumed (not saved) before the saving can emerge' (p. 45). Crozier, then, is attacking the orthodox view that an increase in saving can only be achieved by an equivalent reduction in consumption. But is he actually saying that an increase in consumption will lead to an equal increase in saving, or merely that consumption and saving are positively related? We are not given any clue more pointed than the passage above.

Crozier's underconsumptionist theory is similar to, but much less carefully explained than, Hobson's. Indeed he is apt to quote Hobson's name and assert his conclusions as a substitute for direct analysis.[50] And, like Hobson, Crozier struggles impaled on his failure to distinguish between saving and hoarding. The following, for instance, is intended as an attack on *saving*: 'If all the world turned misers, the wealth of today . . . would in ten years, say, have reduced itself for each individual to a piece of prairie land, a potato patch, a wigwam, and a bear's skin' (*Wheel of Wealth*, p. 115).

Crozier's one major difference from Hobson is on the issue of protection. Indeed Crozier claims that it is because Hobson prefers, for the economy, the simile of an animal body (thus *The Physiology of Industry*) and he, Crozier, prefers that of a wheel, that they end up on different sides of the protection controversy. Since Crozier's account of the issue is notably unrelated to his general view of the economy, it is hard to assess this claim.

Crozier paints with a broad brush. Sometimes he does so defiantly, as if to pre-empt any critical notice of the lack of analytical nicety.

> [Price is determined by] the pace with which quantities of commodities are thrown on the wheel and taken off again at any given point of time . . . [To go further into analysis would be] to focus your subject matter too microscopically for the purpose of a science of Political Economy. (p. 413)

The political and ideological judgements, too, are uncomplicated and liable to be tinged with defiance. Crozier was no nostalgic reactionary; indeed his apparent lack of any strong preference for the actual over the ideal makes it difficult even to classify him as a conservative. But he does have the twentieth-century conservative's confidence that the tide has just begun to turn against liberalism, against (in this case) 'laissez-faire, abstract liberty and equality, the sovereignty of the ballot box and universal suffrage, negro franchise, Utilitarianism, scientific materialism, and the sovereignty everywhere of *abstract* instead of *concrete* ideals'.[51] Only a man of strongly conservative cast of mind would put *laissez-faire* and Negro franchise on the same list. There is no generalised discussion of capitalism (though there is a generalised attack on socialism – Crozier voices the highly original sentiment that it would kill the goose that lays the golden eggs). But entrepreneurs are criticised, and so is Walker for praising them. 'Had he read, as I have recently done, the inner history of the Standard Oil Company, he would have perceived to what set of poor tricksters, inflated into greatness by his own imagination, he had given not only the nominal, but the real primacy of the industrial world.'[52] And Marshall is attacked for giving the rich comfort and legitimising their wealth; his doctrine that labour and capital are substituted for one another as relative prices change is

> a most comforting doctrine for the Rockefellers and Astors of the world, inasmuch as it gives them assurance that however colossal their fortunes may be, they at least have earned them; and however much appearance the labourer may have of being 'sweated' what he is paid is really all that he has earned.[53]

But, though Crozier doubts not that workers are exploited, the truth, he says, is that 'they must forever be exploited in greater or less degree by their own incapacity, ignorance and delusions'.[54] And his complaints about 'millions spent ... on the education of millions whose combined heads no education will enable to turn out a product equal to that of half-a-dozen really great minds'[55] casts some slight shadow of doubt on his sympathy with working-class aspirations.

X

Crozier is an enjoyable writer. Nicholson sneered at his style and the length of his sentences, but Crozier as a writer has twice Nicholson's vitality (and twenty times Marshall's). And whatever his shortcomings as an economist, his central conception – the wheel of wealth – today opens the macroeconomic half of the best-selling British economics text book of all time.[56] With Keynesian (or, if you prefer, Friedmanite) hindsight, we know now that a rise in consumption can, depending on what caused it, lead to either a rise or a fall in savings; Crozier's insistence that it always caused a rise is thus no more misguided than the orthodox belief that it always caused a fall. This does not make Crozier a good economist: his main significance lies in the fact that so bad an economist could get published at all. Economic professionalisation in 1907 had reached an intermediate stage where you could be further outside the pale than ever before or since. We have been travelling away from the pale for the last four chapters; and we have been travelling away from good economics. Marshall was a better economist than Cannan or Nicholson. They were better economists than Cunningham; Cunningham was better than Crozier. It may be argued that our criteria of good economics are Marshallian, and hence the correlation between being a good economist and being near the centre of Marshall's clinging cobweb is a tautology. To protest our own lack of enthusiasm for neoclassicism would be an answer of sorts. To abandon all talk of good and bad economists would be another kind of answer; but this would inevitably lead, sooner rather than later, to a simple assertion of the very point which ought to be proved or disproved in court – that Marshallian orthodoxy ruled economics independently of merit. The only satisfactory thing to say is that it is hard to envisage a set of criteria in which the order of competence given above would be changed. Cannan, as an economic theorist, can only be classified as a less acute version of Marshall: Nicholson as a more 'classical' version who offered an alternative form of moral uplift. Cunningham was certainly a better historian than any Marshallian gave sign of capacity for being: but even those who see historical sense and historical knowledge as the economist's most precious possession must recognise that Cunningham was writing programmes for a historical economics rather than historical economics proper.

But we are forgetting Macleod, who cannot be placed in the basement with Crozier, but upon whom orthodoxy impinged even less. Crozier may have attacked the orthodox position with (at times) very bad arguments. He may have misunderstood the nature of particular orthodox doctrines. But Macleod's misunderstanding of the nature of the whole neoclassical school of thought has a sweep and grandeur missing from Crozier's pedestrian blunders. How did an often acute economist go so wrong? Macleod's writings, which pile on the pugnacity until an abusive apotheosis is reached in his last book, certainly convey a man whose isolation and obstinacy are feeding on each other and slowly suffocating everything else. But it is doubtful whether a purely psychological explanation will do. Crozier picked the right time for being outside the pale. Macleod picked the right time for being out of touch. Any earlier, and there would have been nothing so definite, self-conscious and weighty to be out of touch with; any later, and, even to be an economic outsider, he would have had to be a trained economist.

Macleod, then, is a partial exception to the tendency of ability and orthodoxy to correlate with one another. Yet in another sense, that illogical pharase 'the exception which proves the rule' is for once appropriate here. For the one outsider we have seen so far who seems to have had the ability to fight neoclassicism, had he drawn close enough to see what it was, is also the one outsider who, fundamentally, was not really heterodox at all. Deductive, whiggish, static and – at least in spirit – mathematical, he stands out as three-quarters caricature, one-quarter critic, of economics' ruling faction. For a real and unmistakable exception to the rule, we must look at Hobson.

7

Hobson's choice

J. A. Hobson is best known today as an underconsumptionist predecessor of Keynes, and as a critic of imperialism. In the former of these two roles, especially, he is of major relevance to the theme of this book. *The Physiology of Industry* (1889), written jointly with the businessman and mountaineer A. F. Mummery, was the ideal book at the ideal time to launch a career as an economic pariah. Its uncompromising transformation of thrift from a moral and economic good to a threat to work and wealth struck at both halves of the coalition of science and virtue currently, and laboriously, being sculpted into 'Marshallian economics'. Retribution was immediate. The London Extension Board refused to allow Hobson to lecture on political economy. The Charity Organisation Society withdrew Hobson's existing invitation to lecture. Hobson was never to hold an academic post, or be elected to the Political Economy Club, or (until old age) hear anything but the most occasional, half-hearted and condescending praise from more respectable economists.

To present Hobson, however, as a man whose career was blighted purely by heresy, let alone one single heresy, would be too simple. Even the writer who has made the handsomest posthumous amends to Hobson believes that 'he would in any case have been lucky to establish himself as an academic economist in view of the sheer lack of rigour or respect for academic standards in much of his work'.[1] This is fair comment, and, as an explanation of Hobson's low professional standing, it is especially relevant as regards his periodic assaults on neoclassical welfare economics. For whereas his underconsumptionist writings were apt to be thrown scornfully aside after a rapid check to make sure that he had not yet been seduced into sense (so that, paradoxically, much faulty analysis went uncriticised), his works on social welfare were seen as good sociology even in quarters which rejected their economics. There was, therefore, a sympathetic and interested response to books such as *The Social Problem* (1901), *Work and Wealth* (1914) and *Wealth and Life* (1929).

Consequently Hobson's contributions to welfare economics – though neither then nor now the main source of his fame – were, for good or ill, particularly important in placing him in the context of the emerging economics profession; this chapter will therefore focus primarily on Hobson the welfare economist. There are a number of other reasons for doing this. First, the fact that developments in welfare economics in general are especially relevant to the professionalisation of the subject as a whole. This will be argued formally in the next section of the book, but it is hoped that some evidence for the contention will emerge in the present chapter. Secondly, despite the Hobson boom of recent years, his welfare economics has so far received little attention. Last and most important, nowhere else are the main features of Hobson's thought – the influence of Ruskin, the evolutionist tendency, the sense that society is an organism, the critique of classical and neoclassical economics, and the quest for a supra-individual valuation of goods and activities – so comprehensively displayed. This chapter will first sketch Hobson's intellectual pedigree, then take a direct look at his welfare economics and finally examine the latter's relationship to his general view of society.

II

Hobson's three biographies, *John Ruskin, Social Reformer* (1898), *Veblen* (1936) and *L. T. Hobhouse* (1932, with Morris Ginsberg) acknowledge his three main intellectual debts. From Hobhouse he derived much of his institutionalism – Hobhouse's political philosophy exists to ask what institutions will reconcile freedom and order, by encouraging people to fulfil themselves in ways which will maintain a stable yet progressive society. In pursuing the answer to this question Hobson, like Hobhouse, pictured society as a living, evolving organism. Its goal was an organic harmony sustained by, and sustaining in collective reasonableness, a people whose mutual respect and sensible exercises of freedom together generated peace and stability. The means of this goal was the evolutionary process by which reason displaced instinct as a guiding force; and the sociologist, the economist, the reformer and the statesman were all there to help this process along where possible. Evolutionism is never far away in Hobson's economic writings; and it is as great a reconciler in his economics as in Marshall's. Indeed in Hobson's case it is no mere methodological convenience of minor substantive import, but a vital criterion by which to judge, in terms of the ultimate good, the claims, where they competed, of immediate order and immediate liberty.

Veblen's influence on Hobson can be left to reveal itself in the course of this chapter. Ruskin's – the earliest of the three influences – had better be taken now. There was much of Ruskin that Hobson rejected. The younger man's enthusiasm for evolutionism (detested by Ruskin) opposed him to Ruskin's static, utopian and historically absolute model of good society. Hobson was equally opposed to Ruskin's designation of a political elite as the source of social reason. In Ruskin's world, the men of reason owed it to the mass to try and adjust its values to the requirements of the ideal society. They discharged this responsibility by philanthropy, by setting an example of good conduct and if necessary by coercion. In Hobson's view the first of these 'duties' generally did more harm than good (indeed *Work and Wealth* argues that conspicuous consumption is almost innocuous compared with organised charity), the second might come from social change but would never initiate it and the third was likely to take misguided forms even if exercised in a totally disinterested spirit (which he thought improbable).

These political differences between the two men led to two important economic ones. In the first place, Ruskin's rejection of evolutionary ideas lead to the value theory of *Unto this Last* (1860), with its assertion that utilities were eternal and immutable. Of this claim Hobson commented that 'the value of anything may vary infinitely according to the stage of development an individual or a society has reached'. Secondly, this same relativistic belief of Hobson's coupled with his postulation of, and respect for, sound social instincts of valuation linked his 'human standard' of value to his political thought in a way that Ruskin's was not.

But the differences are less important than the similarities. Hobson enthusiastically adopted Ruskin's axiom that 'There is no Wealth but Life.' From *The Evolution of Modern Capitalism* (1894) through to *Confessions of an Economic Heretic* (1938) he consistently attacked classical and neoclassical economics for failing to take a 'human view', for its blindness to the harm done by some 'goods', the demeaning and dehumanising tasks which millions were expected to carry out and the waste and oppression resulting from the existing distribution of wealth. Ruskin, Hobson's biography proclaimed, had seen all this; he had, in 'truly scientific' style, reduced the concepts of money-measured cost and utility to terms of human effort and use. And whatever Ruskin's mistakes, Hobson continued, orthodox economists were hardly in a position to criticise him.

> It has been humorous to hear the dull drudges of commercial economics speaking contemptuously of an economist whose logic is far keener than their own, and whose work will hereafter be recognised as the first serious attempt in England to establish a scientific basis of economic study from the social standpoint. (*John Ruskin*, p. 121)

III

Hobson, like Marshall, saw evolution in terms of reason displacing instinct and habit. By reason, however, he did not mean what Marshall meant. To Marshall, reason signified the calculating habit of thought buried somewhere in every individual, and his welfare economics embodied this judgement both in a positive and in a normative sense. Its methodological basis was a group of unconnected individuals each satisfying a given set of tastes with maximum efficiency, and its declared objective was to locate that output and distribution which would raise as many people, as soon as possible, into this desirable state of consciousness. Most of Marshall's followers implicitly or explicitly shared his conviction that the economist's task was to assist the once-and-for-all liberation, by material prosperity, of the working man from the grasp of custom, ignorance and prejudice.

Hobson's attitude to the question of reason in economic life is more complicated. When he is speaking, for instance, about the effect of industrialisation on man's mental habits, he sounds very like Marshall.

> It appears to have done more to rationalise and to socialise men than all the higher and more spiritual institutions of man, so far as such comparisons are possible. It has rationalised man chiefly by compelling him to exercise foresight and forethought, to subdue his will and train his active faculties to the performance of long and intrinsically disagreeable tasks, in order to realise some more and more distant object of desire, and by obliging him to recognise the vigorous laws of causation in his calculation.[2]

But such mechanical processes are the only aspect of human life which Hobson deems amenable to purely quantitative, inorganic scientific generalisation. In general, his definition of economic rationality is broader and vaguer. As in Marshall, the criterion is the increase of wealth. But to Hobson the increase of wealth is a matter for art rather than science. As has already been said, he adopted, wholesale, Ruskin's dictum 'There is no Wealth but Life.' And even if one holds that this criterion permits fairly easy identification of a simple increase in wealth, it certainly makes a welfare judgement between two potential and mutally exclusive increases likely to be very difficult. Which of the two will do most to increase the fullness of Life for the most people? And who is qualified to be the judge? Hobson's answer to the second question is the 'social mind', on which he relied both to instil rationality into the valuations of producers and consumers, and to advise his own valuation as an economist.

To Hobson, the social mind is the ultimate arbiter of social welfare, its decisiveness coming from the similarity of individual minds. The illusion that human valuations differ greatly exists only because dissimilarities interest men more than uniformities. And while Hobson sees an 'intelligently ordered community' as one which will 'allow for eccentricities of personal valuations outside the general agreement and conventions', such valuations are secondary, relatively risky and often wilfully perverse.[3]

But the social mind also operates at a more fundamental level than that of discrete economic valuations. Society 'operates through an equipment of instinctive channels towards its own survival and development and the survival and development of its species' (*Work and Wealth*, p. 352). Hobson's collective name for these instinctive channels is the 'general will'.

> This general will . . . urging the individuals to the fulfilment of a purpose that is but slightly theirs, and is not mainly that of the existing generation, but which embodies the general purpose of the species or some wider purpose of a still larger organic whole, can only be realised for thought and feeling as a single current of will implying and conferring unity of life upon the species or the larger unity . . . [It] remains what it was in primitive tribal life, an organic instinct. (pp. 352–3)

Advancing reason fortified all this, improving the individual's understanding of the way the wider organism works, bringing his thoughts and feelings 'into vital communion . . . with the thoughts and feelings of the race, of humanity, perhaps of the larger organic being of the kosmos' (p. 356). This process – like all evolutionary processes – is an interactive one: as sociability comes increasingly to be the prime criterion of survival, a rational order develops which itself helps to further this. Men come gradually to realise that they possess deeply sociable instincts which must be satisfied even if the immediate consequences are individually irksome. This is not only a key to Hobson's identification of individual fulfilment with social order, but also gives him a more satisfactory definition of economic rationality, allowing it to recognise actions neither obviously self-interested nor, in his view, fundamentally altruistic.

> each man's fair contribution to the routine labour of the world, though irksome to him, is not injurious but serviceable to his 'human nature'. Thus interpreted, it stands on the utility, not the cost, side of his account... He is a social being and this social nature demands recognition and expression in economic processes. (p. 360)

This is the main function of the general will in economic life: to transform personal egoism and inertia into a corporate spirit of industrial mutual aid.

The trouble with Hobson's argument is that his identification of the socially conventional with the collectively desirable is an assumption and not a proof. Indeed he openly excuses himself from having to assess the standards of rationality achieved by social valuation:

> How far instinctive dispositions, how far some 'common sense', how far reason, respectively, are instrumental in this harmony, is a question that need not here further concern us. If we prefer, we may say that Nature, working through these channels, provides for human welfare. (*Wealth and Life*, p. 57)

This last assertion surely requires of Hobson that he first give logically independent definitions of nature and human welfare, and then show how the unfolding plans of the one conduce to the other. He does neither, hence the statement that nature provides for human welfare is tautologous. Tautological axioms, however, are sometimes justified by their results. How good the reasons are for this one, we cannot judge until we have seen it in action.

IV

Hobson's conception of the individual and social organisms, together with his definition of reason in economic life, leads on to his attack on the foundations of marginalism. His individual producer and consumer, like Marshall's, are abstractions from reality, wanting only to increase their wealth. It is the definition of wealth that differs. And because, in Hobson's view, the individual's wealth is something unquantifiable and indivisible, he is not being rational if he loses sight of this totality and starts trading-off isolated satisfactions at the margin. Hobsonian man, in other words, consciously aims at a particular standard of life, and sees the expenditure of his income as an integrated pattern by which to reach this grand design. In what sense, we must ask, does this involve the principle of maximisation?

In the last chapter of *Work and Wealth*, Hobson enlarges on his theory of consumer behaviour by means of analogy. An artist painting a picture, or a cook baking a cake, he points out, are not guided by the desire to equalise the benefit from the last strokes of red paint and green, or from the last egg and the last spoonful of flour. Each has a complete and indivisible conception of what he wants to create, and the ingredients are seen, not as commensurable quantities, but as essentials for the attainment of a particular overall quality. The same applies to a complete life:

> So far as I act like a free, rational being, not a creature of blind custom and routine, I employ all my personal resources of knowledge, taste, affection, energy, time and command of material resources, in trying to realise my ideal of a good or desirable life. (p. 333)

But it may be argued against Hobson that whether or not an individual has a clear ideal of a desirable life is irrelevant. As long as scarcity exists, then, however complex the interdependence of costs and utilities (and this is all that Hobson is speaking of when he refers to the *individual* as an economic organism) he will take priorities on the basis of what will least harm his overall standard of living if foregone. This is simple utilitarian welfare maximisation; it is only the task before the consumer that Hobson has complicated.

Hobson himself admits, moreover, that his psychology still involves the idea of marginal equivalence:

> it is quite true that the delicacy of the culinary art will in fact be displayed in deciding whether to put in another handful of raisins, another egg, or a spoonful more sugar . . . so far as an economical use is made of materials or means of any kind for the attainment of any end this marginal equivalence is *implied*. The scientific analysis of any composite arrangement, mechanical, organic, conscious, *involves* this marginal assumption. It is an axiom of all economy whatsoever. (*Work and Wealth*, p. 332)

Any pattern of behaviour which logically implies the marginal value equivalence of different means must surely be interpreted as an attempt to maximise something. But what Hobson's theory of economic behaviour does rule out, he claims, is the notion that there is any 'special importance or causal determination' attached to a marginal unit of anything; that is, that the principle of marginal equivalence can be used to 'explain' consumer behaviour. This is true. It is not, however, a valid objection to marginal utility theory, because marginal utility theory has never claimed anything different. Jevons' theory of consumer behaviour has an identical structure to Hobson's. Both postulate a central behavioural principle which implies (1) a particular pattern of expenditure; (2) a form of marginal equivalence. In both systems the second implication *characterises* the first; in neither does it seek to explain it.

Hobson's other main criticism of the marginal principle is that it assumes 'that the human mind can and does get rid of qualitative differences by referring them to a quantitative standard' (*Work and Wealth*, p. 333). But, once again, this charge fits marginalism only in the sense in which it also fits Hobson's own thought. What marginalism in fact assumes is that the mind has a rough ordinal standard of strength by which to compare its desires, and that two desires of different ethical or spiritual quality can nonetheless be said to be felt equally strongly. It asserts that the human mind does not *need* to get rid of qualitative differences because, for certain purposes, the economist can compare intensities and ignore qualities of feeling. Hobson nowhere makes out a case that this is not so. He is mildly sarcastic about the proposition that if he has 7s 6d and gives 5s to the Famine Fund and buys a 2s 6d ticket for a concert, then he has 'performed the very delicate spiritual operation of reducing my humanitarian feelings to common terms with my love of music, and to have struck the balance ...'[4] But he does not actually deny that some such mental operation is performed; and in the earlier *John Ruskin, Social Reformer* he flatly asserts that it is: 'It must be at once conceded that we can and habitually do make comparisons of desires widely differing in kind and degree by reference to money ...' (p. 60).

Thus Hobson's organic conception of welfare leaves intact the basic premisses of orthodox welfare economics; nor does it destroy the legitimacy of quantitative methods. It is a pity that he chose to present it as a strictly logical attack on neoclassicism's theoretical foundations; for his practical and ethical indictment of what marginalism implied and failed to imply left his fellow critics standing. That this was so, however, owed nothing to ideas of indivisibility – whether of collective standards, social structures or individual satisfactions. What was so productive was Hobson's careful working-out of the forms of mutual dependence and suggestion between individuals who nonetheless felt and thought separately, and his conclusions as to which of these resulted in mutual benefit, which in social exploitation and which in all-round waste.

V

Work and Wealth begins with some sharp criticisms of the idea that all labour should be treated as cost and all consumption as utility. Such criticisms were not new. Heterodox economists had long attacked the classical stereotype of man as totally idle and covetous, pointing to the pleasure inherent in moderate and suitable work. Ruskin made much of it in *Unto this Last* and later in *Munera Pulveris*; Smart even claimed that man 'lives the only life worth living *while* he works' and complained of 'a tradition which looks on labour as a primal curse'.

> To speak of the labour of the merchant, the employer, the farmer – of any one, in fact, who has reasonable hours, who has some pride in his work, and who has some object in it – as 'pain', is, in my view, a serious abuse of language.[5]

But the sharpest and most constructive critic of the 'work is pain' equation was Thorstein Veblen, who attacked its proponents not for contemporary inaccuracy – he thought the axiom was all too sadly correct for most people – but for lack of concern about why work had become drudgery and what could be done about it. Thus *The Instinct of Workmanship* indicted the machine age for suppressing men's need to shape and control their work by means of personal skill and artistry, and attacked orthodox economics for a methodology which perforce omitted this loss.

Hobson's intellectual debt to Veblen is revealed in his biographical study of his work. His own message was a dual one. First, he listed the kinds of pleasure derived from different kinds of work. *Work and Wealth* suggests that the human cost incurred by artists and inventors alike is negative. Even work for an employer may have positive utility 'where it belongs to genuine education or apprenticeship, or where there is close sympathy and mutual understanding between superior and subordinate' (p. 53). But where the worker is merely the tool of his master, the enforced subservience of his mind and will will be a heavier cost to him than the physical effort of his labour. On behalf of the great majority of the working class, Hobson argues vigorously and with feeling, making a long excursion into industrial sociology to diagnose the main sources of human cost as repetitiveness of work, loss of freedom and initiative due to division of labour, and the machine worker's inability to appreciate the social utility of his labour.

Secondly, Hobson drew on Veblen's work to argue that an industrial system which denied the 'pleasure bonus' inherent in all actions which possessed survival value was undermining its own constructive evolution. The short sketch of the origins of industry which forms the second chapter of *Work and Wealth* is intended to show that every rudimentary craft displays 'the promptings of vital utility laying the foundations of an economy of efforts and satisfactions which furthers the organic development of the individual and the race'; and that the evolutionary impulse has benevolently entwined distinctively economic motives with 'other motives and activities, sportive, artistic, religious, social and political'.

Hobson's study of consumption, drawing analogous classifications and the same evolutionary message, is by far the most elaborate and scientifically framed of all attempts at a radical alternative to conventional welfare economics. He assaults the one-sidedness of the classical and neoclassical schools alike in concentrating wholly on the science of production and neglecting that of consumption: 'When the products of industry pass over the retail counter, economic science almost entirely loses count of them. They pass from sight into the mysterious maw of the consumer' (p. 6).

Hobson holds this omission to invalidate orthodox economics from top to bottom. In *Work and Wealth* he lists 'a large proportion of stimulants and drugs', bad literature, bad art, bad recreations and the services of prostitutes and flunkeys as glaring examples of the kind of 'utility' which is injurious to society and to the individual consumer alike; while *Wealth and Life* takes the neoclassical school to task for relying on the rationality of the consumer in all circumstances to justify their approach. To restore the balance between the two sides, we need a census of consumption 'comparable in volume of information and degree of reliability with the best modern census of production'; and economics must also distinguish between 'changes in standards of consumption initiated by individual consumers and extended by imitation, and changes brought about from the producer's side by businessmen through advertisement and salesmanship' (p. 310).

Next, Hobson shows that a human valuation of production and consumption must take account of their interdependence both within the individual and between individuals. Conceding that orthodox economists have not wholly ignored the fact of complementarity in consumption, he explains the neglect of its obverse in the field of production:

> the division of labour has, however, gone so far in modern industry as to obscure what should be the equal significance of a human standard of production; a varied day's work should by its organic composition reduce the total disutility and incorporate elements of positive utility.[6]

But at least as important is the interaction *between* production and consumption. On a man's work, its duration, amount of physical and mental effort and its ability to stimulate his mind and fire his enthusiasm, depends his capacity to enjoy his wealth (and in this respect, too little work can impoverish, just as too much can). In particular, Hobson says that increasingly specialised and mechanical work has its dangers at a time of increasingly complex consumption.

> The Organic Law presses here insistently. It would be going too far, doubtless, to assert that he who can produce one thing can only consume one thing. But everyone familiar with the finer arts of consumption will admit that a consumer who is utterly unskilled in the production of these goods cannot extract from their consumption the full enjoyment or utility which they contain. (*Work and Wealth*, p. 237)

Conversely, the conditions of consumption (amount of leisure, skill in using commodities etc.) will make a given working day easier or more difficult.

VI

To express business costs in terms of human costs, the economist must know three things: the human efforts involved, the capacities of those who make these efforts, and the distribution of effort among them. This last factor, Hobson suggests, has been neglected by industrialists and economists alike – there is no general awareness even of the current *monetary* costs of imposing so many unequal burdens on workers with equal capacity to bear them or vice versa, or of distributing the burden so unequally in time over the same set of workers. Conventional welfare economics scarcely even tried to examine this question, far less attempted to translate it into terms of human toil. Because this particular charge is pressed most heavily against A. C. Pigou, we must now briefly anticipate his main appearance in chapter 8.

'The strongest and most serviceable part of Dr. Pigou's analysis', noted Hobson in 1926, was his demonstration that economic welfare increases with a more even distribution of consumable goods. Why did he not do the same for the distribution of productive effort? Hobson sees a mysterious mental barrier, but finds a clue to its nature in 'the curious treatment of "costs" which has crept into the Cambridge doctrine, formerly confined to the theory of free trade'.[7]

Let us look more closely at Hobson's objection to the idea of opportunity cost. 'The doctrine that the real cost of anything is the foregone utility of other things', he claims, 'perversely rules out all human considerations related to the supply side of exchange, by substituting an indirect and strictly irrelevant test for a direct and relevant one.'[8] This is clear enough. But things become obscure when we take it side by side with the accusation, made two pages previously in the same work, that in Pigou's terms 'economic welfare is ... confined to utilities or satisfactions of consumption'.[9] The correct method of assessment, Hobson says, is to take the total stock of goods and subtract the net dissatisfaction attending its production from the total satisfaction which it affords in consumption.

The point is that Pigou's method and Hobson's are formally identical and indicate the same optimum, *provided* that in the former we go beyond the Walrasian General Optimum and equalise marginal utility of income between consumers as well, and provided that we also include leisure as a commodity (purchased by foregoing income). Then:

(1) Each individual's marginal utility for one time-unit of leisure (which necessarily equals his marginal disutility for one time-unit of work) divided by the monetary reward for one time-unit of work, will equal his marginal utility of income. Hence he will be maximising his personal surplus in the Hobsonian sense.

(2) All individuals, enjoying the same marginal utility of income, will be subject to the same marginal disutility of work. Hence there is no way of increasing the *social* surplus of utilities over efforts by adjustments at the margin.

But did Hobson see this identity or not? His criticism of the 'Cambridge doctrine' can be interpreted in two ways. It could indicate that he entirely misunderstood Pigou, and believed his formulation of the problem to omit half the facts by ignoring costs altogether. Or it could merely accuse Pigou of adopting a euphemistic circumlocution which pushed real human pains, and in particular their alarmingly uneven distribution, out of sight.

Either way, however, *Free Thought in the Social Sciences* makes it clear that Hobson disliked the opportunity-cost theory, not so much because he distrusted the psychological assumptions of the marginalists, but rather because he wanted welfare economics to demand, and help to guide, immediate social reform. And, clearly, Hobson's formulation of the problem of optimisation was very much more direct in its social implications. It was not so much that the Walrasian General Optimum caused – or permitted – many economists to forget about its relativity to a particular distribution, and of the possibility that a non-optimal situation might give more total welfare than an optimal but distributively inferior one. Rather he charged that, even if urgently aware of the importance of distribution and willing to make value-judgements about it, the orthodox welfare economist must still make certain omissions which together crippled the value of his work:

(a) By failing to emphasise the positive utility of moderate labour, and instead focusing his attention on the point at which the wage rate is just insufficient to call forth more work, he blurs the crucial distinction between that labour which wholly benefits the individual and social organisms alike, and that which may well do both of them damage.

(b) He may flatly assume total rationality on the consumer's part, may add the afterthought that this should not be taken for granted or may even give a list of examples of harmful consumption. But his power to demonstrate the social causes of malconsumption and suggest social remedies for it is largely destroyed by his own hand. This is partly due to the assumption of tastes as given, and the definition of reasonableness as the isolated individual mind's ability to calculate quantities accurately. But above all the marginal economist is powerless to underline the interdependence of malproduction and malconsumption. His treatment of production and consumption as unrelated activities, his treatment of producer and consumer as unrelated individuals, combine to give an elaborate mathematical camouflage to two simple, basic and logically related social evils: the maldistribution of the national surplus (defined by Hobson as that part of the national income over and above the sum needed to maintain all factors of production at maximum efficiency) and the labourer's last hour of work. The rising marginal disutility of labour as the day proceeded, together with the falling marginal utility of the later, and hence less necessary, goods produced, meant that the period which added most to human costs resulted in a product most of which was likely to be wasted by the rich, quite apart from its liability to leave the worker too tired to enjoy what leisure he had. It is only the clear consideration of the last hour's product, of its production and consumption, from the social standpoint, says Hobson, that exhibits the waste which it involves.[10]

VII

If the 'central directive power of organic development' acted infallibly, claimed *Work and Wealth*, economists would have no problems to solve. But 'error, waste and sin' were witnesses that this was not so. Consumers were often exploited, usually ill-informed, invariably wasteful; and Hobson believed that the economists, instead of resting a weight of advanced analysis on the shoulders of a perfectly rational, independent-minded and fictitious consumer, should try to identify the social factors which distorted the wise evolutionary instructions he was built to receive, assess the results of such distortion and suggest remedies.

We have already noted the value which Hobson placed on industrial life as a source of more disciplined mental habits. But what was newly required of the consumer exceeded the additional reasoning powers he had been given:

> As reasoning man with his more complex life has more chances of going wrong than lower animals guided by their instincts along a narrower life, so with each advance in the complexity of human life these chances of error multiply. (p. 119)

This was not because reason was an inferior instrument to instinct. It was an improvement. While instinct was adequate in an absolutely uniform environment, reason dealt better with 'changes and eccentricities'. The real reason why 'error and waste increase with the development of human society' was that a smaller proportion of humanity's energy was needed for survival, a greater share for 'specific and individual progress', and here it was easier to make mistakes. Moreover the desire for pleasure was easier to corrupt than the instinct of survival. The industrial flood of non-necessary goods had stimulated the vices of conspicuous consumption, of emulation of the tastes and habits of the rich by those who could barely afford the necessaries of life, of trivial and pointless activities designed to burn up the surplus energy of those who had no need to work and of monopolistic coercion of wants. It had allowed cheap and unreliable household goods and adulterated foodstuffs to flourish. Above all, by giving men work which baulked their creative instincts, tied them in subservience to their machines and reduced their humanity in the broadest sense of the word, it had killed their intuitive sense of balance between production and consumption.

Hobson's hopes of improving this situation rested on 'enlightened common sense'. The valuations of wants and activities by those who possessed this quality he believed to be uniform enough to furnish the economist with unambiguous standards. But *whose* common sense? Hobson was no straightforward paternalist: *Work and Wealth* made it clear that neither those who currently ruled, nor those who currently wrote, were necessarily to be trusted. Hobson regretted 'the excessive part played by certain highly-conscious and vocal interests of the commercial and intellectual classes in the art of government'. Accordingly 'the most pressing task of civilisation in the self-governing nations of our time was to spread the area of effective enlightenment so as to substitute the common sense of the many for that of the few, and to make it prevail'. And so far as the common sense of the many was 'sufficiently intelligible, sufficiently sound', it supplied 'a valid standard and a valid calculus of social values' (p. 322).

Hobson returned to this theme in the final pages of *Work and Wealth*, trusting in education and closer, more reliable communications for the 'rationalisation of the general will'. But he also ended the book on a warning that a 'calculus of social values' could be no more than a qualitative affair. Yet this, in Hobson's eyes, involved no sacrifice of precision: for he did not believe that orthodox economics could provide quantitative exactness in the first place. It had, he conceded, tried extremely hard, imputing money's infinitely divisible and fluid character to factors and components, and drawing up continuous supply curves 'based on the accumulation of such infinitesimal increments effected by minute rises and falls of price operating on the agents of production'. But such mathematical niceties, he claimed, reflected nothing about an actual working economy. The true unit of supply was 'the representative business', and the representative businessman was neither needful nor capable of attaining such microcosmic sensitivity. Hence a rise in supply price must attain 'a certain size and security' before it could bring into action a new representative plant. Short-term fluctuations in demand, it was true, might be met by 'speeding-up, or overtime, or other fuller use of existing factors of production'. But even these increments were of considerable size.[11]

The best one can say of this dismissal of the neoclassical approach is that it needs much more careful justification than it gets. Hobson is not here attacking the marginalists' identification of rationality with utility-maximisation. (He never did. *Work and Wealth* criticised – unsuccessfully, we have suggested – another neoclassical view: that of the relation between total utility and its separate sources.) Nor is he dissenting from orthodox economists' tacit equation of utility-maximising with profit-maximising where the entrepreneur is concerned. He is judging the more empirical question of how far entrepreneurs are able to carry out the neoclassical idea, and how far their not doing so invalidates the logical constructions built on the assumption that they do. But if deviations due to factor-indivisibilities and difficulty in identifying small fluctuations in demand are random and relatively small, an aggregative welfare analysis can reasonably assume them to be self-cancelling and hence list among its own virtues the precise measurement of market values.

Hobson ignores this possibility. Nevertheless it is hard to assert that his welfare precepts translate less usefully into policies for the State than do, for example, Pigou's. It is at least arguable that Pigovian welfare economics sacrifices a breadth of vision which the policymaker needs in exchange for much greater accuracy than he can use. As a guide to policy, welfare economics may well gain more than it loses by recognising specific and socially explicable abuses of the arts of production and consumption, and making an admittedly rough reassessment of certain market values in that light. Unless the virtues of industrialism and growth should ever unanimously be taken for granted, there will always be economists who make Hobson's choice.

VIII

Marshall's opinion of Hobson has already been seen.[12] Maynard Keynes said much the same things in considerably more brutal language:

> One comes to a new book of Mr. Hobson with mixed feelings, in hope of stimulating ideas and of some fruitful criticisms of orthodoxy from an independent and individual standpoint, but expectant also of much sophistry, misunderstanding, and perverse thought. In some of his books the first elements greatly predominate. In his latest book now before us, the latter prevail almost throughout. The book is a very bad one, made much worse than a really stupid book could be, by exactly those characteristics of cleverness and intermittent reasonableness which have borne good fruit in the past.[13]

These strictures are deserved – *Gold, Prices and Wages* (1913) is among Hobson's least clear-headed books. But it hardly seems fair that 'being Hobson' should have become a Cambridge synonym for muddled thinking;[14] and, indeed, Keynes tried to make amends to Hobson after his own conversion to underconsumptionism. *The General Theory* contains high praise of Mummery and Hobson's *The Physiology of Industry*. Privately, however, Keynes drew a distinction between Mummery, whose contribution to the book had 'probably' been the 'outstanding' one, and Hobson, who 'never fully understood [Mummery] and went off on a side-track after his death' (Keynes to Kahn, 30 July 1935).

And in any case Keynes' patronage came too late to shake Hobson's image of himself as a permanent economic outsider – as Hobson's autobiography, *Confessions of An Economic Heretic* (1938), clearly shows. In fact, Hobson stands out as one of the most isolated major figures in the history of economics. At Cambridge he was read only so that condescending reviews might be written in the *Economic Journal* – no Cambridge figure ever admitted he had *learned* anything from Hobson. Outside Cambridge, Cannan and D. H. Macgregor both praised *Work and Wealth* as a broad social study, but insisted that Hobson, whatever he himself imagined, was saying nothing embarrassing to neoclassical economics. Such close intellectual associates as Hobson had were none of them primarily economists. And he had little constituency among the lay intelligentsia either. For much of the time they could not follow him; and they could not follow him because the professionalisation of economics was raising the level of argument to a point where even dissidents were compelled to speak an esoteric language. Consequently *The Times*, reviewing *The Economics of Distribution* (20 September 1900), complained that Hobson's style was 'almost as abstract as Ricardo's', and that his attempts to illustrate his theories with examples from everyday life were 'sometimes as difficult to understand as the text which they are intended to elucidate'. *The Manchester Guardian* (unkindest cut of all) accused Hobson of being too deferential towards marginalism. But it was the *News of the World* – rather a different paper in those days – which summed up Hobson's predicament in a sentence. 'The book appears to be a theoretical justification of common sense against abstract theory.'[15]

This is an uncomfortable position for anyone to have to occupy. It is to be doubted, however, whether Hobson made the best of it. He may have had to ascend to a moderately high theoretical plane in order to assail high theory. But he did not have to adopt the turgid, over-elaborate style of exposition which characterises so many of his books and contrasts so sharply with his journalism and his autobiography.

IX

When all is said and done, Hobson must be ranked among the great economists. His contribution to our understanding of imperialism, his persuasive – if flawed – defence of the idea that a general glut was possible, and his demonstration that the economic ideals of Ruskin were compatible with assured analysis, make him one of the most original and versatile figures in the history of economics. As a political thinker, as well, Hobson is a figure of some importance. Here he has only recently begun to get his due. But Peter Clarke's *Liberals and Social Democrats* (1978) makes ample amends for previous neglect of Hobson's non-economic ideas; Michael Freeden's *The New Liberalism* (1978) goes even further, depicting Hobson as the intellectual leader of the whole 'new liberal' movement, the one man with the boldness and breadth of vision successfully to integrate evolutionary and organic doctrines with existing liberal thought and, in doing so, give it a new and urgently needed lease of life.

How did Hobson manage to do all this? *Did* he manage to do all this? It is a passage from Hobhouse's *Social Evolution and Political Theory* which supplies the key.

> The turning point in the evolution of thought, as I conceive it, is reached when the conception of the development of humanity enters into explicit consciousness as the directing principle of human endeavour ... In particular, it can be seen to be the conception necessary to give consistency and unity of aim to the vastly increased power of controlling the conditions, external and internal, of life, which the advance of knowledge is constantly yielding to mankind. (p. 155)

This theory of Hobhouse's, Freeden says, was 'crucial' in providing philosophical justification for the collectivist hankerings of the 'new liberals'. The idea that society at some point in its development became a self-conscious entity, with both the will and the means to direct its own further evolution, not only legitimated the idea of the social mind, but also gave it, as its 'natural' function, the task of directing social reform. And this specifically 'legitimated the task of the social reformer who, by showing ways through which man could rationally control and change his environment and himself, was taking an active part in evolution' (Freeden, p. 89).

But was the resulting social philosophy still a form of liberalism? Freeden not only insists that it was, but also credits Hobson with 'a very fine attempt at laying down a new basic liberal formula to replace the antiquated maxims of J. S. Mill concerning self- and other-regarding interests.'[16] Freeden is commenting on the following:

> The unity of... socio-industrial life is not a unity of mere fusion in which the individual virtually disappears, but a federal unity in which the results and interests of the individual shall be conserved for him by the federation. The federal government, however, conserves these individual rights, not, as the individualist maintains, because it exists for no other purpose than to do so. It conserves them because it also recognises that an area of individual liberty is conducive to the health of the collective life. Its federal nature rests on a recognition alike of individual and social ends, or, speaking more accurately, of social ends that are directly attained by social action and of those that are realised in individuals.[17]

That Hobson's work transcended the crude and misleading dichotomy of egoist and altruist has already been seen, but the 'very fine attempt at a new basic liberal formula' set out above reads to this writer, he must admit, as a rather undistinguished restatement of an old basic illiberal formula. How can the doctrine that the only ends that matter are 'social' ones, and that individual liberty should be allowed only so far as it is conducive to the health of collective life, be described as 'liberal'? What would Hobson have to say, to qualify in Freeden's eyes as 'illiberal'? Presumably he would have had to argue that individual freedom should be crushed even when it is in the social interest to uphold it!

In fact Freeden's book demonstrates – sometimes intentionally, sometimes, as in the case above, not – that Hobson's political philosophy was a thoroughly authoritarian one. This is something which one does not glean from Hobson's specifically economic work. But, when one does realise how illiberal Hobson's political ideas were, it puts the welfare analysis in a new perspective. Hobson's call for a social valuation of the economic product, taken in isolation, is surely something with which everyone but the most extreme individualist or the most complacent acolyte of industrial capitalism will sympathise. It is surely right that there should be economists who respect people's existing preferences and tell them how they can best be realised *and* economists who take a critical look at the social determination of these preferences, ask who is persuading whom and how, and evaluate, in the social interest, the preferences which emerge. If economists cannot manage even this modest division of labour, there is something wrong somewhere. And, had it not been for Hobson and Smart, theorising in the second tradition would have died with Ruskin.

But, as intimated above, Hobson's 'social valuation' takes on a distinctly *dirigiste* hue after a reading of his political ideas. The authoritarian implications are much fainter in Hobhouse, who seems, much better than Hobson, to represent Freeden's contention that the 'new liberalism' was a matter of individuality replacing individualism. It was Hobhouse who said that 'the heart of liberalism is the understanding that progress is not a matter of mechanical contrivance but of the liberating of living spiritual energy'.[18] The fact that Hobhouse is the 'better' liberal of the two does not, of course, necessarily make him a more important contributor to the development of liberalism, let alone a better political thinker. But our own judgement would be, even on the evidence that Freeden himself presents, that Hobson's true originality does lie where usually it has been thought to lie – in his economics.

Part 3

MARSHALLIAN PREJUDICES

This final section of the book concerns the attempts made by Marshall and some of his contemporaries to detach their economic analysis from its ethical and ideological background. The title, 'Marshallian prejudices', is meant as an advance warning that their efforts were limited in their success.

Chapter 8 focuses on welfare economics as practised by Marshall, Edgeworth and Pigou. Chapter 9 looks at the relationship between economics and ethics. How far did economists, finding themselves a technical role to replace their propagandist one, determine to excise value-judgements from their work? How far did they succeed? As Victorians (and in many cases evolutionists too), most of them were heavily committed to the idea of man's long-term moral progress. How far did their attempt at neutrality on immediate issues escape being coloured by this longer perspective? Chapter 10 examines the related but distinct question of ideological neutrality. (Avoiding normatives does not guarantee the avoidance of ideological bias.) It notes that some orthodox economists came to see economics and socialism as incompatible, suggesting that technical and ideological orthodoxy were intimately linked.

The final chapter focuses on economics, particularly Cambridge economics, in the years between Marshall's retirement and 1914. It ends with some conclusions about professionalisation in general and the professionalisation of economics in particular.

8

Orthodox welfare economics

If economics has typical and untypical branches, welfare economics is one of the latter. Its conclusions cannot be tested. Its evaluations are often arbitrary and based on very partial evidence. Its assumptions are apt to feature the combined fictions of those made by every other economic topic. Nevertheless, it is perhaps in the field of welfare that the neoclassical economists and their opponents revealed most about themselves: their view of the applicability of marginal utility theory, their attitude to conflicts between productive and redistributive considerations, the kind of value-judgements they thought legitimate and their view of the interaction between material and moral progress. Above all it forced them to define their position regarding the scope of economics, and its degree of dependence on other social sciences. Accordingly this book is going to single out for special attention the professionalisation of welfare economics: how it came to make use of advanced theory, achieved a positivist analysis of 'welfare' and attempted to provide more satisfactory links between theory and policy. Essentially the story is of three men: Marshall, Edgeworth and Pigou. All three looked at welfare questions in a heavily neoclassical way. But it is hard to see them (or even to see any two of them) as a neoclassical 'school' of welfare economics. Their approaches are too diverse for that. Indeed, perhaps their most important point in common is that all three, in their various ways, developed and elaborated themes set out by an economist who, to the end of his life, looked at economics from a largely pre-Jevonian standpoint. Sidgwick, therefore, seems to be an appropriate starting-point.

I

Sidgwick, Hla Myint has said, 'succeeded in laying down the foundations of the modern approach to welfare economics in its present form. His beautifully worked out distinction between the Production and the Distribution welfare economics led him directly to consider the possible divergences between the private and the social net products.'[1]

Most of the types of private/social divergence considered by Pigou can in fact be found in Sidgwick's *Principles of Political Economy* (1883). More than any other comparable book, *The Principles* reflects the transitional period when subjective considerations could no longer be omitted from the art of political economy but when the non-specialist was still likely to introduce marginal utility theory informally, by implication, rather than presenting it in all its axiomatic rigour. This rather empirical approach did not allow Sidgwick to make systematic distinction between (1) private/social divergences, (2) obstacles to the efficient use of particular factors and (3) misallocations of wealth simply due to maldistribution of income. Instead, he took all three classes of problem together, providing a list of situations where 'necessary qualifications to the system of natural liberty' were required.[2] Such cases included the non-cultivation of agricultural land owned by wealthy men 'fond of solitude, scenery or sport'; restrictions on inherited wealth which stopped it from being employed in the most 'utile' way; public goods such as lighthouses; scientific discoveries with an ultimate but no immediate market value; cases of monopolistic underproduction; certain possible results of unionisation; cases where it is difficult to adapt supply to an imperfectly known and varying demand; and outlays which would be made if the interests of future generations were given their full weight, but which were not profitable to any existing individual.

Summarising these various cases, Sidgwick distinguished between the results of adhesion to 'blind custom and habit', and the kind of problem that would still occur between individuals possessing perfect knowledge and rationality. The former, he suggested, raise little difficulty for the art of political economy; if the progressive triumph of reason over prejudice were all that was involved, then *laissez-faire* would be the agreed goal, and disagreement would centre on the pace of approach. But even in a community 'where the members generally were as enlightened and alert as we can ever expect human beings to become', collective action would still be necessary and it was the task of the political scientist, if not necessarily of the political economist, to point out the advantages and disadvantages of State intervention as such.

II

Marshall's conception of welfare economics was highly quantitative. The improvement of statistical data and statistical techniques as a basis for welfare calculations was a life-long concern of his. It occurs in 'The Old Generation of Economists and the New' (1897), where Marshall even divides economics into a qualitative past and a quantitative future, calling for the accurate measurement of satisfactions to 'defend the interests of the silent and patient many against the claims of the pushing and clamorous few'.[3] It occurs in a letter to A. H. D. Acland of 1886: 'American experience shows, I think, that a Labour Statistics Bureau may be of great service provided it does not attempt too much.'[4] Here Marshall is recommending that employers and workers at, say, machine-making centres be issued with forms to record wages, overtime, short-time and piecework. From these would be compiled a series of local reports. The most ingenious suggestion, however, is Marshall's contribution to the discussion of Higgs' paper of 1893, 'Workmen's Budgets':

> a great deal of information could be got from the managers of co-operative stores. In many towns a considerable part of the working classes spent nearly the whole of their income in the co-operative stores, and the managers knew the incomes of these men almost exactly. They could estimate pretty well how far a change in a man's consumption was due to a change in his habits or to a variation in his income or the prices of particular goods. Returns from such co-operative bodies would save a great number of those errors which must arrive in private inquiries.[5]

How did Marshall envisage such statistics being used? How, in particular, were they to form a positivistic bridge from economic theory to economic policy? Marshall proposed to use his data to calculate the changes in the sum of consumer and producer surpluses which would result from alternative policies. This task he discussed at some length in the *Principles*, anticipating an uphill struggle on behalf of the consumer against secretive entrepreneurs and trade unions. In particular, the administrator's judgements 'must always be inferior to those which an able business man forms, by the aid of instincts based on long experience with regard to his own business.' But statistics would be a force on the administrator's side.

> It is perhaps not unreasonable to hope that as time goes on, the statistics of consumption will be so organised as to afford demand schedules sufficiently trustworthy, to show in diagrams that will appeal to the eye the quantities of

consumers' surplus that will result from different courses of public and private action. (*Principles*, p. 492)

How seriously did Marshall believe in this possibility? By what steps did he propose to reach it? How far he had to go must have become obvious when, on 6 April 1891, he was reduced to writing to *The Times* as follows:

Now I am going to do a very rash thing, and make a guess at the consumers' net loss which the Post Office inflicts on the public by its one single act of prohibiting private enterprise from starting good and cheap local posts. Putting the population chiefly affected by it at fifteen millions, I should guess that the consumers' net loss is not less than six shillings a head annually ...

According to Marshall's nephew C. W. Guillebaud, the process of disillusionment was slow and painful:

He told me on one occasion that a major disappointment in his life was the recognition, which gradually forced itself on him, that his concept of consumer's surplus was devoid of important practical application, because it was not capable of being quantified in a meaningful way. At the outset he had high hopes that it could have had practical application, and for many years he had wrestled with it, but had finally reached the conclusion that it was a theoretical but not a practical tool in the economist's workbox.[6]

Marshall's disillusionment would have come as no surprise to Hobson, who had predicted from the start that the machine would never leave the ground. Hobson's criticism, however, had centred less on the unquantifiability of consumer's and producer's surpluses than on the triviality of what was to be quantified. As we saw in the previous chapter, Hobson denied that a money measure of human costs and satisfactions could yield serious criteria for policy changes. And against this charge Marshall's defence was odd and unconvincing. He admitted by implication that money as a yardstick of utility could only identify an economic optimum relative to a given income distribution: 'Its most important failure from the social point of view lies in its frequent allotment of a higher remuneration for a small service rendered to a rich man than for the relief of an urgent need on the part of a poor man.'[7] This conceded, Marshall could invest his welfare economics with social significance only by resorting to the claim that fiscal changes generally have the same effect on different income groups. This, as was seen in chapter 4, was a focal point for Nicholson's critique of Marshall. More recently Mark Blaug has called the assumption 'astonishing'. We would not disagree.

It is true that this was not the only way that Marshall tried to deal with the contention that social need does not necessarily correspond to economic demand. Book 4 of the *Principles* (the 'biological' book) uses the logic of evolution to transcend the forces of 'static' supply and demand altogether. Marshall begins by conceding that

> the struggle for survival may fail to bring into existence organisms that would be highly beneficial ... because ... in the economic world the demand for any industrial arrangement is not certain to call forth a supply, unless it is ... offering adequate payment or some other benefit to those who supply it. (*Principles*, p. 242)

Thus, he says, the desire of employees for a share in the management and a portion of the profits, or the desire of clever youths for good technical education, may go unheeded. But Marshall then calls economic biology to the rescue, finding grounds for long-term optimism in the nature of the evolutionary process: 'Those races, whose members render service to one another without exacting direct recompense, are not only the most likely to flourish for a time, but most likely to rear a large number of descendants who inherit their beneficial habits' (p. 242).

Marshall, then, made two very disparate responses to the challenge of Hobson's 'human valuation'. But the first of these responses involved him in a grotesquely implausible assumption, while the second bade him take leave of his carefully assembled marginalist framework altogether. The verdict on Marshall's writings on welfare economics must be that they are theoretically unsatisfactory and practically inconclusive. The overall picture is of a categorised list of exceptions to the optimising behaviour of the market, footnoted by a list of methodological objections to performing such an exercise at all, and delivered with much less conviction than the homilies, justified as usual by evolutionary metaphor, on what conduces to welfare by virtue of being, in Marshall's opinion, 'a wholesome activity'.

> Any step towards equality which increases wholesome activity on the balance I welcome from a cosmopolitan point of view, even if it violates so called rights of property and involves a hastening to that check of population which must come ultimately. My objection to socialism, and especially that putrid form of it, which condemns family life, is that it tends to diminish activities.[8]

Leaving aside the final sentence, this does not sound so very different from Hobson's approach to welfare economics. Did Marshall deserve, in the field of welfare, the professional recognition which was denied to Hobson? The time has come for some direct comparisons.

III

Let us begin by looking at some common criteria by which economists in the age of Marshall, whether orthodox or heterodox, typically judged redistributive questions. One, the effect of the proposed change on the level of population, can be ignored for the present. Neither Sidgwick, nor Marshall nor Hobson seriously advanced a possible consequential rise in population as an argument against any of the reforms which they considered. The other main criteria can be listed as follows:

(1) The proposition that the marginal utility of income for each individual declines as his income rises, and hence that the total utility of two or more individuals with the same tastes and abilities will be maximised by an equal distribution of a fixed total income.
(2) The proposition that there is an overall correlation, however small and uneven, between individuals' *present* levels of income and their capacity, at *any* given level of income, to add to the total happiness of society, including their own.
(3) The effect of the proposed redistribution on the physical and mental efficiency of the working man.
(4) Its effect on the supply of investible funds.
(5) Its effect on the supply of entrepreneurial effort.

The second criterion (2) is in fact an aggregation of two separate factors. The first is the effect of a redistributive change upon those utilities and disutilities which men derive from the wealth of others, e.g. the benefit to society from the maintenance and development of knowledge and culture by the rich, or the disutility caused to members of the poor by their resentment of conspicuous inequalities. The second is the possibility that the tastes of rich individuals may, on average, yield them more intense pleasure per unit of income than those of the poor. No. (2) accounts for both of these.

It was the conflict between (1) and (2) which caused economists the most difficulty. The liberal economist's dilemma was that he could not make fully commensurable, much less resolve, the perpetual confrontation between two mutually vulnerable adversaries: the equalising implications of Benthamism, hard and precise yet brittle and dogmatic, and his own personal experience, moral attitudes and political convictions. For a utilitarian and an economist, synthesis was only possible through a rationalistic, perhaps even mathematical, formulation of the latter, and attempts to do this looked, and in fact were, crude but not simple, mechanistic but not particularly logical: reeking rather of arbitrariness and even smugness in their assumptions. On every count but that of possible ideological convenience, Benthamism minus its leveller's sting was palpably inferior to the original.

We need, however, to consider the interrelationship of all five criteria. For while scientific accuracy depended on success in making these five factors quantitatively commensurable, yet keeping them logically distinct, a persuasive social programme depended on reducing as many of them as possible to a simple and compelling common denominator. And Marshall and Hobson both found such a denominator in the psycho-physical theory of consumption, that is, the set of distinctions, broadly common to Sidgwick, Marshall and Hobson, between necessities, comforts and luxuries.

This distinction dominates much of the *Principles*; and it does so because of Marshall's belief in the work ethic. It was this belief which gave him such a low opinion of consumption which merely gave temporary pleasure without contributing to a man's creative and productive powers. In Marshall's work, therefore, the idea of diminishing marginal utility of income derived its main force from the figure of a consumer who first satisfied his 'real' and intense needs (those wants whose basic rationality was guaranteed by their contribution to his working life), then turned to less important wants and, if rich enough, derived very low or even negative satisfaction from the last part of his income. In other words, Marshall forged a powerful logical and emotional link between the marginal-utility argument and the efficiency argument for greater equality (criteria (1) and (3) above), enabling the two, for most purposes, to be taken together as one. And by suggesting that one man's luxury might be another man's necessity, Marshall also manages to link in criterion (2).

For the sake of giving definiteness to the ideas it may be well to venture on estimates of necessaries, rough and random as they must be. Perhaps at present prices the strict necessaries for an average agricultural family are covered by fifteen or eighteen shillings a week, the conventional necessaries by about five shillings more. For the unskilled labourer in the town a few shillings must be added to the strict necessaries. For the family of the skilled workman living in a town we may take twenty-five or thirty shillings for strict necessaries, and ten shillings for conventional necessaries. For a man whose brain has to undergo great continuous strain the strict necessaries are perhaps two hundred or two hundred and fifty pounds a year if he is a bachelor: but more than twice as much if he has an expensive family to educate. (*Principles*, p. 70)

Marshall, then, simplified the accepted economic criteria to be applied to radical social proposals, stressed their similarities and subsumed them under as few headings as possible. But Hobson took this process much further. In effect, he simply lumped all five criteria together with the unsupported assertion that the surplus, if ideally distributed, would exactly cover the economic organism's requirements of maintenance and growth. This assumption gave him a simple and universal remedy for industrial evils. 'The abuse or uneconomical use of the surplus product is the source of every sort of trouble or malady of the industrial system, and the whole problem of industrial reform may be conceived in terms of a truly economical disposal of this surplus' (*The Industrial System*, p. 78).

By making his concept of the surplus the very basis of his distribution theory, Hobson achieved a single – and politically very persuasive – touchstone of judgement. As we have just seen, Marshall's approach to the theory of consumption also gave a cutting-edge to the notion of diminishing marginal utility. But his redistributive standards were vaguer and less determinate. For Marshall a distributive optimum must share out the national income so that as much of it as possible contributes to the individual working lives of its recipients, but also sufficiently unequally to give the entrepreneur an adequate reward and to maintain the necessary supply of investible funds. Perhaps it is a pity that Marshall, unlike Hobson, does not say whether the national product is exhausted in meeting these conditions. On the other hand Hobson is obviously making a guess, and probably an ideologically motivated guess at that. There is no particular reason to think Marshall could have done any better.

IV

Edgeworth's overall contribution to economic theory cannot receive its due in a chapter like this. (Schumpeter makes a persuasive case for ranking Edgeworth above Marshall in terms of theoretical originality.) Our concern will be with Edgeworth's analysis of the welfare implications of different tax policies.

In England, interest in the theory of taxation had virtually died out with McCulloch. The bibliography of specialist works in the American economist Seligman's survey *Progressive Taxation*, published by the American Economic Association in 1893, mentions only one English work written in the forty years past, and that of very minor importance. But the 1890s saw a partial revival. In 1892 there appeared C. F. Bastable's classic, *Public Finance*, which was widely read, lengthily reviewed and enthusiastically praised. About the same time Edgeworth was discovering what was to become the most congenial of all fields for him. And Marshall's argument for the taxation of industries operating under decreasing returns to scale, and for subsidies in the opposite case, looked like the herald of general success in applying marginal utility theory to public policy.

To the modern reader, much of the work done on taxation in the 1890s and 1900s sounds curiously old-fashioned and pedantic. The competing claims of the 'return of benefits' and 'ability to pay' theories of taxation were universally discussed in a highly ethical and legalistic spirit. In general, economists took their cue from Bastable, who did not regard taxation as a branch of applied political economy at all, but as 'a part of the far wider subject of public finance'.[9]

But the problem studied most intensively was one which called for a direct application of welfare economics. This concerned the distribution, according to wealth or income or both, of the total burden on taxation; and here it was usual for precise ethical principles to support large numbers of possible fiscal interpretations. The most favoured rule was that of 'equal sacrifice', and the majority of economists interpreted this as meaning that everyone should sacrifice the same *proportion* of his total utility. The Dutch economist Cohen-Stuart (in 1889) was the first to show mathematically that, depending on the shape of the individual's marginal-utility-of-income curve, this was compatible with progressive or proportional or regressive taxation. And it is not altogether clear what the implications of equal sacrifice were for Bastable: having said that it does not necessarily result in progressive taxation because not all men's wants are equal, he continues:

Between the system of payment as recompense for state services which would naturally lead to regressive taxation, and the system of progression resting on the idea that sacrifice should be equalised, the intermediate method of taxation in proportion to income is on the whole the best standard for regulation. (*Public Finance*, p. 306)

Perhaps the only lesson of this passage is that Bastable, like some of his colleagues, was prone to choose his principle of sacrifice on the basis of its fiscal implications, rather than the other way about.

Whatever the angle of viewing, it is hard to see fiscal theory at this time as a successful attempt to apply the principles of welfare economics. Rules would be laid down, and models of considerable complexity and mathematical skill erected over them. But when economists' arguments reached the stage of proposing actual fiscal laws, they were apt either to plead insufficient factual evidence, or to discard their painstaking theoretical work in favour of unquantifiable considerations of a 'commonsense' nature. Seligman's book is a good example of this. Rejecting the 'return for benefits' theory on grounds of incalculability, he adopts the 'ability to pay' theory and considers in turn the various distributive principles. Picking that of equal sacrifice, for no apparent very good reason, he reproduces Cohen-Stuart's proof that this will not necessarily lead to progression. But in the last chapter, he declares himself for progression nonetheless, justifying this with the arguments that, on the productive side, having a lot of money makes it easier to get more, and, on the consumptive side, a proportional rate will not exempt the minimum of subsistence.

Neither did Edgeworth have any illusions about the difficulty of finding out, even approximately, what equal or minimum or proportional sacrifice actually involved. Perhaps that is why he never tried very hard, resting content with taking the mean of others' guesses about this. There was some reason, he said, to believe that marginal utility varies inversely with income; but many (Montesquieu, Paley, Say) had believed that it falls more steeply than this. Since no one had held it to be less steep, he continued, let us average out the opinions we have, and conclude that it falls more steeply, but not much more. If this is so, even the doctrine of equal sacrifice requires progressive taxation.[10]

Edgeworth's grounds for nevertheless preferring the principle of minimum total sacrifice were as down-to-earth as the foregoing is casual:

The only certain limit to the application of equal sacrifice – viz, that more than the necessary minimum of taxation should not be raised and more should not be required from the higher incomes than would bring down all above a certain level to that level – is greatly in excess of practical limits. Is it not simpler to dismiss the disputed principle of equal sacrifice, and to adopt as the norm of taxation minimum sacrifice tempered by a regard for the growth of wealth and other advantages above enumerated?[11]

Edgeworth followed this with a demonstration of J. S. Mill's confusion on the subject, and then a curious passage where he seems to be instancing a lasting confusion among economists between equal and proportionate sacrifice, and hence recommending minimum sacrifice as easier to understand.

'As a general stated rule', Edgeworth concluded, minimum sacrifice is best. First: 'It enables us to pierce the metaphysical mist which has been raised by the question: Why should the principle be adopted? The question is not embarrassing to those who regard minimum sacrifice as a deduction from the greatest-happiness principle.'[12] And secondly, 'the want of clearness in reasoning from the principle of equal sacrifice, for, to get any conclusion, some attempt must be made about the rate at which the increase in utility diminishes with the increase in means'.[13] In short, Edgeworth was claiming that he supported the minimum sacrifice principle because it had a widely understood ethical basis and an unambiguous fiscal consequence – progressive taxation. And, having established this conclusion to his own satisfaction, he went on to support Ireland's claim that it was currently (1897) over-taxed, noting that even the principle of equal sacrifice was enough to justify this assertion. Edgeworth's discussion of Ireland's desirable contribution to the Exchequer is a good illustration of his approach to fiscal questions. The tentativeness of the theory is matched by the vagueness of the evidence. Edgeworth begins by warning that the principle of minimum sacrifice is weakened by 'other considerations not admitting of precision'. After listing eight such considerations, he pleads that to evaluate these items would be out of place in a discussion of pure theory, and that he will assume 'for the purpose of illustration' that they are insufficient 'to make the consideration of sacrifice of no account'.[14]

Edgeworth then went on to note the difficulty of discovering Ireland's taxable capacity relative to England's. Giffen, he noted, had put the ratio at 1 : 53 in 1886 and 1 : 41 in 1895; Lough put it at 1 : 72.8. Bastable had said that it was 'quite hard enough' to estimate the ratio of total incomes and 'quite hopeless' to try to discover the amount of 'free' income.[15] Edgeworth swept this confusion aside: it was approximate enough, he said, to take the average of the various estimates.

This mixture of hesitancy and arbitrariness is typical of Edgeworth's writings on fiscal theory. We shall argue in the concluding section of this chapter that it was Edgeworth's mental habits and personality which stopped fiscal theory being professionalised. But that case will be easier to make out after Edgeworth has been compared with Pigou.

V

Pigou was the first British economist to use the General Optimum as a framework for policy recommendations. *Wealth and Welfare* (1912) set the State the aim of equalising the marginal social products of factors in all their alternative uses, by means of a system of taxes and bounties, thus achieving optimality. This was a sharply different approach from Marshall's. Focusing on the effects of very small changes in output in different industries gave the economist a far more exacting task than did Marshall's broad surplus analysis.

Nevertheless, there is much in *Wealth and Welfare* which owes nothing to marginal analysis; the extended discussions, for example, of those social/private divergences which arise from various tenancy laws, or from the relation between employer and worker (p. 150–1); of individual services uncompensated by financial reward (p. 158); or the decasualisation of labour for steadier employment (p. 309); and of alternative schemes for national insurance (p. 408). And where – as often happens – Pigou runs marginalist and empirical arguments side by side, he seldom indicates his opinion of their relative importance. He says, for instance, that total welfare is increased by anything which makes the working man's income less variable, even if it makes the incomes of the better-off more variable. The reasons given for this are: that demand-curves are convex to the origin, that variable income may damage physical health, that periodic unemployment may affect a man's psychological fitness for work and that the temporary labourer inevitably feels insecure. But no attempt is made to rank these in order of importance.

This is because Pigou cannot quantify the effects he needs to measure. Thus his discussion of a national minimum wage peters out into the recommendation that it should be 'at such a level that the direct good resulting from the marginal pound transferred to the poor just balances the indirect evil brought about by the reduction of the dividend'. But to be able to estimate this the economist needs 'a mass of detailed information, much of which is not, in present circumstances, accessible to students' (p. 396).

Hence, for all their different theoretical stances, Pigou actually applied welfare economics in much the same way as Sidgwick had. There were cases, admittedly, where Pigou's superior grasp of the nature of an economic optimum enabled him to correct Sidgwick's reasoning.[16] But in policy-making terms Pigou's advance over Sidgwick was not mainly one of theoretical sophistication. The most real difference is that between a philosopher generalising about the nature and criteria of state intervention and a professional economist considering the possible steps towards a welfare state.

In Pigou's case, however, it was not just the difficulty of applying the concepts of marginal private and social product which gave *Wealth and Welfare* its empirical flavour. The axioms on which its analysis rested and, even more, Pigou's stated ideas of what these propositions implied, shifted his emphasis away from a fixed-resource framework and towards the study of the effects of changes in the supply of factors.

Pigou's three axioms are as follows:

(1) if a cause is introduced, which makes for an increase in the aggregate size of the dividend, providing that the absolute share of no group of members, in terms of the commodities which that group is accustomed chiefly to consume, decreases, the economic welfare of the community as a whole is likely to be augmented. (p. 20)

(2) economic welfare is likely to be augmented by anything that, leaving other things unaltered, renders the distribution of the national dividend less unequal. (p. 24)

(3) if a cause is introduced which diminishes the variability or inequality in time of the dividend, and especially of that part of it which accrues to the poorer classes, the economic welfare of the community as a whole is likely to be augmented. (p. 32)

What kind of analysis will mediate between these propositions and actual policies? The key to what must, and what need not, be done comes in the second chapter of part 2, in which Pigou seeks to show that anything which increases average output per head will ultimately make everyone better off, regardless of attendant changes in the *distribution* of the output. How does Pigou reach this conclusion?

(1) He admits that an increase in capital per head can either raise or lower labour's *relative share*; but even here he is eager to show that a rise is more likely than a fall. He argues that if we think of machinery as the joint embodiment of labour and waiting, then it becomes apparent that any rivalry between 'capital' and labour is in fact a rivalry between labour-and-much-waiting and labour-and-little-waiting. He then declares himself 'content to accept Marshall's authority' that the competition between labour in general and waiting in general is 'of small importance relative to the benefits which labour derives from obtaining cheaply the aid of capital' (p. 84).

(2) Turning to the effect of embodied technical progress on wages, Pigou divides innovations into three classes: capital-saving, neutral and labour-saving. These affect factors' shares by altering relative scarcities: only the third category can make distribution less even, and even labour-saving innovations (says Pigou) are likely to raise the *absolute* wage. It is conceivable that the latter might fall (he continues), but the price-elasticity of demand for labour will normally be high enough to prevent this happening. And if we are dealing with an industry whose products are largely bought by the workers, so much the better; the wage earner will also benefit from the falling costs.

(3) Finally Pigou mentions the possibility that some workers may be injured by an increase in the efficiency of others. But he dismisses it briefly, saying that:

(a) The relationship between different kinds of labour, like the relationship between labour and capital, is more complementary than competitive.
(b) Workers injured by the increasing efficiency of others may be able to change their jobs.
(c) In any case, incidents within 'the broad group labour' are of 'subordinate interest'. (p. 93)

It is hard to see why one worker's gain at the expense of another is of 'subordinate interest' to welfare economics; indeed, the whole of (3) must surely rank as one of the most staggering pieces of complacency in the history of economic thought. But that is not the point. The point is that Pigou – rightly or wrongly – believed that anything which raised productivity ultimately made everyone, or virtually everyone, better off; and believed it firmly enough to make his second axiom (the distributive one) largely redundant. For if we do believe that any increase in productivity anywhere in the economy ultimately increases everyone's welfare then, in the absence of social time-preference, the only logical thing to do is to ignore distribution and think only of output. And the almost complete lack of attention paid to time-preference in *Wealth and Welfare* is one of its most remarkable features. Here Pigou differentiates himself from Marshall, who took a less consistently long-term view. In his evidence to the Gold and Silver Commission of 1888, for instance, Marshall claimed that if a fall in prices did not *much* diminish the total productiveness of industry it should be welcomed, because it tended to cause a 'better' (i.e. more equal) distribution of wealth.[17] Compare Pigou's longer perspective:

> Transferences which diminish the national dividend ... if their annual amount is kept constant, must have the effect of diminishing the real incomes of the relatively poor, to such an extent that their earnings *plus* the transference made to them will ultimately be less than their earnings alone would have been, had no annual transference been made.[18]

It is because Pigou consistently takes this view that part 3 of *Wealth and Welfare*, though presented as an examination of possible redistributive measures, is scarcely a discussion of redistribution at all. It is mainly a discussion of the effect on production of those measures which *happen* to be redistributive. Transferences which diminish the national dividend, whatever they do to distribution, are bad; transferences which increase it are good.

So Pigou's second axiom (economic welfare is likely to be increased by anything that, leaving other things unaltered, makes income distribution more equal) only finds work to do in the 'knife-edge' case where a transference has a neutral effect on production. And death duties are the only major transference which Pigou puts into this category. He presents a few minor ones: but even they are diffidently recommended, in sharp contrast to his confident support for increases in output judged to be neutral distributively. The reason is that, on Pigou's assumptions, the smallest misjudgement of the effects on the supply of productive factors of a change in distribution will loom cumulatively larger until all the good resulting from the change is undone, whereas the grossest neglect of the interests of a section of the community will ultimately cease to matter if there is overall progress towards higher output.

The crucial difference between parts 2 and 3 of *Wealth and Welfare* is not that the former examines possible reforms in a 'productive' light and the latter in a 'distributive' one. The message throughout is to sacrifice everything, or nearly everything, to growth. The really important difference is that part 2 can conduct much of its analysis in a neoclassical spirit, that is within a framework of fixed resources, whereas this proves impossible in part 3. Why this distinction? It occurs because Pigou believes there are few cases where reallocation of existing resources to increase output is detrimental to their long-term supply. Hence part 2 can discuss static resource reallocation and largely ignore dynamic considerations. But a more even distribution of income, Pigou believes, can affect the supply of factors either way. Inevitably, then, dynamic considerations dominate part 3. Thus the part of *Wealth and Welfare* which purports to be about once-and-for-all transfers of income is just as production orientated, but much less 'neoclassical', than Pigou's direct discussion of changes in output.

The tone of *Wealth and Welfare*, however, is less anti-egalitarian than some of the preceding discussion may suggest. Pigou presents a fair number of cases in which the claims of growth and the claims of equality point in the same direction. One of his strongest convictions was that investment in human beings was more important, and more productive, than investment in machines;[19] consequently the question: who is to invest in the poor? is a central theme of much of Pigou's work. *Wealth and Welfare*, recognising that the poor themselves lack the means to invest properly in their own capacities, and that those who can lend them the means are discouraged by their inevitably small share in the eventual return, calls both for a comprehensive system of national insurance (p. 366) and for further redistributive taxation (p. 370). Finally Pigou discusses the question, not of a national minimum money wage, but of 'a national minimum of conditions below which [the government] refuses to allow the fortunes of any citizen in any circumstances to fall'. This for Pigou is the most difficult of all distributive questions: none of his three axioms enables a judgement on a measure which will tend to diminish the national dividend, but which is 'likely for an indefinitely long period to increase the aggregate real incomes of the poor' (p. 393).

This being so, Pigou's prescription is a vague one. For the relief of extreme want he quotes the 'agreed opinion' of 'practical philanthropists' that whatever transferences are needed must be made 'without reference to possible injurious consequences upon the magnitude of the dividend'.

This policy of practical philanthropists is justified by analysis, in the sense that it can be shown to be conducive to economic welfare as a whole, if we believe that the misery that results to individuals from extreme want to be indefinitely large; for, then, the good of abolishing extreme want is not commensurable with any evils that may follow from the diminution of the dividend. (p. 395)

The question remains: What national minimum will do most to increase total welfare? Pigou's difficulty in identifying this standard has already been seen. But it does not concern us here: what matters is that the eradication of extreme want – a condition which Pigou does not try to define – is the only immediate objective compelling enough to defy his implicit identification of maximum welfare with maximum output.

VI

The object of welfare economics is to provide a theory of economic policy. Hence the great virtue of singling out welfare economics for special attention is not just that it is relevant to our first and second criteria of professionalisation,* but also that it relates them to one another. The professionalisation (I)** of welfare economics made an indispensable contribution to the professionalisation (II)*** of economics as a whole. One can go even further. Until Pigou constructed an engine of analysis specifically designed to furnish policy recommendations, professionalisation (I) and professionalisation (II) tended to pull economics in opposite directions. Marshall's career can be seen as an attempt to avoid this awkward reality. He succeeded in creating a lasting distinction between insiders and outsiders in terms of theoretical expertise. But he did not satisfy the second criterion of professionalisation; all he did – all he tried to do – was to keep its demands at bay, by insisting that theoretical sophistication and practical relevance were allied, not rival, considerations.

To satisfy criterion (1) and criterion (2) demanded more than this; it demanded that theory and policy be integrated and yet kept independent at the same time. They had to be integrated in the sense

* Training in an advanced body of theory inaccessible to laymen; monopoly of defined specialist functions (in this case the function of giving policy advice). See p. 3.

** i.e. professionalisation in terms of the first criterion.

*** i.e. professionalisation in terms of the second criterion.

that theory had to contribute enough to policy to make the latter look like more than just another set of personal opinions. They had to be independent in the sense that the theory had to be of some use to economists with a variety of views on policy questions – if it was not, its chances of creating a solid and lasting professional grouping were, at the least, very much reduced.

This elusive balance between integration and non-integration was achieved by Pigou. (In this respect *Wealth and Welfare* reads as a brilliantly successful *tour de force*.) Edgeworth neither achieved it nor tried to. Diffident, indolent about collecting and evaluating information – we have already seen him on two separate occasions preferring to average out other people's guesses of a quantity rather than find out for himself – and thoroughly 'unleaderly' (the word is Schumpeter's), he made very little attempt to persuade anyone that his advice gained much from his algebra. Yet, objectively, Pigou's policy recommendations have as little to do with his theorising as do Edgeworth's – less, in fact. Edgeworth, after all, did derive the case for progressive taxation from the principle of declining marginal utility. There is nothing as new, direct and important as this in *Wealth and Welfare*.

But if, in Edgeworth's work, theory and policy were insufficiently integrated to professionalise fiscal theory as Pigou professionalised welfare economics, in Hobson's work they were insufficiently independent. His analysis has little to offer anyone who does not share his objective of the redistribution of the 'non-productive surplus' so that it becomes productive. This is the crucial difference between Hobson's welfare economics and Pigou's. Pigou ended up with a basic policy objective as simple as, or simpler than, Hobson's – to maximise output almost wherever possible. But this policy conclusion is optional even within the framework within which Pigou looked at the economy. In Hobson's case the policy conclusion *is* the framework.

The distinction here is the Marshallian one between developing an analysis and developing an engine of analysis – which is the same as the modern dichotomy between a theory and a research programme. This difference is notoriously hard to pin down. Nevertheless, after what we have seen of Pigou's and Hobson's writings on welfare economics, it might be plausible to say that the former created a research programme and the latter a theory. And it is here that we reach the nub of the issue of policy's simultaneous integration with, and independence from, theory. The point is that it is very difficult to strike this balance. The value-judgements needed to translate a theory into a policy recommendation are nearly always either too contentious for the economist's opinion to look any more valuable than anyone else's, or too uncontentious for economists who dislike the policy to be able to disown it without attacking the competence of the theory, and hence the theorist. By contrast, a research programme gives its exponents a way of making policy recommendations which differentiates them from outsiders even when they are disagreeing with each other on specific policies.

So Pigou professionalised welfare economics because (unlike Hobson) he created a research programme, and also because he lacked Edgeworth's disarming readiness to wipe, ostentatiously, the theoretical slate clean before proceeding to policy matters. Fiscal theory exemplifies a field ripe for professionalisation but which, for idiosyncratic reasons, did not become professionalised. An advanced body of theory was available. A clear distinction existed between the economic approach of Edgeworth and the legalistic one of Bastable. Yet Edgeworth himself was full of praise for the older approach. Not only did he write two highly deferential reviews of Bastable's book, but he upheld the Italian school of public finance – which treated the subject as a branch of law rather than of economics – for what he called its 'Germanic' and 'philosophical' interest in definitions.

But we must still ask, first, why Pigou was able to create an engine of analysis for welfare economics and, secondly, why he wanted to. The obvious answers, first, that he was a very good economist, and secondly, because he wanted to make economic theory more useful, will take us much of the way. But there is more to be said than that. Pigou's analytical framework – as he himself admits – is only valid on the assumption that economic welfare, with specified exceptions, is a broadly reliable guide to total welfare. Marshall and Pigou both make this assumption. But in Marshall's case it is a substantive assumption – Marshall makes it because he believes it to be true and, indeed, spends considerable time justifying it empirically. In Pigou's case it is a *methodological* assumption explicitly made so as to make the subject-matter tractable. This is the attitude of a specialist; and it was Marshall's drive to professionalise economics which gave his successors specialist attitudes which he either no longer could acquire, no longer needed to acquire or had never wanted to acquire for himself. Pigou represents only the half-way mark of this process.

Unlike the next generation, the generation of Kahn and Hicks, he was not ready to isolate economic activities without explanation and then leave it entirely to others to evaluate the social usefulness of his specialist analysis of economic welfare. But, unlike the previous generation (Marshall's), he did not feel he had to try very hard to justify the isolation of economic from other activities. Marshall's *Principles* begins by trying to *show* that what is good for economic man is normally good for 'total man'; Pigou's *Wealth and Welfare* begins by *postulating* this.

We seem to have ended up with the conclusion that Pigou professionalised welfare economics because he was a professional economist. Yet this is neither vacuous nor trivial. It underlines the fact that the professionalisation of economics started with general theory and, once established there, created an entry qualification that attracted the future professionalisers of the various specialisms within the subject.

And, in any case, Pigou's readiness to identify economic with total welfare cannot be ascribed solely to his professional attitude toward the subject. Pigou would not have made his methodological assumption unless he had really believed that there were a great many cases in which increases in economic welfare could be put down unproblematically as increases in total welfare. And the need to believe this, in order to write professionally about welfare economics, imposed an ideologically selective filter on the economics profession.

Why? The point is that the assumption (in cases where the contrary was not obvious) that changes which affected economic welfare affected total welfare to roughly the same extent was an essential act of neoclassical faith. Without it, marginal welfare analysis did not appear to provide returns which justified the intellectual outlay. But there were various types of economist to whom this assumption was unlikely to appeal. It did not appeal to critics of industrial society, for obvious reasons. It did not usually appeal to economists sceptical about the consumer's real power to make the best use of his income, like Hobson and Smart. Its materialism repelled devout Christians like Devas and Cunningham, who took the prevailing moral standard of wants and activities as the only true indicator of welfare. And it seldom appealed to evolutionary relativists, to whom an increasing national income was far too simple a criterion of progress. Yet its attraction was also small for those with a fixed and utopian conception of a good society. Their sharply defined picture of how the community should be for all time gave them unusual confidence in pronouncing on questions of total welfare and they saw no point, even in an economist's role, in studying a single aspect of it. In this way, as in no other, the influence of Ruskin lived on.

Inability to share the standard neoclassical assumption about economic and total welfare required an economist to write about his subject very differently. What he included and what he omitted both contributed to a perspective which the Marshallian school found cloudy, partisan and amateurish. The economist who took nothing for granted about the meaning of changes in economic welfare committed himself to discuss anew the place of economic activities in society every time he took up a new economic question. And in a majority of cases this was a substitute, rather than a framework, for economic reasoning.

Not to be a political liberal, therefore, was a professional disadvantage for an economist: not an insurmountable one, but a disadvantage nonetheless. The technical orthodoxy which underlay professionalism drew most of its supporters from a fairly narrow ideological base. But that does not prove ideological, or ethical, bias in their work. To assess these questions, we must move on to our third criterion of professionalism – the possession of a professional ethic. For, paradoxically, the main professional ethic at issue was that of ethical neutrality.

9

Economists and ethics

Is positive economics possible? There is one kind of value-judgement which is inevitable not just throughout economics, but throughout all science, and this is the preliminary value-judgement that a particular topic is the right one to study. Thus, for example, neo-classical economics studies the consequences, rather than the causes, of people's preferences: in choosing to do this it is saying that restricting economics' scope, and starting the story half-way through, is justified in the interests of greater analytical rigour. Another compulsory value-judgement occurs when the scientist chooses his method of studying his data.

But what of the belief that the economist cannot avoid value-judgements even *within* the framework of his chosen topic? Killed and buried by J. N. Keynes in 1890,[1] reinterred by T. W. Hutchison in 1964,[2] this belief still stalks a spectral path through the anti-texts. Thus one recent radical critic believes that 'ethical neutrality is meaningless' (if it is, so is ethical non-neutrality); another rejects the positive/normative distinction 'because the bourgeois idea of individuals' values existing in a vacuum is pure mystification' (true but irrelevant).

But 'positive', 'normative', 'value-judgement' were words not much used by economists in Marshall's day. How far this caused, and how far it resulted from, their frequent failure to face up to the precise implications of positive economics is a difficult linguistic question. Just as hazardous is the attempt to describe the position of men like Hobson and Cunningham on the question of ethics and economics in terms of such concepts. The interpretation will necessarily not be exact, and even the most deferential of commentators must fear mistakes of emphasis. But the attempt must be made; only by doing so can different economists' stances on positive economics – sometimes confused, often confusing – be both appreciated and compared.

II

Nassau Senior was the first economist to proscribe prescription. In doing so, he was not saying 'As neutral scientists we should not judge' but rather 'As specialist economists we do not know.' Policy recommendation was for 'scientists', but for scientists of legislation. Later economists, however, chose to distinguish between a positive science and a normative art of political economy. There was no questioning the *existence* of this distinction during economics' period of self-appraisal in the 1870s. But economists did disagree how far they should trespass across it. Cairnes forbade all straying. Political economy, he said, could help us form our opinions on social questions by furnishing data, but could never dictate final judgements.[3] Ingram attacked Cairnes, saying that such an attitude 'amounts to an entire paralysis of political economy as a social power capable of producing or confirming in the mass of the community just convictions on the most important of all subjects'.[4]

After 1880 or thereabouts, there was a close correlation between enthusiasm for (and knowledge of) the marginal revolution, and a disinclination to make value-judgements. Nicholson (against marginalism and value-judgements) and Smart (in favour of both) are the only real exceptions. In fact marginalism and positivism fed on one another. On the one hand economists, cast in an increasingly scientific role, became both less interested in and more wary of a political one. Marshall noted and endorsed the declining interest when he told Section F in 1890 that modern economists were freer from party bias than their predecessors, and that this was because their priorities were scientific.[5] Ashley noted and endorsed the greater wariness; he thought that the economist's best hope of retaining scientific status *and* some political influence was to avoid being too obviously political.[6] On the other hand there was some inclination to make a virtue out of necessity; the relative inapplicability of neoclassical theory was best defended by an aggressive hostility to policy prescription by *any* economist.

This leads us round to the other half of the argument: the extent to which marginalism was the *result* of a pre-existing trend towards ethical neutrality. As the nineteenth century progressed, so did the realisation that a trade-off between liberty and equality could not be avoided.[7] Increasingly, economists were forced to choose between making blatantly partisan value-judgements and making none at all.

Economists who chose the latter course had so much the less to lose in succumbing to the formalities of marginalism.

Broadly, then, marginalism and positivism were allies. Yet the marginal revolution did build one bridge between economics and ethics, in that it revived economists' interest in the unsolved ethical problems of utilitarianism. Edgeworth rightly diagnosed the problem of quantitative and qualitative utility as central to the theory of public finance. Here, however, the decline of Malthusianism counted for as much as the rise of marginalism. Marshall in 1893 emphasised 'a change ... which separates the economics of this generation from the economics of the past'.[8] This was the end of the acceptance of the doctrine that redistributive taxation would, in the long run, merely make the rich poorer and the poor more numerous without being richer. With this belief cleared out of the way, economists were freed either to stress or to circumvent the egalitarian implications of marginal utility theory. Most did both.

III

It is impossible to be concise in surveying economists' attitudes to moral judgements between 1870 and 1914. Even a look at a single economist does not necessarily produce a straightforward or tidy picture. We have therefore resorted to choosing a representative sample of eight economists (Ashley, Cannan, Devas, Hobson, J. N. Keynes, Nicholson, Price, Smart) and describing their views in descending order of moral enthusiasm.

Devas opened his *Political Economy* with the statement that economics was purely a branch of ethics. He divided the moral sciences into 'general ethics, dealing with the foundations and nature of morality' and 'particular ethics, dealing with human actions in particular departments'.[9] Consequently he believed that theorising and fact-gathering were only preparatory to the economist's proper business, the ethical inquiry that was to follow. A good economist, said Devas, 'lives and breathes in a moral atmosphere; and if he dips into the great ocean of technical life, it is only like a seagull, to draw forth food for the denizens of the upper air.'[10] Economists, then, should 'leave sterile discussions of words, and sterile calculations concerning impossible conditions, and sterile accumulations of unverified facts; no longer to expose themselves and their anarchy to the mockery of educated public opinion . . .'[11] Instead they should revive

> the liquor question, the dwellings question, the recreation question, and diverse others connected with consumption, not to speak of questions concerned with production and distribution (why, for example, the final confutation and crushing of Karl Marx has to be done over again every twelvemonth) – all these questions could be answered, not by irresponsible and ill-informed journalists, but by the authoritative voice of the college of economists.[12]

Even Devas did not say it was unavoidable that economists should make value-judgements. He did argue, however, that an economist who did not might be cunningly trying for the best of both worlds. 'Most economists have quite wit enough to know what practical results follow from their innocent looking indicatives, and open bias is better than veiled bias.'[13]

Smart concluded his *Studies in Economics* (1895) by enjoining the economist to take 'what we may, without irreverence, conceive as the standpoint of the Almighty Himself'.[14] Yet he was a significant shade nearer to positivism than Devas, believing economics to be parallel, rather than subordinate, to ethics. He urged that philosophy and economics join hands, 'to find out and declare what is the true and right relation of economic activity among the other activities of human life'.[15] Economics, moreover, should be turned into a moral guide for ordinary lives: 'By making clear what certain uses of wealth involve [it] may point an immediately practicable way in which the conscientious person may proceed to clear his own little corner of creation.'[16] And in *The Distribution of Income* (1899) Smart endorsed Mill's contention that the laws of distribution were 'human' laws. This being so 'the economist, almost in spite of himself, is generally called to express an opinion on the results of distribution which, disguise it as he may, amounts very much to an ethical judgement'.[17]

Hobson's position is characteristically complicated; whether he escapes contradicting himself depends on nice points of interpretation. In *Wealth and Life* he gives the issue of economics' relation with ethics extended treatment, and seems to waver between pronouncing positive economics possible but undesirable, and pronouncing it impossible.

Hobson begins by saying that it is generally agreed that economic laws are less binding than past generations thought. But if this is so, then 'the real problems of modern economics are mainly to control economic resources by the intelligent will of man' in which case 'economics, as art' becomes a branch of human conduct.

> This creed demands a change in the conception of an economic science, not in the sense of a direct subordination to ethics, but as involving recognition that every operative 'ought' is an 'is', and must be taken account of in any analysis of economic forces. (p. 125)

So Hobson believes that economists must study other people's values, so far as these count as economic factors. But need economists make value-judgements themselves? The statement 'not in the sense of a direct subordination to ethics' rather suggests that Hobson thinks they need not. But then Hobson goes on to say that, since so many economic aims are moral ones, 'the disposition to deny the term normative to economic science ... is an obstructive procedure which hampers the progress of social science'. Here it sounds as if Hobson has, after all, fallen into the error of believing that, because economic agents make value-judgements, economic analysts must also do so. However, let us follow him further.

Next, Hobson takes up Lionel Robbins' claim that if we introduce distinctively ethical criteria we land ourselves in a region not merely outside measurable facts, but outside agreed facts.[18] While declaring that he himself cannot go as far as this, Hobson concedes that

> economists will generally be in agreement with him in preferring to keep their science within the sphere of actual behaviour and measurable motives and satisfactions ... The relations [this] permits between economics and ethics are hardly more than those of a bowing acquaintance.

But, Hobson continues, the demand for a wholly autonomous economics cannot be entertained:

> We cannot admit as the objective of economic activities either the yield of material goods which these activities produce, or the 'psychic income' which they yield as assessed in terms of current desiredness or satisfaction, without reference to their intrinsic desirability. (p. 127)

Hobson, then, is saying that the idea of desiredness necessarily involves that of desirability. But does he mean that the one in *practice* must involve the other (because their divorce leads to 'pointless' welfare economics of the Pigou variety); or that the one *logically* involves the other? If the latter, then Hobson is reasserting, in different language, the fallacy that the study of other people's values necessarily entails that one put forward one's own.

Finally, Hobson asks whether, given its connection with ethics, economics can survive as a separate science. 'We seem', he says, 'to be landed with the alternatives of attempting to preserve a distinctly economic field of study into which ethical concepts and valuations continually trespass, or else of dissolving economics altogether into an all-embracing ethics or humanism' (p. 133). In other words, Hobson believes that economics' ethical content depends on the extent of its boundaries. But again this is ambiguous: does he mean its *logically necessary* ethical content, or the ethical content it will need to add in order to be saying something worthwhile? If Hobson nowhere takes the trouble to make this ambiguity clear, that is probably because he does not think the issue very important. He was in no doubt that economics *ought* to make ethical judgements: and thus he understandably lacked interest in whether they were theoretically avoidable. And it was Hobson's insistence on making value-judgements in his capacity as an economist, as much as the analytical content of his work, which barred him from respectability in orthodox eyes.[19]

IV

Ashley believed that value-judgements must be made by any economist 'ready to allow that political economy ought to treat material interests as subordinate to the higher ends of human development'.[20] And in a review of L. L. Price's *Industrial Peace*, Ashley poured scorn on Marshall's positivistic urge to make recommendations to public inquiries purely as a private citizen. The public, Ashley said, was as likely to distinguish between the two Marshalls as the public of the thirteenth century to separate Benedetto Gaetani and Pope Boniface.[21]

Price himself thought that an economist who avoided value-judgements would have to be 'more or less than human'. Economists could not be contented to observe the connection of cause and effect without trying to set in motion the cause or to restrain its action. Nor could they contemplate the misery due to bad economic arrangements without seeking to devise and supply a remedy.[22]

Nicholson alternated between arguing that economic analysis can and should be delineated from ethics, and claiming that the economic and the ethical standpoint lead to much the same results anyway. From its opening pages, Nicholson's *Principles of Political*

Economy insists on the 'sharp distinction' between 'economic laws' and 'moral ideas'.[23] However, says Nicholson, it is only natural that, as opportunity arises, attention should be directed to the moral side of economic facts and institutions.[24] It is also traditional: Adam Smith himself interspersed his work with moral reflections even if they are 'essentially *obiter dicta*, and might be omitted without affecting the main argument'.[25] And Nicholson follows the tradition, discussing at length what the ideal distribution of wealth is, before pulling himself and his readers up with the reminder that 'the comparison of ethical ideals' does not fall within 'the positive science' of political economy.[26]

This is one Nicholson speaking. The other Nicholson was an altogether less clinical character who, not content with merely presenting his own political views as neutral economic truths, would then claim the sanction of morality for them too. The following assertion, for example, was intended to show that there is no opposition between 'common-sense morality' and political economy.

> it ought to require no very deep insight to discover that a social order that depends almost entirely on freedom of contract, implies a much higher degree of moral development than is to be found in a society only held together by obedience to authority.[27]

Speaking, of course, as private citizens, we may agree. But to use this statement as an argument for the congruence of morality and political economy is to identify both with economic liberalism. Nicholson's strong ideological preferences will be considered further in the next chapter.

Nicholson represents the last intermediate stage before the insistent positivists. *Cannan* excised the 'ought' from economics at an early age, writing in his 1886 Cobden Essay Prize entry that, although statesmen and politicians might use political economy in forming their conclusions, 'it is no more the business of Political Economy or Economics to tell them what their conclusions should be, than it is the business of mathematics'.[28] Quoting Toynbee's contention that some answer must be given to the pressing questions of the day, and if political economy did not give one, journalism would, Cannan replied, 'Then let journalism', asking what else Toynbee thought it was for.[29] Cannan agreed with Marshall that, while the economist was as entitled to political opinions as anyone else, these opinions should be uttered explicitly as those of an ordinary citizen.[30] By 1902 Cannan was stressing the *tactical* importance of this rule: it was politic to avoid politics and the economist could do so by saying he only explained cause and effect.[31]

As Cannan grew older, he exchanged a passive self-denying positivism for an aggressive and active one. 'The Practical Utility of Economic Science' (*Economic Journal*, December 1902) gave economics the task of reducing the moral content of discussions of distribution, both by showing where ethical arguments are misplaced ('the peacemaking influence of economic theory lies chiefly in the fact that it tends to get rid of that stupid cry for "rights" and "justice" which causes and exacerbates industrial and commercial quarrels') and by showing where they could be replaced by more effective economic ones.

> Moralists and statesmen have long seen the evils of great inequality of wealth, and now, thanks to modern discoveries in economic theory, the economist is able to explain ... that it makes a given amount of produce less useful. (p. 462)

We began with Devas and his intensely ethical 'denizens of the upper air'; with Cannan we are hedge-hopping just above the flat fields of pure positivism. Finally we touch down with *J. N. Keynes*, who not only believed that an economist should make policy recommendations *only* as a private citizen, but abjured this role, even in his own diaries.[32]

V

Laymen in the Marshall era invariably accused economists of too much neutrality rather than too little. Typical was the *Dundee Advertiser*'s review of Hobson's *Work and Wealth*. 'If ... questions of high moral importance do not come within the scope of true political economy, we need not wonder that ardent reformers shun it as a mere trifle.'[33] And the *Church Gazette*'s review of Hobson's *Economics of Distribution* contained a revealing phrase: 'Mr Hobson has not yet advanced to the stage erewhile reached by the great Ruskin, for the probable reason that hardly any serious economist ever can; he is unable e.g., to regard capital as a mere fiction, and usury as a total fraud.'[34] In other words, to be a serious economist necessarily barred you from taking a proper ethical view.

Semi-laymen could be equally severe. Sidney Ball, reviewing Nicholson's *Principles of Political Economy* in the *Economic Review*, said that Nicholson's whole position assumed that economic distribution was a matter of ethical indifference, and that 'if this is so, then economics ceases to be of any practical interest'.[35] Sir Leo Chiozza Money, a member of parliament who did much statistical work to expose the extent of inequalities in Britain, had strong advice for Cannan.

> Do not ask what determines but tell your students both what does and what ought to determine. Tell them of the moral and physical considerations which should lead us to see that fair wages (you remember how Jevons sneered at 'fair wages') are paid. But perhaps you do.[36]

In fact Cannan was one of the few economists who did not talk about fair wages. In general, however, ethical neutrality was permissively interpreted by economists. The role of morality in economics was a much less contentious issue among them than the role of deduction. There was certainly nothing resembling a positive or a normative 'school' of economics. Smart and Devas, it is true, wrote with a very strong ethical flavour; Hobson made so little of the positive/normative distinction that it is not clear whether he believed it existed or not. But in general the line between positive and normative economics was not only accepted by most economists of all schools, but drawn in much the same place, as an exact and absolute distinction but one which might be sinned against in practice when the economist held a strong view about a particular question. No one saw it as unprofessional that an economist should openly recommend policies on the basis of a welfare analysis, freely interspersing theory and prescription throughout his work; no one was likely to see it as unprofessional with the example of Marshall's *Principles* in front of him. While the consensus followed J. N. Keynes, that the economist was entitled to make value-judgements only if he made it clear that he was speaking as an ordinary citizen, the consensus also expected the ordinary citizen to invade his own and each other's works to an extraordinary degree.

In this respect the pioneers of professional economics had more in common with those whom they wished to exclude than with the successors they trained. For though Marshall, Edgeworth, Wicksteed and Foxwell may have been the first generation to professionalise themselves in terms of theory, they were also in another sense the last pre-professional generation. None of them was an economist to begin with; but their own influence on the subject made them the last generation who could come to economics relatively late without being at a grave and perhaps life-long professional disadvantage. And because they came to it late, they brought with them a broader and more developed range of social concerns than their successors did. And there was another reason for this: that as economics changed, so did the average balance of motives which attracted people into it.

But it was not just that economists of the Marshall era were so strongly interested in so many things that they felt obliged to give their private selves an extended hearing. At least as important in pushing ethical judgements to the fore were the developments in ethics itself. Neoclassical economics flourished at a time when the combined influence of Darwin, Spencer and Huxley had made it temporarily reputable to regard ethics as a qualitative science of human development. Thus economists, provided they cast their ethics in an evolutionary mould, did not necessarily see moral judgements as incompatible with the scientific spirit. It is now time for a detailed look at what this implied.

VI

It will have been noticed in the preceding survey that several economists wrote of ethical and economic considerations as if the two were commensurable. Sometimes, no doubt, this was mere careless speech. When Nicholson said, for example, that slavery was unjustified on either economic or ethical grounds, he presumably meant that its abolition had both increased America's wealth (a positive statement with normative implications) and removed an injustice (a normative statement). But sometimes there are signs of genuine belief in the commensurability of economics and ethics. And this was not the fault of the concept of 'normative economics' but the fault of the concept (not invented by economists) of 'positive ethics'.

No one called positive ethics by that name – if they had, they might have seen that it was not ethics at all. It was the side of Social Darwinism which measured the ethical rightness of an action by its effect on, and defined the ethical progress of human nature in terms of, social evolution (however the latter was defined.) Thus T. H. Huxley defined morality as 'a real and living belief in that fixed order of nature which sends social disorganisation upon the track of immorality, as surely as it sends physical diseases after physical trespasses'.[37] This definition of morality, it is true, can be interpreted as falling short of positive ethics. Huxley was not necessarily defining immorality *purely* as 'that which is punished by social disintegration'. But Spencer and Leslie Stephen went beyond Huxley. Spencer held that it was the business of ethics to deduce from history what kinds of actions tend to produce happiness and what kinds to produce unhappiness. However valuable such a study may be, it is not ethics. It is not even on the same plane as ethics, which asks, not what makes men happy, but to what extent happiness is the criterion of good. Stephen made a slightly different mistake in writing a history of the evolution of ethical attitudes and presenting it as a major contribution to moral philosophy.

With Huxley, Spencer and Stephen each pouring his colourful dye into the once-pure well of ethics, it is not surprising that some economists became confused. Even Sidgwick, professional moral philosopher though he was, hovers at one point on the brink of positive ethics. Sidgwick quotes the statement, made 'some years ago by a writer of repute', that 'a man's first and last duty is to see and do those things which the social organism of which he is a member calls on him to do'.[38] If we admit this statement, Sidgwick continues, we admit sociology's claims to reduce the older subject of ethics to a department of itself.

But we would be admitting no such thing. There would still be the ethical question of what the social organism *ought* to call on the individual to do. Admittedly Sidgwick then pulls himself together, going on to say that sociology cannot answer any ethical question and ethics cannot answer any sociological one. But, in the meantime, he has come curiously close to endorsing Social Darwinism's philosophical fallacy.

It was left to L. T. Hobhouse among evolutionary sociologists to make a clear distinction between social development and ethical progress. 'The fact that a thing is evolving is no proof that it has progressed.'[39] And Hobson and Morris Ginsberg, Hobhouse's joint biographers, approvingly drew this lesson from Hobhouse's work.

The scientific problem is to correlate the several aspects of social change and to measure the kind and amount of growth in the light of criteria not necessarily ethical but analogous to those that might be employed by the biologist in dealing with organic evolution. The ethical point is to determine whether the development thus established, if it be established, satisfies ethical standards of value.[40]

But is this passage enough to acquit Hobson of being under the influence of 'positive ethics'? Given that it comes very late in his career, given that even here there is the backsliding phrase 'not *necessarily* ethical', given above all that this passage was actually written by Ginsberg (though presumably read and approved by Hobson), there is considerable room for doubt. And Hobson's own contributions to social science show (as has been seen) an ambiguity as to the relationship between economics and ethics. We have already suggested one possible reason for this – that Hobson, not *wishing* to exclude ethical judgements from his economics, thought the question unimportant. But it is not the only possible explanation. The other one is that his obvious (and uncritically paid) debt to evolutionary sociology extended (equally uncritically) to its conception of ethics. And indeed these two explanations are not necessarily strict alternatives, because it may be that it was precisely Hobson's lack of interest in the positive/normative distinction which held him back from probing and seeing through Social Darwinist 'ethics'.

But this is to digress. The idea that ethics was no more than a science had its greatest impact on those economists who clung hardest to their scientific status. Hobson did not need Social Darwinism to give him permission to write, in his capacity as an economist, about ethical progress. Marshall did.

VII

Marshall's position on the issue of value-judgements was made clear very early on. Economists should condemn what they thought wrong, but economic science had no normative authority. 'Direct decisions on questions of moral principle she must leave to her sister, the Science of Ethics.'[41] Marshall reiterated this position when attacking Henry George;[42] and again in his inaugural lecture at Cambridge. He enlarged on it in the *Principles*, distinguishing between the 'strictly scientific' questions investigated by the economist and 'practical issues which stimulate the inquiries of the English economist at the present time, though they do not lie wholly within the range of his science'. All the latter were strongly ethical:

How should we act as to increase the good and diminish the evil influence of economic freedom, both in its ultimate results and in the course of its progress? If the first are good and the latter evil, but those that suffer the evil, do not reap the good; how far is it right that they should suffer for the benefit of others . . . Taking it for granted that a more equal distribution of wealth is to be desired . . . how far should an increase in the income of the poorer classes and a diminution of their work be aimed at, even if it involved some lessening of national material wealth? . . . etc. etc. (p. 41).

Thus the economist as private citizen had much to do. And Marshall the private citizen was everywhere. He attended Professor Marshall's lectures doggedly; his constant interruptions must have been very frustrating to the latter, who had not come along to tell students that one of the best ways to use their wealth was to buy pictures, exhibit them and leave them to the nation,[43] or to tell them that keeping up with fashion was 'a crime'[44] or that the *nouveau riche* was a trial to himself and to his friends.[45] Marshall the private citizen appeared constantly throughout the *Principles*, arguing for example that there was 'no other so urgent need for bold expenditure'[46] as increased aid to the helpless. He wrote to *The Times*[47] advocating public works to help the unemployed, but opposed old age pensions in the *Economic Journal*.[48] He gave the Royal Commission on the Aged Poor a memorandum on 'Ethical Aspects of Limitations of Poor Relief'.[49] And he told the Cooperative Congress of 1889 that every sensible man would rather have a trade union leader than an ironmaster as a friend. What he used to say to ironmasters has not survived.

There was thus an untidy give-and-take between Marshall the economist and Marshall the private citizen. But Marshall the static theorist and Marshall the economic biologist – whatever we think of the latter – are triumphantly integrated: Talcott Parsons' charge of intellectual schizophrenia fails totally (albeit provocatively). To begin with, it is certainly a mistake to conclude from Parsons' study that Marshall's evolutionary hankerings either did affect, or should have affected, the analytical content of his economics. But one can go further than this. His hankerings did not even affect (and should not have affected) the *value* he placed on his static analysis. The problem which Parsons wishes onto Marshall (that the latter could not compare the effectiveness of different means to an end because he recognised that the end changed with the means) was not Marshall's problem. Indeed, Marshall was perhaps the only neoclassical economist for whom it was *not* a problem. For if we believe that (1) the more efficiently a means reaches today's ends, the better the ends it creates for tomorrow and (2) better ends do not need more resources than worse ones, then the most efficient means are unambiguously the most desirable. And Marshall did make both the above assumptions.

First, he linked the worker's moral progress to his material prosperity. (The very first paragraph of the first edition of the *Principles* was about the influence exerted on a man's character by the way his income was earned. The next was about the influence of that income's size.) This led to the belief that to maximise the quantity of output today would maximise the quality of output demanded and activities pursued tomorrow. And (our second point) quality was a moral variable, and its increase did not imply increasing expense in terms of resources. Indeed the *Principles* suggested that as civilisation progressed so would the number of 'non-purchasable' pleasures.[50] Nor did Marshall think that higher wages in themselves would necessarily cost the community more than lower ones. 'Skilled labour is generally the cheapest where wages are highest.'[51]

To maximise real incomes today, therefore, would raise future aspirations without making them harder to satisfy. Marshall has steered round the neoclassical problem. The corollary, however, is that in Marshall's work every 'static' reallocation of resources has unavoidable ethical implications. This point Marshall stressed himself: 'In all economic questions considerations of the higher ethics will always assert themselves, however much we try to limit our inquiry for an immediate practical purpose.'[52]

Marshall's own distinctive attitudes, as described above, must now be placed against his intellectual background. Utilitarianism and evolutionism – however opposed in other respects – both helped to give ethics a 'scientific' empirical status, even in the minds of those who, like Sidgwick, argued against 'positive ethics'. To make ethical judgements and yet persuade oneself science had not been left behind, the manufacture of biological and evolutionary metaphors was needed. Marshall, like Sidgwick, did not go the lengths of seeing ethics and economics as collateral, logically commensurable branches of an evolutionary super-science. But he did follow the trend of the time in seeing ethics as a study with pronounced empirical content. (How else could he have remarked of evolution:

'*Ethically* it is the successor of so-called Utilitarianism'?)[53] And so the belief that all economic phenomena had immediate ethical implications, wedded to the belief that ethics itself was looking to social science for help, was enough to tempt him both into assuming an ethical role and into reassuring himself that he was not seriously compromising his professional one. Marshall the moralist, dressed up as Marshall the economic biologist, egged on Marshall the ordinary citizen to speak out in public by telling him he was speaking more or less professionally after all.

Nor is this all. Marshall was far from thinking that another half-crown a week for a working man would have a standardised effect on his wants and activities, regardless of who he was, how he got it, and how much freedom he had to spend it as he liked. The resulting overall position – that to deprive was to deprave but that some privations depraved more than others – was such as to maximise the explicit ethical content of Marshall's work. If he had believed there was no link between income and morality he could have written positive economics with a clear conscience. If he had believed that the link was strong, simple and uniform, he could have done the same, allowing the ethical implications to speak for themselves. But, believing that the link was strong, but variable and complex, he was obliged to make a separate ethical assessment of every economic policy and every suggested reform he examined.

VIII

Marshall was more optimistic than any of his contemporaries about the link between income and character. Jevons had been decidedly sceptical. 'There are comparatively few signs that the wages of the working-classes, even when sufficient, are saved and applied really to advance the condition of the recipients.'[54] Cannan (the middle-aged conservative Cannan, admittedly) went out of his way in a lecture to disagree with Marshall).

> 'Poverty causes degradation.' Why put it that way? Poverty is no new phenomenon, and there is no reason consequently to suppose anyone has been degraded.[55]

But the right foil to Marshall's thought is, once again, Cunningham's.

Cunningham, like Marshall, believed the relation between wealth and activities was circular. 'Human energy gives rise to better material conditions and better material conditions afford the opportunity for greater energy.'[56] Unlike Marshall, however, Cunningham assigned strong immediate priority to moral, rather than material, remedies for the condition of the working class. Though agreeing that the plight of the labourer since the industrial revolution had had largely material causes, he asserted that remedies 'must be sought not in any external conditions but in the personal convictions and aspirations which supply the springs of human action'.[57] This belief naturally reduced the value which Cunningham placed on, and hence the space he devoted to, positivistic economic analysis. So did his belief that 'what makes for the comfort of the masses in the present generation does not necessarily result in the material welfare of posterity in the long run'. The paragraph from which the above is taken continues in such a way as to leave no doubt that Cunningham's sentiments derive from his holistic and historicist perspective.

> There are two points of view which must always be distinguished in our minds: the good of society on the one hand, and the welfare of individuals who compose society on the other. While this distinction needs to be drawn even from an economic point of view, it is still more important to keep it in mind when we try to take account of culture and character and other elements in human nature. (*Christianity and Politics*, p. 165)

The implication of this is that moral factors count for enough, and operate in such a way, seriously to downgrade as a worthwhile activity the material comparison of different social systems: a conviction which could only encourage the historian in Cunningham at the expense of the economist.

Cunningham, then, refused to make the identification, largely accepted by Marshall, of economic with total welfare, and this caused his economic writings to be less analytical, more historical and more ethical than Marshall's. Cunningham wrote ethical economics with positive interludes: Marshall wrote positive economics with ethical implications. This reinforces the point made in the previous chapter: that to be a professional economist the first step was to believe, or persuade yourself, that economic and total welfare were closely linked. There we saw it in relation to professional theorising: now we have seen it also in relation to the differing degrees of professional neutrality. It was also briefly suggested, at the end of the last chapter, that the identification of economic with total welfare normally went with liberalism. It is time for the relationship between professionalism, marginalism and liberalism to take the centre of the stage. In the next chapter, it will. This chapter has argued that neoclassical economists did not achieve ethical neutrality, although it is attainable, because they did not try to. The next will argue that they did not achieve ideological neutrality, although they often tried to, because it is unattainable.

10

The ideology of marginalism

For goodness sake don't say that I have 'intense sympathy with the working classes', or am 'a man with broad ethical views' or that sort of thing generally.

(Smart to Cannan – asking for testimonial for the Glasgow professorship, 1896)

Well we can't go into the question of collectivism here. We have gone to seven o'clock and the end of the academical year – are there any questions?

(anon. student's notes on Cannan's lectures, L.S.E.)

An ethically neutral statement can still be ideologically biased. Take, for example, the following remark of Cannan's:

> Among well-to-do people there is not one person in a hundred who will not work more rather than less in consequence of an increase in taxation.[1]

This is an entirely non-normative statement; it contains no imperative. But if, after having read it in context, we decide that is based less on satisfactory evidence than on an unfulfilled wish to believe that more equal distribution does not damage production, then we term it an ideological statement. Indeed the very decision to be ethically neutral may be related to one's ideology. The positive economist may be positive only because he is happy to leave recommendations to politicians. Thus – insofar as neutrality is a criterion of professionalism – professional economists are likely to be chosen from those who either approve of existing society or trust existing politicians to try and do something about it. And an examination of the ideology underlying economic professionalism is all the more important now we have seen how closely professionalisation was linked with the advance of the marginal utility school. For no economic perspective has been so ferociously attacked as the neoclassical one. To its radical critics, past and present, neoclassical economics is an elegant bourgeois cul-de-sac – narrow, exclusive and shut off from the world outside. It is argued that the main effect of neoclassical economics –

perhaps even the main motive for inventing it – has been to divert attention from capitalism's faults and, like Orwell's Newspeak, to narrow the scope of economics until radical changes can no longer even be discussed. Jevons, Marshall and Edgeworth, to their detractors, are prime examples of 'Victorian middle-class hypocrisy', building ornately innocent façades which concealed half-truths and distortions which in turn camouflaged oppression and misery.

Marx, although he outlived Jevons, paid no attention to marginal utility theory. Schumpeter claims – rightly, perhaps – that if Marx had lived fifty years later he would have used marginal analysis as a matter of course. The Fabians broadly approved of neoclassical value theory, at least after Shaw's well-publicised conversion, by Wicksteed, away from a labour theory of value to a subjective one. And Hobson, his autobiography tells us, took some considerable time to realise 'how potent was the influence of victorious capitalism to impress the justice and utility of its procedure upon the dawning science of Economics and to exclude from consideration all attempts to challenge its intellectual domination'.[2]

But, once convinced, Hobson set himself to convince others. A short article in the *University Review* for June 1915 listed eight 'myths' which orthodox political economy had fabricated for the defence of economic privilege.[3] Hobson's eight points added up to a straightforward collectivist critique which made no particular distinction between classical and neoclassical economics. But in *Free Thought in the Social Sciences*, published eleven years later, Hobson did single out both neoclassicism itself, and the mathematical methods associated with it, as 'the modern substitute for that economic man moving in the "simple system of natural liberty" by which vested interests defended themselves against dangerous assaults in the earlier era of modern capitalism' (p. 107).

Hobson saw orthodox economics as only one of the intellectual buttresses of capitalism. His biography of Veblen endorsed the latter's attack on the conventional teaching of history, and demanded 'a veracious history of modern times which might disclose the actual process by which the wealth and power of the ruling classes were attained'.[4] And *The Fight for Democracy* (1917) congratulated Britain's capitalists on their 'servile press, servile schools, servile church, which they utilise to drape their selfish dominion with the gallant devices of national service, imperialism, "scientific management" and other cloaks for class-mastery'.[5]

But our focus is specifically economic. From the later Hobson, at least, there was little interruption in the allegations that orthodox economics was profoundly, perhaps even primarily, apologetic in its purpose. Was it? Let us start with the marginal revolution itself.

II

The idea that a 'ruling class' discarded classical economics because its implications had become too awkward for them has been much challenged in recent years. In *Economic Theory in Retrospect*, Mark Blaug has argued that classical economics is a far better instrument for defending private property than neoclassical economics. In the first place, Blaug says, 'It would be difficult to think of an argument more agreeable to business interests than the classical wages fund doctrine.'[6] Secondly, marginal utility theory brought along with it the uncomfortable implication that equal incomes maximised total satisfaction. T. W. Hutchison's *On Revolutions in Economics*, while reiterating both these points, stresses also that the defects of classical value theory, the growing difficulty in 1870 of explaining market wages in terms of labour's cost of production, and 'the practical impotence of the Ricardo–Mill theories' in the face of monopolies, increasing returns and the problem of public utilities[7] were together more than sufficient to create a widespread crisis of confidence in the classical paradigm. And any change in the political climate associated with the rise of marginalism, Hutchison continues, was a conciliatory change rather than a reactionary one. The extensions of the franchise in 1867 and 1884, the political and legal recognition and establishment of trade unions (1871 and 1875), interacted with attacks on the 'natural' wage doctrine (part of the breakup of the old political economy) and calls for progressive taxation to finance social reform (backed up by invoking the new).

Hutchison's contention that ideological factors played second string in the marginal revolution, being neither a necessary nor a sufficient cause, is true, important and salutary. But one can accept this part of his argument without agreeing that the implications of Ricardian economics were *unambiguously* more conservative than those of neoclassicism. Certainly many (non-socialist) economists at the turn of the century believed Ricardian economics had socialistic implications so close to the surface as to make even an unembellished statement of the doctrine dangerous. Cannan claimed that 'The movement for nationalising land without compensation to present owners, on which Mr Henry George and others have wasted immense energy, would probably never have been heard of, if the Ricardian economists had not represented rent as a sort of vampire.'[8] Ashley suggested that Ricardian doctrines had lost support among conservatives after socialists, with 'much show of reason',[9] had taken them up; and Foxwell noted on the inside front cover of his copy of Ricardo's *Principles* that it was

> the first edition of this disastrous book which gave us Marxian Socialism and the Class War. Deductive playthings of this type, completely divorced from realities, make very dangerous literature for the half educated. It is like giving a child a razor to play with.[10]

Cannan in particular paid much attention to the respective political implications of classical and neoclassical value theory. In *Theories of Production and Distribution 1776–1848* he blamed the current enthusiasm, among quite 'reasonable' people, for confiscating the property of others, on the Ricardian failure to '[give] the distribution of wealth between individuals its proper place, instead of being so exclusively devoted to the distribution of wealth between economic categories such as "labourers", "capitalists" and "landlords"'.[11] Cannan recognised, however, that in at least one important area it was classical economics which was conservatively inclined and neoclassical economics which was more radical. Addressing the British Association in 1890, he praised marginal utility theory for giving a rationale to the 'commonsense' belief that 'roughly speaking, the more equally a given income is distributed, the further it will go in producing economic welfare'. He continued:

> In common thought and speech this is recognised in many ways. It is recognised in the long-standing, and to some extent just, outcry against economists for devoting too much attention to the production of wealth and its distribution among ideal classes and too little to its distribution among individuals.[12]

Cannan, then, is criticising classical economics for diverting attention from the obvious arguments in favour of greater equality. 'Till Jevons wrote', the paper continues, 'the economist had to be deaf to the voice of common sense on this subject.'

> However much he might dislike it, he was compelled to maintain that the distribution of the produce of industry could make no difference to the economic welfare of a nation ... But since the introduction into economics

of the Jevonian theory of value, there is no longer any excuse for taking this narrow view.[13]

So, according to Cannan, classical economics had both revolutionary and reactionary implications, both of which were receiving short shrift from the emerging neoclassical generation. If he is right, then the modern radical claim that the marginal revolution added to the armoury of weapons for holding down class conflict, and the modern 'orthodox' claim that it dispatched many of the self-interested excuses for preserving the status quo, are perfectly compatible with one another. Is it going too far to claim that Cannan settled the argument over the ideological nature of the marginal revolution several decades before it began?

III

But no one has ever argued that the character of the neoclassical movement was fully determined from its birth. In fact we have to deal with three separate issues: the nature of the marginal revolution, how economists subsequently used the neoclassical paradigm and how it used them. Having looked at the first of these issues, we now move on to the second.

Although the marginal revolution came too soon to have been engineered as a 'bourgeois' answer to Marxism, neoclassical doctrines did come to be wielded explicitly against Marx. Though the Austrians took, and retained, the lead in this attack, their message found support in England. Thus the *Economic Review*'s reviewer of Bohm-Bawerk's *Capital and Interest* concluded

there is no question that the labour theory of value is false, that the labourer in general does receive his whole product at its valuation at the time when he receives his wages; that, as labourer, he has no claim upon the interest of capital.[14]

This was written in 1891. Some English economists, however, had already paid serious attention to Marx – albeit not necessarily from a neoclassical perspective. Wicksteed's article 'The Marxian Theory of Value' appeared in *To-Day* in October 1884. Its tone was critical, arguing that prices were not necessarily proportional to quantities of labour embodied in goods (Marx's distinction between value and price is ignored) and that the price of labour often bore little relation to its cost of production. Ashley wrote little of Marx – either in the

1880s or later – but a letter to his fiancée, written some time between 1886 and 1888, and listing those points of Marxist doctrine with which he agreed and disagreed, suggests a fairly painstaking study of Marx's writing.[15] That Marshall was mentioning Marx in lectures in 1886 has already been seen[16] – but there is nothing in his notes to suggest any extensive acquaintance with *Capital*. Certainly Marshall never felt familiar enough with Marx to satisfy his own demanding standards as a lecturer – as a letter to Foxwell (12 February 1906) makes clear.

> I think no one can lecture safely on German Socialism without having studied recent writings, including Marx's *Capital* Vols. 2 and 3, and other posthumous works. I have not read them. But whenever I talk to Germans about Socialism, they come to the front. I have looked at them sufficiently to think that they do not save Marx's position. But I should not be willing to lecture on the subject till I have read two or three thousand pages of recent German literature.

By this time, however, the tone of orthodox economists towards Marx had hardened into unqualified hostility. Nicholson's tirade against Marx has been seen already. Bonar's review of Ramsay MacDonald's *Socialism and Society* tried to combine contemptuous dismissal of Marx with the cheerful determination to believe that thinking socialists had outgrown his influence; 'When socialism was built on the economics of Marx, which was a perversion of Ricardo's, and on his philosophy of history, which was a perversion of Hegel's, the refutation of it was delusively simple.'[17] Cannan, however, was less sanguine about the socialists. 'They are so sunk in the Marxian morass that they can't get out.'[18]

The important point, however – in spite of all the above – is that there was little conscious inclination among English economists to use marginal analysis actively as a weapon against Marxism. Nor is there any correlation between enthusiasm for marginalism and distaste for Marx. Indeed we are not sure if Nicholson, by the force of his opinions, does not achieve, single-handedly, an overall correlation the other way!

But what of attitudes to socialism in general, non-Marxian variants included? With the possible exception of Pigou, it would be hard to classify any neoclassically-minded English economist before 1914 as a socialist. But the same is true of the opponents of neoclassicism. Ashley and Cunningham were conservatives. Hobson occupied the frontier country where liberalism met social democracy. And the three economists who continued to write from pre-Jevonian standpoints, Sidgwick, Macleod and Nicholson, were the most anti-socialist of all. Nicholson and Macleod[19] have been quoted already; Sidgwick told readers of the *Economic Journal* in 1895 that 'no positive contribution of importance has been made to Economic Science by any Socialist writer throughout the century'.[20]

Macleod was out of touch with the mainstream of economic thought. But Sidgwick and Nicholson were not, and the fact that they could evidently feel satisfied with attacking socialism on so crude a level says much about the attitudes of the fellow economists to whom they addressed themselves. We have already seen Marshall, Nicholson and Macleod[21] distinguishing between 'economists' and 'socialists' as though it was to be taken for granted that the two categories were mutually exclusive. The distinction was also made by L. L. Price,[22] and, in a characteristically picturesque passage, by Devas, who warned that, if the 'firm of political economy' hoped to thrive in the future

> we must move our premises into a more respectable neighbourhood; we must artistically decorate our shop front without, and keep a well-assorted stock of Ruskinian goods within. Else we may find our customers leaving us for the socialistic store and ourselves on the way to the bankruptcy court.[23]

IV

Again, however, attempts to use neoclassical doctrine explicitly against socialism were rare. So were attempts to use marginal productivity theory to justify the existing distribution of income; though Nicholson, in 1896, was still using *classical* principles to justify the distribution which would prevail under conditions of perfect competition. His argument was neither tactful nor persuasive:

> A duke might be willing to pay a cook five thousand a year rather than do his own cooking, and a cook might be willing to accept his keep as wages rather than do his own starving, but the actual market price of a cook will be between the two extremes. And the reason is that, under competition, all the cooks (making allowances, of course, by a kind of multiplication table, for differences in quality), for work of the same kind, must have the same wages.[24]

How exactly this is supposed to justify the distribution of income between the cook and the duke is not explained, as Edgeworth was quick to point out. 'Our complaint is against the unequal treatment of the cooks and the dukes. That the cooks fare equally well or badly as compared with each other is a poor consolation.'[25]

Edgeworth's comments illustrate again the generally less conservative outlook of the marginalists compared with the survivors of classicism. Marshall, on the whole, went further than Edgeworth. Though he did not make a great deal of the principle of declining marginal utility as an argument for greater equality, he explicitly rejected the marginal productivity theory as a justification for the status quo, stressing that the market rate for a job had 'no claim to be an absolutely just rate; it is relative to the existing state of things here and now'.[26] But, in general, the tone of Marshall's remarks on redistribution was that greater equality was a cause which should transcend disagreements over economic theory. He criticised 'the maintenance of those rights of property which lead to extreme inequalities of wealth'.[27] He wished 'to see wages increase at the expense of the incomes of the well-to-do classes as fast as possible without causing the latter to strike permanently'; he 'could put up with their striking for a little while'.[28] And he told Bishop Westcott that he would promote redistribution from the rich to the poor 'by every means in my power that were legitimate; and I would not be specially scrupulous in interpreting that word'.[29]

The best-known attempt to use marginal productivity theory to justify the status quo is J. B. Clark's. Clark argued that marginal productivity theory showed that workers and capitalists were paid according to their respective contributions to the total product. Therefore whatever distribution of income existed was a just one. This piece of apologetics is wheeled out so indefatigably, in virtually every radical critique of orthodox economics, that it probably backfires on the radicals. Confronted by J. B. Clark, always J. B. Clark and never anyone but J. B. Clark, the reader is likely to conclude that his kind of ideological statement must be extremely rare in neoclassical writing, or else other examples would have been found. Nevertheless, Clark's idea was not rejected out of hand by all other economists. Edgeworth for one was notably hesitant in his criticisms.

> [Professor Clark says] that the division of total produce effected by the play of the labour market, or which would be effected if the market played freely, constitutes the best possible distribution. Doubtless it is difficult to find a better. Yet there are those who doubt whether a fair share may not be defined

by some other criterion than the produce added by the marginal labourer, whether our author has not too slightly dismissed the aspirations embodied in other definitions.[30]

And Smart's intellectual journey, as the marginal productivity theory and a concurrent belief in the status quo rose, fell, wavered and interacted in his mind, is of some considerable value to the historian. For it demonstrates not only the limited ideological persuasive power of the marginal productivity theory, but also something about the nature and limits of the persuasive power of the whole marginal paradigm.

In *Studies in Economics* (1895), Smart's tone was tentative: he was waiting for a more fully developed theory of distribution before passing judgement on the disproportionate rewards which different classes had drawn from industrialism. However, there are signs, even in *Studies*, that Smart is groping his way towards the doctrine eventually laid down by Clark: 'Distribution of income according to the product created certainly seems, on the face of it, a distribution according to reason ... the latest works of Professor J.B. Clark and Professor Wieser [are] particularly suggestive' (p. 257).

By 1899, when Smart published *The Distribution of Income*, his position had developed. The main message of the book comes in the final chapter, entitled 'Is It a Bad Distribution?' This starts with a robust broadside against egalitarianism and in favour of existing arrangements. Yet after this, the chapter dwindles steadily, until the book fades out on a pianissimo of doubt, evasion and platitude. First, Smart admits that no theory of the distribution of the product among the factors can help us pass any judgement on the distribution of factors among people. This inevitably leads on to the admission that neoclassical theory can provide no arguments of its own against the expropriation of capital. 'If it be objected *in limine* that no justice is possible under private property and free transfer of property, then of course, there is no more to be said ...'[31]

And so to the concluding paragraph:

given private property, the free transfer of property, and the inequality of start which the possession of two factors gives, there is a good deal to be said for the present distribution as a Distribution according to Service. At least there is enough of 'rough justice' in it to make even those of us who feel its imperfections most keenly think twice before we give our countenance to any rival scheme which has yet been proposed.[32]

Thus the only British economist who tried to derive a theory of distributive justice from the marginal productivity theory promptly fell over the fact that the latter did not imply, and could not imply, anything as to how factors of production should be distributed in the first place; and was reduced to vague mumblings that those who basically approved of capitalism should think twice before they abolished it. It is hard to see how anyone else could have done any better; it is therefore hard to see how the marginal productivity theory could ever have been persuasively used as a defence of the existing distribution.

V

But the use to which marginal productivity theory was put is only part of the question. Critics of neoclassical economics, past and present, have also argued that the intricacies of marginal analysis cause people to lose sight of the fact that market 'optima' are relative to the prior distribution of income. So did Wicksteed.

> The market does not tell us in any fruitful sense what are the 'national', 'social' or collective wants, or means of satisfaction of a community, for it can only give us *sums*, and the significance of a sum varies indefinitely according to its distribution.[33]

Critics have argued that neoclassical theory takes wants as autonomous, neglecting the near-coercive powers of producers over consumers through advertising and the like. So did Wicksteed.

> All along the line, from a certain type of ingenious advertiser to the financier (if he really exists) who engineers a war in order that he may arrange a war loan, we may study the creation of wants and passions, destructive of general welfare, for the sake of securing wealth to individuals.[34]

Critics have argued that neoclassicism covers conflicts of interest with a disingenuous veneer of apparent harmony. So did Wicksteed, who accused economists of assuming a coincidence between 'individually gainful and socially valuable occupations, privileges, or positions'.

> And this optimism makes a great deal of economic literature little better than apologetics, welcomed by those whose consciences need a soothing syrup, and cursed by those who realise the 'wounds and bruises and putrefying sores' skinned over by the use of such words as 'productive' 'useful', 'the supply of human wants' and the rest.[35]

Above all critics have argued – and this point to some extent incorporates all the others – that the atomistic premises of neoclassicism falsify reality by abstracting the relations of exchange between individuals from their social context. So did Wicksteed.

> these things ... derive their whole significance from their social and vital bearings, and ... the categories under which we discuss them conceal rather than reveal their meaning.[36]

However, it is important not to make too much of the fact that one neoclassical economist anticipated neoclassicism's modern critics. For Wicksteed stands out very much on his own. Marshall, it is true, warned about 'the mirage which is caused by the fact that the comfort of a few rich men sometimes has a higher bidding power in the market than more urgent needs of many poor'.[37] But it cannot be claimed that it was exactly typical for neoclassical theory to come packaged with a warning about its omissions and their consequences.

And even if all neoclassical economists *had* been Wicksteeds, would it have made much difference to the persuasive effect of their theories? We spoke earlier of the distinction between economists using marginalism and marginalism using economists. It is time to see what this distinction means.

VI

To make such a distinction at all may seem odd to some. It implies that a body of theory can bind an economist so tightly to a particular world view that he ends up an instrument of political views alien to his own. We believe this is true: but it is a proposition which needs painstaking defence.

If economists can be unaware of their own political motives in making statements – and unless this is conceded ideology collapses into propaganda or lying or both – then it is hard to believe that they are always conscious of the political implications of paradigms. Paradigms, moreover, are ideologically persuasive chiefly when their political implications are subtle enough for readers not to notice that they are being persuaded at all. If readers, why not writers too? But when an economist is *not* conscious of his paradigm's ideology, its connection with his own ideology becomes much looser. Up to a point, it is true, a paradigm is an ideologically selective personnel filter. A paradigm has a conservative ideology if it pushes aside, as not amenable to its brand of analysis, facts which conventionally imply radical conclusions. Since radicals are likely to see precisely these facts as socially important and hence worth studying, they may reject the paradigm as not providing adequate returns (in terms of social significance) to justify the intellectual outlay. But not all economists have strong ideological convictions, and not all economists decide what to study on grounds of social significance. Consequently not all economists will refuse to serve paradigms with ideologies distinct from their own.

Moreover, the gulf between paradigmatic and personal ideologies is widened by anything that inhibits economists from choosing their paradigm to fit their politics: and the professionalisation of economics under an exclusively neoclassical banner did exactly that. Economists who cared about professional recognition had to accept a world view which might or might not correspond to their own. And an economist whose beliefs really did correspond to the ideology of marginalism could no longer be certainly convicted of ideological motives in choosing his paradigm: there was always the possibility that professional ambition was the real cause.

Of course, the economist who uses a paradigm is not wholly straitjacketed into a particular patter of emphasis. He can, if he wishes, point out the paradigm's narrow focus and show his readers the areas of which it says nothing. But this is usually a limited exercise with still more limited effects. In the first place, professional assertiveness prompts economists to play up the scope and usefulness of their theories: thus the less attention given to matters outside their boundaries, the better. Indeed, to emphasise exceptions and qualifications to a theory, levels of explanation beyond its depth and economic realities outside its scope, is to sow doubts about whether the mental investment was justified.

Moreover, economists have good professional reasons to adopt exactly the type of paradigm which, when unqualified, gives the most misleading picture of reality – a mathematical paradigm which claims general applicability. Esoteric economics' attraction is that it excludes laymen from participation, and to some extent from criticism too. But esoteric economics gives a particularly biased picture of the world. Why?

The higher economic theory ascends, the more universality it claims. As mathematical rules of behaviour float clear of the agents, events and institutions which embedded them they lose their separate identities. All maximisations, all constraints, all markets take the same form. It should also be noted that professionalisation would give an incentive to greater universality even without high theory as the link. The paradigm on which professional authority rests cannot afford too many no-go areas.

But the more universal economics tries to be, the more dangerously selective it becomes. Economics can only expand its extensive margins at the expense of its intensive margins. This has nothing to do with economists having limited time– the remedy for that would be more economists. It is because the more universal the laws, the less they have to say about particular events, and to select a few aspects of a complex situation on the basis that these few aspects will translate readily into mathematical symbols is a certain recipe for bias.

None of this would matter so much if economists did justice to the exceptions, limitations and qualifications to their paradigms. But, as we have suggested, they have reasons for not doing this. And even when they do it, the impact may be less than they intended. First principles in study, like first experiences in life, leave the strongest impressions. To construct a perfectly competitive model of the economy and mention monopoly as an exception to this will produce a very different picture from the converse. To write about the Permanent Income Hypothesis, mentioning on the last page the severe difficulties in measuring permanent income, will produce a different effect from mentioning this drawback from the start.

Indeed this writer doubts if economists' qualification of their own theories does anything to dislodge them from their readers' minds. Faced with, say, a standard account of the neoclassical theory of the firm, with a few half-hearted 'real-life' exceptions tacked on to it, the reader may merely congratulate the writer on his realism, open-mindedness and intellectual honesty, and take the paradigm as being all the more authoritative. Listing exceptions and qualifications may also make the reader feel that the more that is wrong with a paradigm, the more must be right with it, to have justified so much trouble in exposition.[38]

Economists, then, seldom struggle effectively against the world view inherent in the paradigm they choose. Economic paradigms – classical, Marxist, neoclassical, Keynesian – differ above all in their philosophical points of departure – the knowingly simple views of the world which initiate their journeys towards reality. An economist is constrained both by his philosophical point of departure, and by the pattern of factual emphasis to which it leads. His attempts to round out the picture are likely to stick less firmly in readers' minds than the picture's methodological essence will. And such attempts will be enfeebled by the process of professionalisation – undermining the paradigm's exclusive authority will also undermine that of the profession. Professionalisation moreover, favours just that type of paradigm that takes a particularly selective view of the world.

Thus, in choosing his own methodological point of departure, the economist determines his believers' scientific destination. It remains to be shown how extensively he determines their political destination too.

VII

Take, for example, an economist arguing for a mixed economy. He might start by describing how a perfectly competitive market economy works, then remove various simplifying assumptions (such as perfect competition) and then instance areas where State regulation, planning or nationalisation are desirable. Or he might start with a hypothetical planned economy, then remove various simplifying assumptions (such as the perfect knowledge of the planning authority) and then instance cases where private enterprise should have its head. But the two books will have different political impacts. The first book will, implicitly if not explicitly, put the burden of proof on to socialism. Cases where the facts are unclear, or where the arguments on either side are incommensurable, will carry the implication 'no definite grounds for intervention'. In the second book the burden of proof, and the destination of unclear cases, will be in the other direction.

Reinforcing this is the fact that the neoclassical paradigm (which starts with a market economy) is best at uncovering reasons why government intervention is *not* needed in a particular case. Neoclassically-trained economists do to some extent gain the faculty of spotting market imperfections. But most market imperfections are visible enough anyway. The neoclassical telescope primarily helps the economist to see why superficially undesirable features of capitalism do *not* lead to a loss of welfare, or why the State's remedy may be worse than the disease. Incomes policies, minimum wage laws, anti-pollution laws (rather than taxes), laws to halt the 'brain drain', are all 'commonsense measures' whose rationale is reduced by neoclassical analysis. The nature of the neoclassical paradigm fits it best to the task of showing up cases where, contrary to 'common sense', government intervention is not desirable. Cases where neoclassical analysis justifies intervention are nearly always cases where 'common sense' already justifies it.

But in fact the first of these books (the one starting with a market economy and chronicling grounds for State intervention) is not hypothetical. It is *The Economics of Welfare* by A. C. Pigou, and, of its 800 pages, the vast majority deal with cases and recommendations for intervention by government, either on the side of production or distribution. Fundamentally, however, Pigou *is* upholding capitalism in that he is concerned – must be concerned, given his choice of paradigm – with how a free market attains socially desirable ends. This task, it is true, is undertaken partly to expose cases where the market should be supplanted. *The Economics of Welfare* contains more criticisms of unfettered capitalism than it does of socialism. But to categorise it, either in intention or in effect, as primarily a critique of capitalism would be misleading. Exceptions do not cease to be exceptions just because they last for 800 pages.

So, by constraining the economist's choice of facts, the neoclassical paradigm constrains his political message. Thus it must be accredited with an ideology of its own. And this is in spite of the fact that its practitioners had a wider range of personal opinions than their classical predecessors. This last fact has received some comment. Schumpeter said that after 1870 the English economist understood enough about the nature of theory to realise how much room was left for any social creed he chose. A. W. Coats has argued that the corpus of theory which grew up after 1870 *replaced* a common ideology as a unifying force. It is also likely that the very success of utilitarianism as a public doctrine destroyed its properties as professional cement for economists. There could hardly be an excited gleam of comradely recognition between utilitarian rationalists when it had become almost deviant to be anything else.

And so far as theory did replace political attitude as the economists' badge of membership, the result was that economics looked less united and hence – paradoxically – less authoritative to the outsider. A united policy conclusion is no stronger than a united theoretical base (indeed it is perhaps absurd to compare their dissimilar strengths at all) but it looks as if it is. Consensus out of diversity is persuasive, diversity out of consensus is disenchanting. By the outsider, the tree of economics will always be judged by its fruits, not its roots. (Why 'insiders' are odd enough to think otherwise is, of course, the main theme of this book.)

In the previous chapter it was argued that theoretical expertise replaced political commitment both by driving it out and by filling the gap its prior retreat was already leaving. It is hard to say – and perhaps there is no great need to say – which of these processes was pre-eminent. They interacted, and with a chemical inexorability. The more ready an economist was to accept that his political creed was his private affair, the more enthusiastically he could throw his weight behind the propagation of theoretical orthodoxy. And the more he conformed as a professional, the more he acquired a scientific status which turned his thoughts from a public political role. By 1914 enthusiasm had ceded to theory far more than it had originally meant to yield, and theory had appropriated from enthusiasm more than it had originally meant to take.

VIII

But just as there were diversities of outlook within the orthodox camp, so there may have been common ideological presuppositions which transcended its limits. There was certainly an ideological underpinning to the intense moralism which united most economists of all persuasions. It should also be considered whether there was a sectional ideology common and exclusive to the academic profession. Finally, we would like to examine the contention that *all* economics is in some sense 'liberal'.

One would need a pretty crude mind to write off all Victorian middle-class preaching at the workers (however unctuous some of it sounds today) as a mere class manoeuvre designed to elevate the importance of changes of heart and downgrade that of changes in the economic system. But an emphasis on individual moral self-improvement clearly did suit middle-class interests fairly well. If character was what mattered, material privileges were correspondingly less important. It might be objected to this that, by emphasising how much improved character owed to increased income, Marshall solved nothing. But in Marshall's mind a little extra income went a long way – indeed the stage of undesirable 'comforts' was soon reached. So Marshall the materialistic moralist's egalitarian demands, though urgent, were also fairly limited.

What, though, of the distinctive ideology – if any – of the academic profession? Marshall praised university life for its freedom from bias: the academic economist, he said, had 'no class or personal interests to make him afraid of any conclusion which the figures, when carefully interpreted, may indicate'.[39] In general, however, there seems no reason to think that academic employment either freed economists from outside ideologies or gave them a generalised 'ideology of academia'. Any correlation between university teaching and indifference to public affairs appears to have come about only because both were correlated with a specialised approach to economics. It was being an economic specialist, not being a don, that made the difference.

But it has also been alleged that economists of all theoretical persuasions have always worked, and still do work, under the aegis of a transcendent and largely inescapable liberalism. The assertion – it is Myrdal's[40] – has obvious parallels to this chapter's claim that neoclassical economists, try as they might, could not escape the intrinsic ideological implications of their theories. The difference is that Myrdal is not confining himself to one particular group of economists.

Can the idea be sustained that all economics has a common and inescapable methodological core which infuses it, willy-nilly, with a 'liberal' character? This writer does not think it can. Liberalism is the ideology which draws together the belief in the possibility and desirability of individual freedom, the belief that the State has no rights other than those which its citizens choose to grant it, the belief that the right to own property is both important in itself and also the only secure basis of other liberties, and the belief that most people are, at least potentially, the best judges of their own interests. What exactly are the fundamental assumptions, common to economics, which are supposed to conduce to these beliefs? Methodological individualism? Only if you leave out the entire Marxist tradition and most of the macroeconomics that has been written since 1936. The assumption that all economic bargains between individuals are free exchanges which benefit both parties? This assumption counts for little outside the classical and neoclassical schools.

It is certainly true that, in the classical period, economists tended to see their science as the vehicle of liberal values. (*The Economist*, founded in 1841, was so called not because it was intended to concentrate on economics, but because it was intended to express liberal views.) And this was recognised after the classical period ended. The Rt. Hon. Grant Duff, Governor of Madras, addressing Section F as its president in 1881, referred to 'the distrust excited in many minds by our parents, science and liberalism'. It is also true that English socialists often resembled their liberal compatriots more than they did their continental comrades. The empiricism of their outlook, the utilitarianism of their rhetoric, were the sources of Engels' vituperative attack on Bernard Shaw.

But the fact that classical economics can be seen, among other things, as part of a liberal crusade, and the fact that in *England* the distinction between socialism and liberalism later became increasingly blurred, hardly add up to grounds for asserting that a penumbra of liberalism somehow clings to economics whatever the nationality, school of thought and political views of the economist. And when Myrdal goes on to back up his claim (which by now has extended beyond economics) that 'even the severest critics of liberalism find it difficult to free themselves from its fascination',[41] the examples he chooses do his argument more harm than good. To exclaim, open-mouthed, that some liberal presuppositions even extend to *American trade union leaders* (as though these were the *ne plus ultra* of revolutionary socialist consciousness – and this in 1953!) is hardly the way to persuade anyone that liberalism is inescapable.

Definitions, of course, are free, and if you defined liberalism eccentrically enough, you *could* make it sound inescapable. (Hegel's delightful definition of freedom as 'the opportunity to obey the State' could perhaps be adapted to describe a new Hegelian 'liberalism'.) But this hardly seems a useful exercise, and in any case it is not what Myrdal is trying to do. Someone once said that the trouble with liberals is that they can never quite believe that, underneath it all, everyone else is not a liberal too. Myrdal seems to be taking the more unusual position of attributing liberalism to everyone *except* himself.

So, *contra* Myrdal, there is no reason why, for example, modern macroeconomics should have a liberal bias. Indeed until it can incorporate, *at a basic analytical level*, the less-than-perfect foresight and information of the State, its Gestalt picture will, regardless of its more 'monetarist' practitioners' wishes, impart a collectivist bias, just as microeconomics' continuing failure to do full justice to imperfect information in the market imparts a liberal bias. (The fact that economists have a vested interest in extolling the wisdom of the State, because a powerful State demands more economists, is a separate issue.) And there is no reason to accuse historical economics of liberal bias either; in fact one could argue that Thorold Rogers was trapped in a holistic 'paradigm' regardless of his own views, just as Pigou was trapped in an individualist one. But the fact that ideological bias can operate in more than one direction is something which some economists prefer not to think about, much less write about. The most blatantly ideological writing in economics is that which is about ideology. How else but ideologically can one explain, for instance, the remarkable claim by two Cambridge economists that the marginal revolution was got up to divert attention from the Paris Commune?

None of this is meant to detract from the profound ideological importance of the marginalists' methodological assumption of individual autonomy. So far as this assumption caused economists and their audiences to lose sight of the role of social structure in determining individual wants, the coercive powers and persuasive techniques of producers and above all the grossly unequal bargaining powers of the two sides of the labour market, it helped supporters of capitalism to skate lightly over much that was inconvenient to their case. Janos Kornai, however, has suggested there was another side to the coin.

> One of the basic ideas of the General Equilibrium school is that the economic system should be constructed in such a way that production, the utilisation of resources, is adapted to the needs of the consumer. Production should serve man and not the opposite. This is a beautiful, humanistic idea, the importance of which cannot be stressed sufficiently.[42]

Hutchison goes further. To him neoclassical theory implies 'not merely that production should serve the needs of the consumer, but that individuals, and not party bosses and bureaucrats, should be the judges of what their own needs as consumers and producers are'.[43]

But does neoclassical theory imply that individuals should be judges of their own needs? Conversions to the view that individuals should be judges of their own needs must result either from an increased belief in individual freedom as an end in itself, or from an increased belief that the free consumer will succeed in maximising his utility. There is nothing in the neoclassical paradigm to sway anyone in either of these directions.

However, neoclassical economics does have a libertarian bias insofar as its neglect of the determinants of wants will repel a disproportionate number of authoritarian (and totalitarian) economists. An economist who wants governments to tell consumers what they ought to want will be concerned to find out which of consumers' wants should be frustrated or discouraged. But marginalism, in neglecting the determination of wants, does nothing to illuminate the question of our authoritarian. Consequently, he is apt to see the neoclassical paradigm as unhelpful, and reject it. If, therefore, the corpus of neoclassical writing has libertarian implications, this is not because of anything the paradigm implies, but because it restricts the subject-matter of economics in a way which libertarians will find less unacceptable than authoritarians. It does not possess a libertarian ideology of its own, but is practised by those who do.

But it may seem like hair-splitting to say that marginalism's pro-capitalist bias is inbuilt whereas its libertarian bias derives from its exponents. It is unlikely that the distinction matters very much in practice. Suffice it to say that neoclassical writing has had, and still does have, a libertarian anti-socialist tendency: and whether you put an 'and' or a 'but' between those last two adjectives could depend on your own ideology.

11

The Marshallians and the Pigouese

Woe unto you, Edwin, woe unto you – age and a curse on your innocent head – for you are the cause of my undoing. Understand then, that having lectured faithfully according to 'the Principles' for four years running, I threw them over-board last year and lectured off my own bat, attacking D[iminishing] R[eturns] & Rent & C[onsumer] S[urplus], and quoting freely from The History of the Theories of Production and Distribution.

Three days ago, I got a letter from Mrs. Marshall, asking me to come to tea today, when she would tell me of some criticisms she had heard about my lectures. I went. The ladies, she said, could never guess what was coming next, I didn't keep to the Principles & I had called the Indians 'niggers'. Warmly repudiating the last charge & as yet unsuspecting, I admitted that I had strayed from the Principles because the men found my original lectures rather uninteresting. Mrs. M. looked very pained, murmured that nothing could be straightforward enough for beginners & that a good grounding was all-essential. I promised that I would announce in advance my line of treatment – and rose to go, when to my surprise she asked if I would not like to see HIM – 'just for a few minutes only'.

He was in the tent (I hadn't seen him, except for a moment, since I was married) and he began,

'Many years ago you said something, which I never understood. There was company present and the matter was too controversial – what did you mean by saying that general laws were useless and that everybody should ask himself: How exactly does the matter affect me? Does rent enter into my costs of production, if I am a farmer ... ?'

Now, never in my life have I mentioned theory in the sacred presence, so at first I tried to tell the truth and said – 'I really can't remember ever having ... ' 'Oh yes you did. I remember it distinctly. It was the sort of thing Cannan says. Clapham has just written a most eulogistic & I must say, I think, very inappropriate review of Cannan's new book ... ' Truth failing, I had recourse to straight lies – explaining how much Malthus had suffered from the Malthusians & from Harriet Martineau, how all the early economists were really in favour of the factory acts, how ... etc. etc.

The gloom lifted from his brow. 'Oh! I am so relieved we've had this out and that is really what you did mean.'

I then hurriedly rose, but he stopped me and I interjected after a minute or two more 'I'm a great admirer of Bowley. I've been walking with him in the

Lakes, he's such a human statistician.' 'Yes,' said M, delighted, 'He's just like Ricardo. Ricardo you know was the most human of people, at the back of the whole labour movement in those days. Bowley and Ricardo both remind me of an egg: a brittle surface without, but when you prick it – well, well ...'

Gritting my teeth to avoid convulsions, I told him that Bowley was the greatest economist next to himself – and bolted ...

To think of it! For five long years I have lived in the great man's favour & now I am dethroned, back into the abyss into which I dropped when I became a research student in London 'to come under influences which should not be risked without grave and weighty deliberations'. I have the letter still, & if it isn't your fault, it's Sidney Webb's.

Cheer me with a p.c.
Yrs CRF

(*Fay to Cannan, 13 October 1913*)[1]

II

Marshall spent the last weeks of his professorship ensuring that Pigou, not Foxwell, would succeed him. His recorded remarks at the time – including his not especially soothing letter of condolence to Foxwell on the morrow of the election – imply that he was motivated by admiration for Pigou rather than dissatisfaction with Foxwell.[2] Marshall, however, outlined his objections to Foxwell when, in December 1908, Higgs proposed that money be raised to found a second chair in political economy for Foxwell's benefit. In the first place, Marshall told Higgs, it was his opinion that professors should normally retire at 60; secondly, 'the speciality of Cambridge teaching is to develop faculty and leave judgement to be formed later ... a lecturer who imposes his judgement on youth is not acting up to the best Cambridge tradition'. Thirdly, Foxwell's judgements were 'apt to turn in opposite directions at six months' notice', his judgement on finance, in particular, being 'extraordinarily bad'.[3] For these reasons, Marshall told Neville Keynes, he could be at most 'benevolently neutral'; and if, the professorship founded, the question should arise of whether it should go to Foxwell or Clapham, 'I must speak for Clapham.'[4]

The final insult to Foxwell came in 1916, when Pigou pleaded before a military tribunal that his call-up would leave no one in Cambridge capable of doing his job. He was exempted. After an angry letter from Foxwell, the military representative of the tribunal appealed against Pigou's exemption on the grounds that he could be replaced by Foxwell. At the subsequent hearing Clapham, representing Pigou, made it clear that Pigou's previous plea should not have been constructed as a reflection on Foxwell's competence – it was merely that Foxwell, though resident in Cambridge, was already holding a chair at University College, London, and would be unable to do Pigou's work as it should be done. It was not enough, Clapham said, for Foxwell to offer to do 'not less than the average work for a Professor'. With every member of the Economics Faculty except himself occupied in the war effort, Pigou had been doing far more.[5] Foxwell was not mollified. He had already accused Neville Keynes of 'dressing up' his minor reservations about occupying two professorships at once 'in such an embroidery of exceptions as to make it equivalent to a refusal'.[6] Now he remained convinced that he was being rejected as a replacement for Pigou not because he had another job but because he was Foxwell.[7]

It is very hard not to sympathise with Foxwell, a good economist pushed by the influence of Marshall from the front to the back row of the emerging profession. Four letters by Foxwell to J.N. Keynes, written approximately at ten-yearly intervals, together chart the whole process. The first indicates that, before Marshall's return to Cambridge in 1884, it was Foxwell who had been the leader in the battle for professional standards of competence.

> The Fawcetts are at the bottom of most of [Moorson's] errors, as invariably happens. The most curious is his almost complete omission of any treatment of interest as distinct from profits – and his very bad theory of wages – both thoroughly characteristic of the Fawcetts ... the Syndicate is not careful enough in the appointments it makes ...[8]

But by 1892 Marshall had already begun to propel Foxwell towards the sidelines.

> As I disagree very profoundly with Marshall on many points, especially in regard to Ricardo, Mill, Economic method and consumption – I thought it better that someone occupying a more central position should write the guide.[9]

Already, then, Marshall had succeeded in defining a 'central position' as one which accorded with his own. Foxwell's letter to Keynes of October 1900, revealing his annoyance at the favour which Marshall from the first showed to Pigou, has already been seen.[10] Finally in 1912, Foxwell confided bitterly to Keynes that

> I have no doubt [Marshall] is glad now, as he always has been, that others should help in work which himself despises and neglects, I mean in providing for the poll men, for examinations, and in correspondence with the outside

world. But for the people who thus oblige I believe he has in his inner feelings a very honest contempt ...[11]

It is not surprising in the circumstances that Foxwell gradually transferred both his energies and his loyalties from Cambridge to University College, London.[12]

III

Pigou was a very different kind of economist from Marshall. He had been taught political economy as an undergraduate; he had begun to specialise in economics at a very early age; and it is likely that this more professional background was at the root of his much more 'professional' treatment of the relationship between economic and other activities. It was argued at the end of chapter 8, and it is reiterated now, that *Wealth and Welfare*, with its initial *methodological* postulate that changes in economic welfare indicate equivalent changes in total welfare, was a major landmark in the professionalisation of economics. The book, however, can still be seen as a development of the Marshallian tradition, unlike Pigou's first two economic books, both of which, in their different ways, had marked departures. *The Riddle of the Tariff* (1903) was an assertion that both economic and political arguments favoured free trade. Thus the penultimate chapter concluded:

The economic argument against Mr. Chamberlain's policy is a strong one. To many, however, the political argument seems, in the side-light thrown upon it by history, to be still stronger, and, by itself, to make imperative the rejection of the ex-Colonial Secretary's scheme. (p. 100)

It is not recorded what Marshall thought of this would-be authoritative pronouncement by his most valued pupil. But, given what we have seen of his own attitude to the protectionist controversy,[13] given also his letter to Neville Keynes in which he expressed the hope that the controversy would die down because he wanted to lecture on the issue,[14] one might guess that he found Pigou's book somewhat indiscreet.

The Riddle of The Tariff was a harbinger of Pigou's life-long readiness to go into battle over policy questions. And, with Pigou's *œuvre* in front of us, we can see that Marshall's grudging and nervous attitude to topical issues was more a personal aberration than a forerunner of a general professional detachment. Marshall has dominated this book so much that we should perhaps remind ourselves how eccentric his position was, even within a disciplinary context largely of his own making. Anyone with no knowledge of the history of economics, opening this book at random on page 62, and reading that Marshall especially valued Neville Keynes as an economist because the latter lacked interest in economic affairs, would surely think that a 'not' had been left out somewhere. Even Edgeworth merely said that students should not be able to discover what their lecturers' opinions were on policy questions: Marshall actually worried that his lecture-subjects might become topical! Such devotion to detachment was unique: it has had no followers.

The Riddle of the Tariff, then, represents a return to the traditional norm, a reassertion that the economist was, and should be, involved in the issues of the day. There are many places where policy is extracted directly from theory without qualifications, and there are no disclaimers that Pigou is speaking as a 'private citizen'. But *Principles and Methods of Industrial Peace* (1905) is even more of a landmark, standing out as the first solid attempt to professionalise specifically a particular area of applied economics hitherto open to laymen. The analysis of wage fluctuations which constitutes part 2 of the book is, admittedly, only a little more theoretically and mathematically advanced than Marshall's treatment of the subject in the *Principles*; in the context of a book aimed at a topical problem, however, it is a major innovation. But it was the mathematical appendixes to the book which aroused the most interest. Oddly enough, L. L. Price, who had criticised the main text for stepping too close to 'the boundary which separates the legitimate use from the perilous abuse of mathematical economics',[15] then went on to praise these appendixes for being in the spirit of

> those more recent developments of economic theory of a mathematical type, with the brilliant conclusions of which the Cambridge teacher, of whom Mr Pigou, like many others, is proud to confess himself a pupil, has earned the gratitude of all economists of his generation by making them familiar ...[16]

Candidly, however, Price revealed the reason for his uncritical remarks.

> We acknowledge ... that our own unfortunate ignorance of mathematics precludes us from appreciating the technical apparatus used in the appendices ...[17]

It is unlikely that any mathematically-minded economist was either cynical enough, or concerned enough about criticism from Oxford, to act on the moral which emerges from this review article. But the moral is quite clear – if you are going to be mathematical at all, be mathematical enough to flummox your potential critics.

IV

How do the writings of the young Pigou relate to those of Marshall's other pupils? Pigou stands out for his determination to use advanced analysis for the purpose of policy recommendation – a determination which eventually led to *Wealth and Welfare*. Was Marshall's enthusiastic approval of Pigou – and his strenuous efforts to have him succeed to the Cambridge chair – an indication that he believed neoclassicism's policy-making harvest was at hand? Whatever the differences between Marshall and the young Pigou, both were intellectual leaders of their respective generations. Pigou succeeded Marshall as the professionalising influence on Cambridge economics, though he never matched, and never tried to match, Marshall's national efforts.

Certainly Pigou's unabashed use of mathematics and graphical methods gave him a theoretical sophistication which in the early years of his professorship was unchallenged in or out of Cambridge. Most of Marshall's pupils clung tenaciously to the 'literary' style of exposition of the *Principles*, often without the graphical and mathematical footnotes and appendixes with which Marshall had achieved greater precision. Thus, for example, Sydney Chapman's *Political Economy* (1912) eschewed graphs and formulae throughout, leading to passages such as the following:

> the price of a commodity will be the price at which equal quantities are demanded and supplied, provided that a slight addition to the supply would mean a supply price above the demand price, and a slight reduction of the supply would mean a supply price below the demand price. There may be, but there is not likely to be, more than one such price. It is only possible when increasing returns rules, and if it does, is least likely when demand is inelastic. (p. 75)

In the pages of the *Economic Journal* too, Pigou, together with Edgeworth, stood out as the theoretical leading light. He stood out more plainly for the fact that the *Journal*'s second decade was, at best, one of stagnation. Gone were the days of 1894, when A. W.

Flux had demonstrated in the course of a mere review that payment according to marginal product would exhaust total product if and only if returns to scale were constant. But if the *Economic Journal* in the 1900s gave the impression of a profession marking time, the *Economic Review* showed how unprofessional a supposedly specialist journal could still be. It took the *Review* eighteen years to carry an article either using or criticising marginalist theories. Finally there appeared W. W. Carlile's 'The Present Position of Marginal Utility Theory' (July 1908), which was handicapped by the author's failure, even when considering a man buying ten loaves of bread, to understand the difference between total and marginal utility. Only three more theoretical articles appeared before 1914: H. W. B. Joseph's 'Karl Marx's Theory of Value' (January 1910) was unobjectionable if unexciting, but Hobson's 'Marginal Productivity' (July 1910) consisted of choosing a production function such that factor payments would more than exhaust total product and presenting this as a refutation of marginal productivity theory. Hobson, as we have seen, had the year before presented an eminently reasonable critique of marginal productivity theory which Marshall never adequately answered. Did taking up the pen to write for the *Review* somehow bring an economist bad luck? Price's extraordinary review of Crozier's *The Wheel of Wealth*, which he found full of 'persuasive reasoning of uncommon quality' (*Economic Review*, April 1907), would appear to confirm this tentative hypothesis.

The final article of the three was by J. A. Smith, an Oxford philosophy professor, whose critique of Marshall's *Principles* led to the comments by Cannan we have seen already.[18] Smith courteously sent his article to Marshall, but Mrs Marshall intercepted it and passed it to Fay, who gave it to Pigou. As Cannan expected, Pigou declined to answer Smith himself, but nonetheless made his own point by asking an undergraduate, Philip Sargant Florence, to do so. Looking back in 1981, Professor Florence did not recollect it as one of his more difficult assignments.[19]

V

Another way of assessing economics as it stood in the years immediately before 1914 would be to look at the differing degrees of professionalisation of the different branches of the subject. It has already been seen that Marshall seized the chance to turn value theory into a professional monopoly, that Edgeworth had the chance to do the same for fiscal theory but turned it down, and that Pigou, by 1905, was extending the tentacles of professionalisation towards labour economics. But a 'great man' theory of professionalisation would be as inadequate when comparing the different branches of economics as when looking at the whole process. Some economic areas dropped ripely into the professional net with a minimum of shaking; others resisted actual, and would have resisted all conceivable, attempts to harvest them for specialists only. To pursue this line of argument we must invent a cumbersome new set of terms, and draw the rather fine distinction between a primary and a secondary professional economic orthodoxy.

There are two kinds of economic orthodoxy: those based on a command of theory beyond the reach of an outsider, and those based on a particular opinion on a policy question. A theory-based orthodoxy is, by our first criterion of professionalism, a professional orthodoxy. An opinion-based orthodoxy, however, cannot by itself create a new professional status for the school of thought which holds it. The most that it can do is reinforce a theory-based orthodoxy by coinciding with it in terms of membership. But perhaps 'coincides', with its connotations of randomness, is the wrong word here. What has more often happened is what happened in the controversy over protection which began in 1903. Here the theoretical divide was widened by the conflict about what economists' responsibilities should be in such a situation: whether they should confine themselves to strictly economic arguments, or whether they should examine the political consequences as well. This conflict itself reflected different degrees of professional self-consciousness, which in turn stemmed from different theoretical attitudes and attitudes to theory. In this way a theory-based orthodoxy tends to create – at two or three causal removes – a series of opinion-based orthodoxies.

We would therefore suggest the following typology of orthodoxies. A primary professional orthodoxy is based on a theoretical paradigm capable of supporting a programme of research, uniting those economists who share its partisanship, regular use and comparative mastery. The secondary professional orthodoxies, though dependent for their effect on the primary ones, feature a consensus on some policy question which, because it involves non-economic arguments, admits of a distinctively limited 'professional view'. This implies, and is intended to imply, that the purely technical questions of economic policy, because they impose the same strictly economic terms of discourse on everyone, have less power to create genuinely professional orthodoxies. When they do so, they do so by chance. The obvious example in our period is in the field of money and banking. In the bimetallic controversy of the 1870s and 80s it *happened* that most of the professionalising sector of economics was on one side. Because of this, and because the logical consistency of their arguments tended to be more reliable than their opponents' ones, monometallism flourished briefly, at least in the minds of some, as a touchstone of professionalism. But monetary issues, lacking both advanced theoretical foundations and obvious extra-economic implications,[20] could not be lastingly professionalised, and when the bimetallic controversy ended, its inner circle lost their specifically monetary credentials. So far as they retained specially authoritative status, it was now based on their overall reputation as economists.

And – still more important – the idea that a bimetallist somehow has dubious standing as an economist was in any case confined to non-economists. There is not a single recorded remark either by Marshall or by any other non-bimetallist (except, inevitably, Macleod) which casts aspersions on the professional competence of bimetallists as bimetallists. One contributor to the *Economic Review*, W. W. Carlile, even picked up the idea that there was a professional orthodoxy the other way, and it was the monometallists who were the victims of professional prejudice. There is no evidence for this view either, but the fact that it could be held by a keen, if erratic, student of economics ought to dispose of any suspicion that there was a professional orthodoxy hostile to bimetallism.

The correspondence which surrounded Smart's appointment to the Glasgow chair is significant in this respect. Sir Matthew Pollock Fraser, Assessor to the University's Rector, wrote to Cannan asking his advice. Certain members of the University court, said Sir Matthew, felt strongly that no bimetallist should be appointed to the chair. He wanted to know 'whether bimetallism as against monometallism or the reverse should be made a test of reason of disqualification to the chair of Political Economy'.[21] Cannan's reply – that such a disqualification, either way, would be an outrage – reflects a general view among economists that there were no professional and unprofessional attitudes to monetary questions. There were, of course, logical (i.e. internally consistent) and illogical theories, but – Neville Keynes' single stricture on Palgrave aside[22] – academic economists did not try to place bankers on the wrong side of this distinction. (They had no justification for so trying – though that, conceivably, might not have stopped them.) Nor, in general, did they challenge the hegemony of 'practical' men in monetary writings. According to Fay, the Cambridge Tripos in the years before 1914 consisted of 'potted Marshall and sugared sticks of Hartley Withers'.[23] The remark emphasises both the low priority Cambridge gave to teaching monetary economics, and its lack of interest in professionalising it.

VI

The battle to professionalise economics was primarily a battle between those who saw it as a discipline comparable to the natural sciences and those who saw it as an adjunct to immediate social reform, and, in explaining the victory of the former over the latter, both the absolutist 'trait' method and the historical-relativist method in the sociology of the professions have their value. The absolute approach shows why, other things being equal, an occupation like economics is dominated by its advanced theorists who, by means of their superior status, tend to determine the direction of future research; the historical-relativist approach focuses on the fact that other things seldom are equal.

The widespread adoption of the neoclassical paradigm established a necessary and sufficient basis for professional economics as we have defined it. But this does not deny the importance of the social and historical setting. Even if one sees the marginal revolution itself as an endogenous intellectual conversion, it was its social context that made it so crucial to professionalisation. By 1870 it was no longer possible to emulate the traditional professions and build a monopoly of specialist practice on a foundation of high social status, ratified by an appropriate degree from the right institution. This status professionalism, as it is generally called, was giving way to the technically based professionalism characteristic of an industrial society. In economics, as we saw in the case of Marshall versus Hobson, the professionals' claims to superiority over outsiders were sometimes unfounded. But, excessive or justified, they could not have been made at all had they not grown out of a hard-won technical achievement which by and large bestowed the ability to command the terms of theoretical debate.

We have already discussed the close relationship between the professionalisation of economic theory and the growing predominance of the academic economist. The synchronisation of these two developments gave the emerging profession an immediate established status as part of the existing academic profession. Thus from the start it had the power to decide its own methods of practice, training requirements and standards of qualification, and its own definitions of what was and was not relevant to successful economics. This enabled it to follow its own inclinations in stressing the value of, and devoting personal resources to, its more abstract elements. Developing these, ascribing central importance to them, questioning the practical skill and judgement of those who lacked a thorough training in them, reinforced the professional economist's control over his own fate, his critics' fates and his audience's imagined needs. Concentration on theory resulted in the neglect of problems only slightly touched by it. Particular needs were apt to be defined as imperative because particular solutions were the specialist's monopoly; and as the untrained layman fell further behind the leaders of the discipline in his ability to understand the answers, his judgement on the relative worth of examining the different questions also became less confident.

How far the priority which the Marshallian school of economics gave to the development of price theory represented a conscious drive towards secure professional autonomy is a very hard question to answer. Undoubtedly other motives are involved in all such cases. To possess an ability denied to all but a few, to belong to an esoteric closed shop selling a scarce commodity and monopolising a task at which outsiders are seen to fail, is gratifying as end in itself. And it should not be overlooked how much less time-consuming it was for the economist to make a professional reputation through theoretical brilliance rather than through dull and dogged factual work.

But neither of these factors will by itself lead to the kind of *cumulative* bias in favour of high theory which economics developed over the years. This can be attributed to a process which, once again, is common to many disciplines. It is that a high degree of abstraction in professional training may be especially useful for grading entrants in terms of general intellectual calibre. This is certainly the message of those invaluable tutorial notebooks to be found among the Marshall Papers. From Marshall's comments on 200-odd pupils, recorded between 1895 and 1902, it is clear that he regarded the mathematicians so highly not because he had any great opinion of mathematical economics as such – his correspondence with Bowley makes it clear that he did not – but because he saw their analytical sophistication as symptomatic of a generalised intelligence which would triumph over more pedestrian rivals even in pedestrian fields. But if prowess in high theory is seen as the best indicator of overall potential and if a discipline attracts enough would-be recruits to be able to choose between them, then each generation will recruit a successor a little more theoretically inclined than itself. For the old generation, by and large, transmits an image of the subject likely to attract potential successors of the same average stamp as itself. But not all of these will be recruited, and if the more theoretical ones are on the whole preferred, the professional median will shift successively towards greater abstraction.

This process is likely to be irresponsibly independent of the merits and demerits of the theories concerned. Where a slow-maturing but potentially fruitful paradigm is involved, a strong professional drive towards theorising may be needed to achieve equilibrium against laymen with a measure of control whose interests demand concrete results fast whatever the scientific price. But in the context of a degenerating research programme, the main function of a body of advanced theory may be merely to uphold the status of its practitioners and to fish the stream of recruits for the talents most fitted to perpetuate this monopoly, whatever the social cost.

Which of these two pictures best describes the Marshallian orthodoxy in the years immediately before 1914? Neither of them describes it very well – the neoclassical 'paradigm' has never had enough empirical content to be comfortable in any of the garments provided by Popper or Kuhn or Lakatos. Even if it is interpreted as predicting the impossibility of mass unemployment, it is doubtful whether it can be brought face to face with enough uncontested evidence to allow it either to pass or to fail any test but the most primitive falsificationist one, which all theories fail anyway.[24] And this reflection brings us back to the question which we posed, at the beginning of chapter 2, about the cumulative nature of the neoclassical research programme. Then we asked whether it was the marginal idea, or the people it attracted, which gave orthodox economics four decades of purposeful progress along a single path. Now we must ask whether it was the marginal idea, or the people it attracted, which directed the path to so inconclusive a destination.

The answer in this case – unlike the answer in the original case – is that there is little point in trying to separate the two factors. Like co-operating factors of production, their contributions to the total product are not separable; and it is this fact which is the measure of the professionalisation of economics between 1870 and 1914. By 1914 the economics profession was responsible for the character of its entrants; and the neoclassical paradigm was largely responsible, not just for the preoccupations of the economics profession, but also for the fact that there was an economics profession at all. Yet the fact that personalities were becoming less important was largely due to one personality. How did Marshall, retired and a full-time scholar at last, look back on his professionalising achievement? The answer is that we hardly know. His letters as professor had bristled with exhortations, complaints and evaluations which together gave a graphic picture of the economist's duty towards economics as a professional insider saw it. It is understandable that retirement should have diminished this flow. But it is surprising that retirement should have ushered in virtual silence.[25]

Denied Marshall's own views on the matter, how should *we* view his achievement? His greatness as a teacher is not in doubt: Chapman's unpublished autobiography describes the inspiring experience of being the pupil of so outstanding, and so enthusiastic, a master; so does Maynard Keynes' tribute in the *Economic Journal*:

> The pupil would come away with an extraordinary feeling that he was embarked upon the most interesting and important journey in the world. He would walk back along the Madingley Road, labouring under more books, which had been taken from the shelves for him as the interview went on, than he could well carry, convinced that here was a subject worthy of his life's study. Marshall's double nature, coming out informally and spontaneously, filled the pupil seated by him with a double illumination. The young man was presented with a standard of intellectual integrity, and with it a disinterestedness of purpose which satisfied him intellectually and morally at the same time. The subject itself had seemed to grow under the hands of master and pupil as they had talked. There were endless possibilities, not out of reach.[26]

But Marshall's intellectual leadership extended far beyond those he actually taught. It is best assessed by returning, briefly, to economics' anxious period of self-appraisal in the 1870s.

In the years following 1870, the discussion over the scope, method and ends of political economy was essentially a prospective one. New goals were needed (because of the growing difficulty of defining economics' significance by identifiable public ends), old assumptions were shaking (because of the decline of classical value theory) and leadership was temporarily absent (because Mill was dead). These facts impressed themselves on all schools of thought. So far as an English *Methodenstreit* took place, it contested less what economics was than what it ought to become. No longer a symbol of reasoned progress, economics in the 1870s and 80s seemed only to symbolise the difficulty of constructing a guiding system of social science from atomistic premisses.

Of English economists other than Marshall, both Edgeworth and Jevons made gestures in this direction. But the former went too far to be realistic and the latter not far enough to be interesting. It is, of course, interesting to speculate whether Jevons, had he lived, would have come to believe in the vision of a theory of economic policy on a subjective value basis. But there is little or no evidence that he ever desired to think of applied economics other than classically.

The historical economists, too, had a programme; but what they actually achieved was a disappointment even to themselves. As a contribution to economics 'proper', little empirical work materialised. Neither, of course, did Marshall's life's work live up to his claims about what was possible in economics. But in his case it was not necessary to his prophetic role. Policy recommendations scientifically based on measurable welfare criteria might be a vision which retreated faster than the prospector advanced. Economic biology might be of uncertain meaning. But no one, least of all Marshall, claimed that their realisation was imminent. Whereas the historicists called for facts, Marshall stressed the danger of committing oneself to them before the theoretical foundations had been made strong. Thus procrastination seemed to represent failure for a historicist, but something like admirable restraint in the work of a Marshallian.

Marshall, then, was the one credible prophet; and to appreciate this is to take a functional view of his personal authority. His leadership of British economics rested not so much on his greatness as an economist, or on any conscious self-aggrandisement he might have been guilty of, as on his appropriateness to his time. His temperament, the direction of his interests, his persuasive optimism about the future of economics were all needed to give a sense of direction. A theory of economic policy based on advanced analysis, the application of evolutionary ideas, an independent economics syllabus in universities and colleges, were aims which many economists wished to achieve. It was shown in chapter 2 that, in the case of each of these, Marshall had additional reasons of his own to make it his objective. By his correspondingly greater energy and persuasiveness, as well as intellectual stature, he distinguished himself from the field, and acquired a larger-than-life appearance. Disquiet over the apparently hedonistic basis of much economic thought served only to enhance his authority. Temperamentally opposed to hedonistic psychology, he would probably in any case have expunged its overtones from his economics. In the circumstances, his moral preoccupations provided economists with both an answer to the charge of hedonism and a substitute for an overtly political role.

During Marshall's lifetime, the belief that economics was something both cumulative and incomplete came to dominate the outlook for the dominant school. This owed much to the growing institutional structure of degree courses and economic journals. To feel the need to say something new no longer required a rebellious or particularly original outlook. It became a normal and expected part of the economist's professional role. The journals had to be filled, and with something more than journalism; the academics were expected to do original research. But not only did Marshall play an important and direct part in the setting up of such institutions; he also did much to create an awareness that they were needed. The ideals which he supplied to the Cambridge Economics Tripos have been seen. But, more generally, the urge to institutionalise innovation depended on the – perhaps difficult – confidence that the neoclassical model was not subject to sharply diminishing returns. Few if any objective guidelines exist as to what ex ante constitutes diminishing returns in the social sciences: the criteria are personal, generally tacit and swiftly adjustable. Misguided or not, Marshall's youthful sense of the inexhaustible was quietly picked up by others and turned into bricks and mortar: and this institutionalisation formed a virtuous circle with the growth of the attitude that what was new was normal.

Biographical notes

Ashley, Sir William James (1860–1927). Educ. St Olave's School, Southwark and Balliol College, Oxford. Fellow of Lincoln College, Oxford, 1885–8; Professor of Political Economy, Toronto, 1888–92; Professor of Economic History, Harvard, 1892–1901; Professor of Commerce, Birmingham, 1901–25.

Bagehot, Walter (1826–77). Educ. Bristol College and University College, London. Editor, *The Economist*, 1860–77.

Bastable, Charles (1855–1945). Educ. Fermoy College, Cork and Trinity College, Dublin. Professor of Political Economy, Trinity College, Dublin, 1882–1932; Professor of Jurisprudence, University College, Galway, 1883–1903; Professor of Jurisprudence, Trinity College, Dublin, 1902–32.

Bonar, James (1852–1941). Educ. Glasgow Academy, Glasgow University and Balliol College, Oxford. Examiner, Civil Service, 1881–1907; Deputy Master of the Canadian Branch of the Royal Mint, 1907–19.

Cairnes, John Elliot (1823–75). Educ. Trinity College, Dublin. Whately Professor of Political Economy, Trinity College, Dublin, 1856–61. Professor of Political Economy and Jurisprudence, University College, Galway, 1859–65; Professor of Political Economy, University College, London, 1866–75.

Cannan, Edwin (1861–1935). Educ. Clifton College and Balliol College, Oxford. Lecturer, L.S.E., 1897–1907, Professor 1907–26.

Chapman, Sir Sydney John (1871–1951). Educ. London University. Lecturer, University College, Cardiff, 1899–1901; Professor of Economics, University College, Manchester, 1901–17; Board of Trade 1918–27; Chief Economic Adviser to the government, 1927–32; Chairman of British Arc Lamp Carbon (War Emergency) Pool and Controller of Matches, 1939–44.

Clapham, Sir John (1873–1946). Educ. Leys School and King's College Cambridge. Fellow of King's, 1898–1904 and 1908–46; Lecturer in History and Economics, Cambridge 1898–1902; Professor of Economics, Leeds, 1902–8; Professor of Economic History, Cambridge, 1928–38.

Crozier, John Beattie (1849–1921). Educ. Galt Grammar School and Toronto University. Doctor of Medicine, historian and economist.

Cunningham, Ven. William (1849–1919). Educ. Edinburgh Academy, Edinburgh University and Caius College, Cambridge. Ordained 1874; Cambridge University Extension Lecturer 1874–8; Lecturer in History 1884–91; Tooke Professor of Statistics, King's College, London 1891–7; Chaplain, Trinity College, Cambridge, 1880–91; Vicar of Great St Mary's 1887–1908; Archdeacon of Ely 1907–19.

Devas, Charles Stanton (1848–1906). Educ. Eton and Balliol College, Oxford. Received into Roman Catholic Church 1867. Occupation given in *Who's Who* as 'private study'.

Edgeworth, Francis Ysidro (1845–1926). Educ. at home, at Trinity College, Dublin, and Balliol College, Oxford. Tooke Professor of Political Economy, King's College, London, 1888–91; Drummond Professor of Political Economy, Oxford, 1891–1925; editor of the *Economic Journal*, 1891–1926.

Fawcett, Henry (1833–84). Educ. K. C. S. London, Peterhouse and Trinity Hall, Cambridge. Seventh Wrangler, 1856. Fellow of Trinity Hall 1856–84; Professor of Political Economy, Cambridge, 1863–84; Liberal M.P. 1865–84; Postmaster-General 1880–4.

Foxwell, Herbert Somerton (1849–1936). Educ. Queen's College, Taunton and St John's College, Cambridge. Fellow of St John's College, Cambridge, 1872–1936; Professor of Political Economy, University College, London, 1881–1928. Described his own library as 'the most important library of works on political economy in Europe'.

Giffen, Sir Robert (1837–1910). Educ. Glasgow University. Assistant editor, *The Economist* 1868–76; Controller-General of the Commercial, Labour and Statistical Departments, Board of Trade, 1882–97.

Goschen, Viscount (Rt. Hon. George Joachim Goschen) (1831–1907). Educ. Rugby and Oriel College, Oxford. Conservative M.P. 1863–1900. First Lord of the Admiralty 1871–4 and 1895–1900; Chancellor of the Exchequer 1887–92.

Hewins, William Albert Samuel (1865–1931). Educ. Wolverhampton School and Pembroke College, Oxford. Director of L.S.E., 1895–1903. Conservative M.P., 1912–18. Under-Secretary of State for the Colonies, 1917–19.

Higgs, Henry (1864–1940). Educ. University College, London. Civil Servant 1881–1921; Secretary of Royal Economic Society, 1892–1905.

Hobson, John Atkinson (1858–1940). Educ. Derby School and Lincoln College, Oxford. Author and journalist.

Ingram, John Kells (1823–1907). Educ. Newry School and Trinity College, Dublin. Fellow of Trinity College, Dublin, 1846; Professor of Oratory and English Literature, 1852; Regius Professor of Greek, 1866.

Jevons, William Stanley (1835–82). Educ. University College School and University College, London. Assayer to the mint of Sydney, Australia, 1854–9; Professor of Logic and of Political, Mental and Moral Philosophy, Owens College, Manchester, 1866–80.

Keynes, Lord (John Maynard Keynes) (1883-1946). Educ. Eton and King's College, Cambridge. India Office, 1906–8; Fellow of King's College, Cambridge, 1909–46; editor, *Economic Journal* 1911–44.

Keynes, John Neville (1852–1949). Educ. Amersham Hall School, London University and Pembroke College, Cambridge. Lecturer in Moral Science, Cambridge, 1884–1911; University Registrary, 1910–25.

Leslie, Thomas Edward Cliffe (1827–82). Educ. King William's College, I.O.M. and Trinity College, Dublin. Professor of Jurisprudence and Political Economy, Queen's College, Belfast, 1853–82.

Macleod, Henry Dunning (1821–1902). Educ. Eton and Trinity College, Cambridge. Barrister.

Marshall, Alfred (1842–1924). Educ. Merchant Taylors and St John's College, Cambridge. Fellow of St John's 1865–77 and 1885–1908; Principal, University College, Bristol, 1877–83; Lecturer in Political Economy, Balliol College, Oxford, 1883–4; Professor of Political Economy, Cambridge, 1885–1908; served on Royal Commission on Labour, 1891–5.

Nicholson, Joseph Shield (1850–1927). Educ. Edinburgh University and Trinity College, Cambridge. Professor of Political Economy, Edinburgh, 1880–1925.

Palgrave, Sir Robert Harry Inglis (1827–1919). Educ. Charterhouse. Banker. Editor, *The Economist*, 1877–83; editor, *Dictionary of Political Economy*, 3 vols. 1894–1914.

Pigou, Arthur Cecil (1877–1959). Educ. Harrow and King's College, Cambridge. Fellow of King's, 1900; University Lecturer in Economics, 1904–8; Professor of Political Economy, 1908–43.

Price, Bonamy (1807–88). Educ. privately and at Worcester College, Oxford. Master at Rugby, 1832–50; Drummond Professor of Political Economy, Oxford, 1868–88.

Price, Langford Lovell Frederick Rice (1862–1950). Educ. Dulwich and Trinity College, Oxford. Fellow of Oriel College, Oxford, 1888–1923; University Reader in Economic History, 1909–21.

Rogers, Rev. James Edwin Thorold (1823–90). Educ. Oxford University. Private tutor, Oxford, 1846–59; Professor of Economics and Statistics, King's College, London, 1859–90; Drummond Professor of Political Economy, Oxford, 1862–8 and 1888–90.

Sidgwick, Henry (1838–1900). Educ. Rugby and Trinity College, Cambridge. Fellow of Trinity, 1859; Knightsbridge Professor of Moral Philosophy, Cambridge, 1883–1900.

Smart, William (1853–1915). Educ. Glasgow High School, Glasgow University. In business until 1884. Lecturer in Political Economy, Glasgow University, 1892–6; Professor of Political Economy, Glasgow University, 1896–1915.

Toynbee, Arnold (1852–83). Educ. privately and at Pembroke College and Balliol College, Oxford. Tutor in Economics, Balliol College, Oxford, 1878–83.

Ward, James (1843–1925). Educ. Liverpool Institute, Spring Hill College, Universities of Berlin and Göttingen, Trinity College, Cambridge. Fellow of Trinity College 1875; Professor of Mental Philosophy, Cambridge, 1897–1908.

Webb, Sidney James (Lord Passfield) (1859–1947). Educ. privately and at the Birkbeck Institute, London. Professor of Public Administration L.S.E., 1912–27. Labour M.P., 1922–9; Secretary of State for the Colonies, 1929–31.

Wicksteed, Rev. Philip Henry (1844–1927). Educ. Ruthin Grammar School, University College School and University College, London; Manchester New College. Unitarian minister; London University Extension Lecturer, 1887–1918.

Notes

1. Economics in the 1870s

1 W. Bagehot, 'The Postulates of Political Economy' (1876), reprinted in R. Holt Hutton (ed.), *Economic Studies* (1st edn 1879), 2nd edn, London, 1895, p. 1.
2 *ibid.*, p. 3.
3 W. J. Ashley, 'The Present Position of Political Economy', *Economic Journal*, December 1907, p. 475.
4 Bagehot, 'The Postulates of Political Economy' p. 22.
5 Political Economy Club, *Revised Report of the Proceedings at the Dinner of 31st May, 1876* (London, 1876), p. 21.
6 *ibid.*, p. 46.
7 The article was by Sir James Stephen, and appeared in the *Edinburgh Review*. H. Sidgwick, *The Principles of Political Economy* 3rd edn, London, 1901, p. 3.
8 The exclusion was proposed by Francis Galton. See F. Galton, 'Economic Science and the British Association', *Journal of the Royal Statistical Society*, September 1877.
9 L. Stephen, *Life of Henry Fawcett* (London, 1885), p. 123. Fawcett, according to Stephen, believed that 'the leading principles of political economy and those which were really valuable were few, simple and therefore capable of an exposition on the level of average intelligence' (*ibid.*, p. 124). We would not claim that Fawcett was wholly wrong about what does and does not matter in economics. (His views are certainly less eccentric than what we can presume to be the views of, let us say, the present editorial board of the *Review of Economic Studies*.) Indubitably, though, his was an attitude unhelpful to the professionalisation of the subject.
10 W. S. Jevons, preface to the second (1879) edition of *The Theory of Political Economy*, pp. 49–50.
11 *ibid.*, p. 10.
12 B. Price, *Practical Political Economy* (London, 1878), p. 2.
13 *ibid.*, p. 16.
14 T. E. Cliffe Leslie, 'On the Philosophical Method of Political Economy', *Hermathena*, 1876, reprinted in *Essays in Political Economy* (Dublin, 1888), p. 189.

15 *ibid.*, p. 186.

16 By a liberal, we simply mean a libertarian who is not a socialist. It has been argued that some 'liberals' are not particularly libertarian; see Kenneth Minogue's *The Liberal Mind* (London, 1963) and, especially, Maurice Cowling's *Mill and Liberalism* (Cambridge, 1963). While agreeing, as to Mill, that anyone who believed so strongly that 'society' should create so definite a pattern of citizen cannot be called a true libertarian, we would extend this to saying that, to the extent he cannot, he should not be called a liberal either. One reason why covert semi-authoritarians like Mill, and overt ones like Hobson (see chapter 7) have been allowed to keep their 'liberal' labels is that there is no convenient word to describe the non-conservative non-socialist reformer. Now if some conservatives and Marxists, annoyed that such reformers not only dominate English public life but also often seem to think that they alone are above ideology, choose to inveigh against a 'liberal consensus', let them do so. But the price of using the word 'liberal' in this way is to lump Hobson in with Hayek. To the historian of economics, at least, the price is surely too high.

17 Some may feel that 'in practice' is too weak here, and that it is inconceivable, even theoretically, that the 'greatest happiness' principle can provide specific guidance about anything. We do not agree with this, but since, if it is insisted on, the remarks to follow in the main text about the vacuity of utilitarianism are true *a fortiori*, perhaps we may be excused from getting into a long and complicated argument.

18 In terms of the kind of mentality it appealed to, it was surely the nineteenth century's equivalent of logical positivism.

19 C. J. Dewey, '"Cambridge Idealism": Utilitarian Revisionists in Late Nineteenth-Century Cambridge', *Historical Journal*, March 1974; Michael Freeden, *The New Liberalism* (Oxford, 1978).

20 Dewey, '"Cambridge Idealism"', p. 76.

21 H. Sidgwick, *The Methods of Ethics* (1st pub. 1874), 2nd edn, London, 1877, p. 176.

22 S. Collini, 'Idealism and "Cambridge Idealism"', *Historical Journal*, March 1975.

23 Freeden, *The New Liberalism*, p. 17.

24 Said to be Green's fundamental belief by his biographer, R. L. Nettleship; and quoted by Dewey, '"Cambridge Idealism"', p. 63.

25 A. Kadish, *The Oxford Economists in the Late Nineteenth Century* (Oxford, 1983).

26 A. Toynbee, second of two lectures on Henry George and land nationalisation, St Andrew's Hall, Newman St, London, 18 January 1883. Published as *Progress and Poverty: A Criticism of Mr. Henry George* (London, 1883), pp. 53–4. Toynbee had six weeks to live.

27 *Essays and Reviews* (London, 1860), Preface.

28 Justly neglected as an economist; less justly so as a sociologist. Mallock's strange career began as an undergraduate with *The New Republic*, in which he poked fun at Matthew Arnold, Pater, Jowett (a very severe portrait), Huxley and other luminaries, all assembled under thin disguise

at an endlessly discursive weekend party. He then went on to write several works of religious and political thought (*Social Equality, Is Life Worth Living?*, etc.) and ended up compiling facts and figures about income distribution and wartime finance. It is rather as if Evelyn Waugh had gradually retreated into the pages of *Lloyds Bank Review*.

29 P. Abrams, *The Origins of British Sociology, 1834–1914* (Chicago, 1968), p. 81.

30 See p. 10.

31 J. E. Cairnes, *The Character and Logical Method of Political Economy*, 2nd edn, London, 1888, p. 20.

32 Thus Lord O'Hagan, president for 1874, described economic studies as 'vital to our wellbeing and progress in the world', 'fruitful in precise and enduring results', and entitled to be called scientific 'if science be needed to deal with subjects and educe results of the last importance to our race, and to accomplish this by drawing, from facts rightly ascertained, lucidly classified, and profoundly considered, conclusions of permanent truth and wide application for the government of human conduct and the increase of human happiness'. W. E. Forster (1873) spoke of the laws of economics with the uncritical reverence professional economists are supposed to, but do not, have; while Sir George Campbell (1876) equated political economy with political sense where the governing of India was concerned (though his speech also had strongly historicist overtones).

2. *Marshall's objectives and Marshallian orthodoxy*

1 See p. 3.

2 *The Rise of the Marginal Utility School* (Kansas, 1960).

3 *Essays in the History of Economics* (Chicago, 1965).

4 Manuscript in Marshall Papers: Mrs Marshall has written at the top 'Saved from the Waste Paper Basket, intended for Preface to *Money, Credit and Commerce*.'

5 *Principles of Economics*, 1st edn (London, 1890) pp. 3–4.

6 *ibid.*, 8th edn (London, 1920), pp. 781–3.

7 *The Present Position of Economics* (London, 1885), reprinted in A. C. Pigou (ed.) *Memorials of Alfred Marshall* (London, 1925), p. 171.

8 Motto on first page of *Industry and Trade* (London, 1919) and a phrase used very often elsewhere by Marshall.

9 'Mechanical and Biological Analogies in Economics', *Economic Journal*, March 1898, p. 43.

10 'The Old Generation of Economists and the New', *Quarterly Journal of Economics*, January 1897.

11 *The Present Position of Economics* reprinted in *Memorials*, p. 155.

12 'The Future of the Working Classes', read 25 November 1873, printed *Eagle*, 1874, p. 22.

13 'The Old Generation of Economists and the New', reprinted in *Memorials*, p. 310.

14 *Official papers by Alfred Marshall*, J. M. Keynes (ed.), p. 209.

15 'The Old Generation of Economists and the New', reprinted in *Memorials*, p. 302.
16 'Some Aspects of Competition' (1890), reprinted in *Memorials*, p. 281.
17 'The Social Possibilities of Economic Chivalry', *Economic Journal*, March 1907, p. 9.
18 *ibid.* p. 14.
19 *A Plea for the Creation of a Curriculum in Economics*, Cambridge private printing, 1902, p. 10.
20 See pp. 39–40.
21 Although the Oxford founders of the *Economic Review*, though broadly distinct from the Marshall tradition, saw economics (properly interpreted) as a positive moral force.
22 See p. 168.
23 Marshall to T. H. Elliott, 25 May 1906.
24 Draft memo dated 23 September 1903, Marshall Papers.
25 K. S. Inglis, *Churches and the Working Classes in Victorian England* (London, 1963), p. 257.
26 'A Reply to "The Perversion of Economic History"', *Economic Journal*, September 1892, p. 509.
27 See *Economic Teaching at the Universities in Relation to Public Wellbeing* (Cambridge, 1902).
28 With one very important exception – the support which marginal utility theory lent to the case for progressive taxation. See chapter 10.
29 See appendix, pp. 55–6, for examples of these.
30 Marshall to Foxwell, 14 February 1902.
31 *ibid.*
32 From Marshall's notebook of his tutorial pupils, 1895–1902, Marshall Papers (Large Brown Box), Marshall Library.
33 Marshall to Keynes, 16 August 1897.
34 *Principles*, 8th edn (London 1920), p. 776.
35 Marshall to Keynes, 16 August 1897.
36 It was in connection with this dispute that Marshall said that Hobson was 'perhaps apt to underrate the difficulty of the problems which he discusses'. See p. 49.
37 Marshall to Bowley, 3 March 1901.
38 Marshall to Keynes, 16 August 1897.
39 Tutorial Notebook, 1895–1902, Marshall Papers.
40 Marshall to Keynes, 17 October 1897.
41 Marshall to Keynes, 28 October 1888.
42 Marshall to Keynes, 30 January 1902.
43 Though not, perhaps, the ideal ally.
44 Marshall to Foxwell, 29 January 1902.
45 Marshall to Foxwell, 12 February 1906.
46 See his letters to Keynes about the latter's *Scope and Method of Political Economy*.
47 See chapter 5.
48 First of three lectures on Henry George, Bristol, 20 February 1883, printed in *Western Daily Press*.

49 Lecture notes, 'Socialism and the Functions of Government', dated 7 June 1886, Marshall Papers.
50 Marshall to unidentified recipient, 2 December 1889, Marshall Papers.
51 *Principles*, 8th edn (London, 1920), pp. 586–7.
52 Marshall to unidentifed recipient, 2 December 1889.
53 Lecture notes, 'Socialism and the Functions of Government', Marshall Papers.
54 *The Present Position of Economics* (1885), reprinted in *Memorials*, p. 156. In some cases this was fair comment. On the other hand Marshall, like any economist, was liable to judge his rivals' displayed skills in terms of their relevance to his own objectives. Thus he risked translating all differences of intention into simple differences of competence, hence into the presumption that he was being more 'economic' than they were. Therefore ideological and technical orthodoxies tended to be linked.
55 Lecture notes, 'Socialism and the Functions of Government', Marshall Papers.
56 'The Old Generation of Economists', reprinted in *Memorials*, p. 309.
57 Marshall to Foxwell, 22 July 1883.
58 'A Reply to "The Perversion of Economic History"', p. 518.
59 Though Parsons much exaggerates the resulting inconsistencies in Marshall's work. See chapter 9.
60 See Marshall to Foxwell, 25 January 1897; also Marshall to Cannan, 22 September 1902, Cannan Papers, L.S.E.
61 However, earlier editions of the *Principles* say the exact reverse. The second edition (1891), p. 73, having doubted whether Mill gave economics exactly the right scope, continues: 'what is wanted is a general principle which shall determine the point in the widening of the scope of economics, at which the growing loss of scientific precision would begin to outweigh the gain of increasing reality and philosophical completeness'. This remained in the next two editions, but was deleted in the fifth.
62 *Principles*, 5th edn (1907), p. 781. See also p. 25 here.

3. *John Neville Keynes, a reluctant lieutenant*

1 Russell to Alys Pearsall Smith, 4 November 1894. Reproduced in Russell's *Autobiography* (London, 1967).
2 Keynes diaries (Cambridge University Library, Add. Manuscripts 7827–7867), 18 January 1873.
3 *ibid.*, 20 February 1873.
4 *ibid.*, 2 June 1873.
5 *ibid.*, 16 August 1873.
6 *ibid.*, 13 December 1875.
7 Whole paragraph based on Keynes diaries, 18 December 1884–31 January 1885.
8 *ibid.*, 15 February 1887.
9 *ibid.*, 13 January 1888. However, Foxwell, in one of the most inaccurate

prophetic passages of all time, pressed Keynes to stay. 'Think of the effect your move may have on your son. He may grow up flippantly epigrammatical and end by becoming the proprietor of a Gutter Gazette, or the hero of a popular party; instead of emulating his father's noble example, becoming an accurate clearheaded Cambridge man, spending his life in valuable unpretentious service to his kind, dying beloved by his friends, venerated by the wise and as unknown to the masses as true merit and worth mostly are' (recorded in Keynes diaries, 16 January 1888).

10 See p. 46.

11 Keynes diaries, 14 December 1884, 24 March 1892, 12 July 1888, 2 July 1886, 26 November 1884, 19 October 1892.

12 *ibid.*, 20 August 1903.

13 *ibid.*, 8 December 1909.

14 *ibid.*, 11 May 1886, 25 May 1888, 24 October 1894, 2 November 1894, 11 December 1899, 15 October 1902.

15 The diaries give a full picture of the Keyneses' domestic life. We are in a world of three hundred presents for a middle-class wedding, pained inquiries into the chastity of servants, hair restorers and bicycle lessons. Keynes found getting off his mount so difficult that, in learning it, he unfortunately lost the knack of getting on. Eventually he turned to Maynard for tuition. We also learn that Maynard (aged 5) became the youngest economist to endorse Marshall's definition of economics as the science of measurable motives. 'He says he thinks he shall call his Mother pounds because he values her so much.' Also entertaining (though not, apparently, to Keynes) are the visits of Keynes' vulgar friend Spokes, who sounds more like Mr Pooter's vulgar friend Gowing than any real-life character has the right to be.

4. *Cannan and Nicholson*

1 *Quarterly Journal of Economics* (1905); reprinted in Cannan, *The Economic Outlook* (London, 1912).

2 Lecture notes on Marshall's *Principles*, 1906–7. Cannan Papers, L.S.E.

3 *Wealth* (London, 1914), p. 117.

4 C. R. Fay, 'Edwin Cannan: the Tribute of A Friend', ms., Cannan Papers, p. 23.

5 *ibid.*, p. 10.

6 *ibid.*, p. 23.

7 Cannan, lecture notes for 1907–8, p. 25, Cannan Papers.

8 *ibid.*, p. 4.

9 Cannan to Fay, 17–30 December 1908, Cannan Papers.

10 Cannan, lecture notes, 1907–8, p. 63, Cannan Papers.

11 Fay's letter is not in the Cannan Papers, but Cannan's 'capitulation' took place in his reply of 30 December 1908.

12 Cannan, lecture notes, 1907–8, supplement for 1909–10, p. 186, Cannan Papers.

13 Cannan to Fay, 28 October 1913.

14 *ibid.*

15 16 May 1914.
16 February 1915.
17 'Godfrey' was a cough mixture, containing laudanum, much used for keeping babies quiet.
18 Adding, however, 'Of course, individual "Socialists" are, many of them, idiots, demagogues, or artists!' Webb to Cannan, 1 April 1889, Cannan Papers.
19 J. A. Schumpeter, *History of Economic Analysis* (Oxford, 1954), p. 830n.
20 Keynes diaries, 28 March 1900.
21 J. S. Nicholson, 'Political Economy and Journalism', reprinted in Nicholson, *Strikes and Social Problems* (London, 1896), p. 165.
22 Nicholson to Cannan, 27 December 1918, Cannan Papers.
23 Nicholson to Keynes, 18 January 1892, Keynes Papers, Marshall Library.
24 Marshall's home in Madingley Road, Cambridge.
25 J. S. Nicholson, *Principles of Political Economy*, vol. 1 (London, 1893), p. 51.
26 *ibid.*, chapter 3; Edgeworth, *Economic Journal*, March 1894; Nicholson, *Economic Journal*, June 1894; Edgeworth, *Economic Journal*, June 1894.
27 Nicholson, *Principles*, vol. 1, p. 414 and vol. 2, pp. 80–1.
28 Nicholson's Presidential Address to Section F in 1893 drew a distinction between Marshall, a first-rate mathematician with a sure enough grasp of the subject to translate his findings into prose and relegate the mathematics to appendixes and footnotes, and Jevons, who 'struggles with the differential calculus as a good man struggles with adversity', and whose mathematical theory of utility 'savours too much of the domestic hearth and the desert island' (*Strikes and Social Problems*), p. 178.
29 Nicholson to Keynes, 27 July 1890, Keynes Papers, Marshall Library.
30 The letter also indicates the reason why: 'I sent Marshall a copy of my book. Generally he sends me in return a printed form with his comments. Judge of my amazement when I receive almost by return a letter in which he says "it will be of exceptional interest and assistance to me as well as a public benefit". What do you think of that? He then goes on to say that there is a lot of Adam Smith in his coming book – in the modern part. Generally Marshall only favours me with the most vague intimations of his labours. What has happened? This change of attitude is at any rate pleasing personally.' The book of Nicholson's was *A Project of Empire*.
31 Nicholson to Keynes; copied into Keynes' diary, 28 July 1885. Nicholson was commenting on Ingram's article 'Political Economy' in the *Encyclopaedia Britannica*.
32 Keynes diaries, 2 June 1885.
33 *The Effect of Machinery on Wages*, London, 1892, p. 132.
34 *Principles*, vol. 1, p. 16.
35 Reprinted in *Strikes and Social Problems*, p. 19.
36 *ibid.*, p. 30.
37 *ibid.*, p. 33.

38 'A Plea for Industrial Liberty', lecture presented at Edinburgh University, October 1892. Published in *Strikes and Social Problems*, p. 147.
39 *ibid.*, p. 147.
40 *Political Economy as a Branch of Education* (Edinburgh, 1881), p. 12.
41 *Historical Progress and Ideal Socialism* (London, 1896), p. 27.
42 *A Project of Empire* (London, 1909), p. 19.
43 'The Reaction in Favour of the Classical Political Economy', reprinted in *Strikes and Social Problems*, p. 189.
44 *ibid.*, p. 185.
45 *Economic Journal*, December 1894, p. 680.
46 *Economic Review*, April 1895, p. 242.
47 *Economic Journal*, March 1921, p. 71.
48 'A Plea for Industrial Liberty', lecture presented at Edinburgh University, October 1892. Published in *Strikes and Social Problems*, p. 143.
49 For what appears to be Nicholson's idea of 'natural justice', see p. 209.
50 *The Effect of Machinery on Wages*, p. 100.
51 Nicholson, *A Dreamer of Dreams*, p. 87.
52 *The Times*, 13 May 1927.

5. Cunningham and historicism

1 Audrey Cunningham, *William Cunningham, Teacher and Priest* (London, 1950), p. viii.
2 *ibid.*, p. 128. Cunningham had been a liberal in his youth but, after engrossing himself in Gladstone's Midlothian campaign in 1879–80, characteristically announced his conversion to the conservative cause.
3 W. Cunningham, *Christianity and Social Questions* (London, 1910), p. 50.
4 Cunningham, 'Nationalism and Cosmopolitanism in Economics', Presidential Address to Section F, 1891. *Report of the Proceedings of the B.A.A.S. 1891* (London, 1892), p. 732.
5 *Modern Civilisation in its Economic Aspects* (London, 1896), p. 50.
6 *Christianity and Social Questions*, p. 99.
7 *Political Economy Treated as an Empirical Science* (Cambridge, 1887); *Modern Civilisation in its Economic Aspects.*
8 *Political Economy Treated as an Empirical Science*, p. 10.
9 *ibid.*, p. 20.
10 Cunningham, 'The Progress of Socialism in England', *Contemporary Review*, January 1879, pp. 251–2.
11 Cunningham, introduction to the *Report of the Industrial Remuneration Conference*, reprinted separately as a pamphlet, Aberdeen, 1885, p. 6.
12 *ibid.*, p. 8.
13 Cunningham, 'The Relativity of Economic Doctrines', reprinted in *Economic Journal*, March 1892, p. 1.
14 A. Marshall, *The Present Position of Economics* (1885), reprinted in A. C. Pigou (ed.), *Memorials of Alfred Marshall* (1925), pp. 166–70. Marshall's inaugural represented, at the least, a substantial shift of

emphasis in his position. *The Economics of Industry* (1879, jointly with Mrs Marshall), had said: 'In backward countries competition exerts but little influence; men do not forecast the future, and deliberately shape their course by a calculation of distant advantages. They rather drift along under the influence of custom, doing the same work in the same way, and for the same remuneration as their fathers did it' (p. 65).

15 Cunningham to Keynes, recorded in Keynes' diary, 27 April 1885.
16 Cunningham, *Politics and Economics* (London, 1885), p. 10.
17 Keynes' diaries, 21 April 1885.
18 Audrey Cunningham, *William Cunningham*, p. 64.
19 Cunningham, 'On the Comtist Criticism of Economic Science', *Report of the 59th meeting of the British Association for the Advancement of Science, Newcastle, 1889* (London, 1890), p. 470.
20 *ibid.*, p. 470n.
21 Cunningham, 'What Did Our Forefathers Mean By Rent?', *Lippincott's Magazine*, February 1890.
22 Cunningham, 'Nationalism and Cosmopolitanism in Economics', *Report of the Proceedings of the B.A.A.S. 1891*, p. 729.
23 *ibid.*, p. 723.
24 'A Plea for Pure Theory', *Economic Review*, January 1892.
25 See p. 62.
26 D. G. Ritchie, 'What are Economic Laws?', *Economic Review*, July 1892.
27 A. Marshall, 'A Reply', *Economic Journal*, September 1892, p. 508.
28 29 September 1892.
29 Cunningham, 'Why Has Roscher had So Little Influence in England?', *Annals of the American Academy of Political and Social Science*, November 1894.
30 Published by the Cambridge University Press, 26 May 1903.
31 A typed copy of the Board's statement is in the Marshall Papers.
32 *Christianity and Socialism* (London, 1909) p. 5. Cunningham had been extremely upset at the way Foxwell had been passed over in favour of Pigou on 30 May 1908, and mentioned the affair from the pulpit the following Sunday. See R. H. Coase, 'The Appointment of Pigou as Marshall's Successor', *Journal of Law and Economics*, October 1972.
33 Cunningham, *Christianity and Economic Science* (London, 1914), pp. 16–17.
34 Even in 'A Plea for Pure Theory' Cunningham did not deny the necessity for causal generalisations; he merely said that they should be confined to economic history and excluded from 'economic theory' as he redefined it.
35 Cunningham, *Politics and Economics*, p. 14.
36 The best summary of Cunningham's position on this issue is not in *Politics and Economics* but in *Modern Civilisation in its Economic Aspects*, pp. 183–8.
37 *The Use and Abuse of Money* (London, 1891), pp. 45–6.
38 *Christianity and Social Questions*, p. 75.
39 *Politics and Economics*, p. 273.
40 *ibid.*, p. 16.
41 Audrey Cunningham, *William Cunningham*, p. 63.

42 'The Failure of the Free Traders to Attain Their Ideals', *Report of the Proceedings of the B.A.A.S.* (London, 1904), p. 751.
43 *Christianity and Social Questions*, p. 74.
44 *ibid.*, p. 13.
45 *ibid.*, p. 5.
46 Augustine Birrell, liberal politician.
47 'The General Election – Prospects of Social Legislation', *Economic Review*, October 1895, p. 515.
48 See the last line of quotation from *Christianity and Economic Science* on p. 110 here.
49 W. J. Ashley, *An Introduction to English Economic History and Theory*, part 1, vol. 1 (London, 1888).
50 Ashley, 'On the Study of Economic History', inaugural lecture, Harvard University, 4 July 1893, reprinted in N. B. Harte (ed.), *The Study of Economic History* (London, 1971), p. 5.
51 *ibid.*, p. 3.
52 L. L. Price, review of R. T. Ely's *An Introduction to Political Economy* (London, 1891), *Economic Journal*, September 1891, p. 609.
53 Cunningham, 'A New Contribution to Economic History: Ashley's English Economic History', *Political Science Quarterly*, 1891.
54 Ashley went to America a liberal and came back a unionist; but in private conversation he called himself an 'evolutionary socialist' to the end of his life (see Anne Ashley, *William James Ashley* (London, 1932). Of the other historicists, the closest to Cunningham in political outlook was Ingram, who saw the connection between religion and politics in terms very similar to Cunningham's (see Ingram's *History of Political Economy* (1st publ. 1888), 2nd edn, 1915, p. 299). But, politics aside, no two historicists were further removed in viewpoint. Remarks by Ingram such as the following must have been anathema to Cunningham: 'The variations depending on difference of race, as affecting bodily and mental endowment, or on diversity of external situations, are secondary phenomena only; they must be postponed in studying the general theory of social development' (*ibid.*, p. 199).
55 Cunningham, 'Political Economy in Relation to Practical Life', *International Journal of Ethics*, January 1893, p. 191.
56 Ashley, 'On the Study of Economic History', p. 9.
57 *ibid.*, p. 10.
58 *ibid.*, p. 6.
59 *ibid.*, p. 8.
60 *ibid.*, p. 4.
61 Ashley, 'The Present Position of Political Economy', reprinted *Economic Journal*, December 1907, p. 481.
62 *ibid.*, pp. 484–5.

6. *Two economic outsiders: Macleod and Crozier*

1 H. D. Macleod, *The History of Economics* (London, 1896), p. 139.
2 *ibid.*, p. 142.

3 *ibid.*, p. 142.
4 *ibid.*, p. 148.
5 Vol. 1, London, 1881; vol. 2, part 1, London 1886.
6 *The History of Economics*, p. 166.
7 *Elements of Economics*, vol. 1, p. ix.
8 *ibid.*, p. x.
9 *The History of Economics*, p. 166.
10 *ibid.*, p. 164.
11 *Elements of Economics* vol. 1, pp. 130–1.
12 *Address to the Electors* (Cambridge, 1884), p. 18. As an afterthought Macleod adds that economics also requires 'a thorough investigation of the history of every country in the world'. This modest proposal sits ill with his dismissals of geographical relativism.
13 *Thoughts on the Forthcoming Election of a Professor of Political Economy in the University of Cambridge* (Cambridge, 1863).
14 *The History of Economics*, p. 107.
15 *ibid.*, p. 108. Compare Marshall, recorded by Neville Keynes: 'Amongst other things he said he would give his right arm never to have learnt any classics; the time that he wasted on classics might so much more profitably have been spent on music, drawing, sculpture, a few modern languages, biology and general culture.' J. N. Keynes diaries, 26 April 1877.
16 *ibid.*, pp. 100–1.
17 *ibid.*, p. 123.
18 'Handloom weavers study geometry; shoemakers are proficient in polemics; tailors especially affect politics . . . If a man being compelled to earn his own livelihood would study, or indulge the imagination, he should seek for the purpose a peculiarly simple subdivision of labour' *Elements of Economics*, vol. 2, p. 176.
19 *ibid.*, pp. 142–52.
20 *ibid.*, p. 194.
21 *ibid.*, p. 100.
22 *ibid.*
23 *History of Economics*, p. 135.
24 *Elements of Economics*, vol. 1, p. 107.
25 Macleod, *Economics for Beginners* (London, 1878), p. 13.
26 *History of Economics*, p. 135.
27 *Elements of Economics*, vol. 1, pp. 254–5.
28 On p. 158, Jevons' 'sunspot' theory of the trade cycle is dismissed as a 'Bedlamite craze'.
29 Macleod, *Theory and Practice of Banking*, 5th edn, London, 1892, vol. 2, p. 93.
30 *Elements of Economics*, vol. 1, p. 298.
31 *Economics for Beginners*, p. 35.
32 *ibid.*, p. 32.
33 *Elements of Economics*, vol. 1, p. 130. My italics.
34 *History of Economics*, p. 164.
35 *Elements of Economics*, vol. 1, p. viii. *The History of Economics* also

claimed (p. 78) that 'there is not much difference in the ideas involved in protection and the slave trade'.

36 *Elements of Economics*, vol. 2, p. 211.
37 Macleod, *On the Definition and Nature of the Science of Political Economy* (Cambridge, 1862), p. 9.
38 *History of Economics*, p. 81.
39 *ibid.*, p. 98.
40 *Elements of Economics*, vol. 1, p. 101.
41 *ibid.*, vol. 2, p. 140.
42 *ibid.*, p. 33.
43 J. B. Crozier, *My Inner Life*, 2nd edn, London, 1908, vol. 2, p. 509.
44 Crozier, *The Wheel of Wealth* (London, 1907), p. 17.
45 *ibid.*, p. 17.
46 *ibid.*, p. 478.
47 *ibid.*, p. 396.
48 *ibid.*, p. 391.
49 *ibid.*, p. 483.
50 See, for instance, Crozier's 'refutation' of Mill's belief that a general glut was impossible. *The Wheel of Wealth*, p. 38.
51 *ibid.*, pp. 479–80.
52 *ibid.*, p. 441.
53 *ibid.*, p. 442.
54 *ibid.*, p. 494.
55 *ibid.*, p. 498.
56 R. G. Lipsey, *An Introduction to Positive Economics* (6th edn, London, 1983).

7. Hobson's choice

1 Peter Clarke, *Liberals and Social Democrats* (Cambridge, 1978).
2 Hobson, *Work and Wealth* (London, 1914), p. 26.
3 Hobson, *Wealth and Life* (London, 1929), p. 51.
4 *Work and Wealth*, p. 326.
5 William Smart, *Studies in Economics* (London, 1895), p. 275.
6 *Free Thought in the Social Sciences* (London, 1926), p. 95.
7 *ibid.*, p. 103.
8 *ibid.*, p. 104.
9 *ibid.*, p. 102.
10 *Work and Wealth*, p. 235.
11 *Free Thought in the Social Sciences*, pp. 119–20.
12 See pp. 49–50.
13 J. M. Keynes, review of *Gold, Prices and Wages*, *Economic Journal*, September 1913, p. 393.
14 This information is from Joan Robinson, quoted in Peter Clarke, *Liberals and Social Democrats*, p. 48.
15 5 May 1900.
16 Freeden, *The New Liberalism*, p. 111.
17 *Work and Wealth*, p. 304.

18 L. T. Hobhouse, *Liberalism*, p. 137, quoted by P. Clarke, *Liberals and Social Democrats*, p. 154.

8. Orthodox welfare economics

1 H. Myint, *Theories of Welfare Economics* (London, 1948), p. 129.
2 Sidgwick, *Principles of Political Economy* (3rd edn, London, 1901), pp. 402–12.
3 'The Old Generation of Economists and the New', *Quarterly Journal of Economics*, 1897, reprinted in *Memorials*, p. 301.
4 Marshall to Acland, 26 February 1886, Marshall Papers.
5 Marshall, *Statistical Journal*, 1893, p. 288.
6 C. W. Guillebaud, 'Some Personal Reminiscences of Alfred Marshall', Marshall Papers.
7 From some jottings on Bernoulli, dated 1907, Marshall Papers.
8 'Economics and Utilitarianism' ms. dated 20 August (no year), Marshall Papers.
9 C. F. Bastable, *Public Finance*, 2nd edn (London, 1895) p. 248.
10 Edgeworth, 'The Pure Theory of Taxation', *Economic Journal*, June 1897, reprinted in *Papers Relating to Political Economy* (London, 1925), vol. 2, p. 110.
11 *ibid.*, p. 114.
12 *ibid.*, p. 117.
13 *ibid.*, p. 117.
14 *ibid.*, p. 119.
15 Bastable, 'Ireland's Place in the Financial System of the United Kingdom', *Economic Journal*, June 1896. By 'free' income, Bastable meant income above the minimum of subsistence – an amount which, like everyone else before and since, he completely failed to define. Bastable thought this minimum, whatever it was, should be exempted from taxation, which should otherwise be proportional. Edgeworth disagreed. Applied utilitarianism, he told Bastable, should not by its gaps frighten economists into safe choices, but by its egalitarian spirit give them the courage to make radical ones. 'The golden mean is not to be attained by creeping cautiously close to the limiting extreme – *nimum premendo litus inquum*. The guiding star of Utilitarianism shines in a direction away from that hard coastline and gilds the bolder course with the light of pure theory' (Edgeworth, quoted from *Papers Relating to Political Economy*, p. 119).
16 Thus Sidgwick, for example, included among the economic consequences of unfettered enterprise cases where an entrepreneur appropriated more than the whole net gain to the community of his enterprise, as when B, by building a better railway than A's existing one, got paid for a large part of the utility that A before supplied (*Principles of Political Economy*, p. 408). Pigou's reply was that the inequality between the increase in B's profits and the increase in total profits was irrelevant; the total product was maximised when one unit of investment was equally productive in either use and, *ceteris paribus*, total private product was

maximised with the same allocation of investment as was total social product (*Wealth and Welfare* (London, 1912), p. 161).

17 *Official papers*, pp. 91–2.

18 *Wealth and Welfare*, p. 393.

19 Pigou, *Socialism versus Capitalism* (London, 1937), makes the suggestion that cutting 'investment in the health, intelligence and character of the people be made a criminal offence.'

9. *Economists and ethics*

1 J. N. Keynes, *The Scope and Method of Political Economy.*

2 T. W. Hutchison, *Positive Economics and Policy Objectives.*

3 J. E. Cairnes, *The Character and Logical Method of Political Economy*, 2nd edn (London, 1888), pp. 39–42.

4 J. K. Ingram, Presidential Address to Section F of the British Association for the Advancement of Science, 1878. *Report of the British Association For the Advancement of Science, Dublin, 1878* (London, 1879), p. 648.

5 A. Marshall, 'Some Aspects of Competition', *Report of the British Association for the Advancement of Science, Leeds, 1890* (London, 1891), p. 903.

6 W. J. Ashley, 'The Present Position of Political Economy', *Economic Journal*, December 1907, p. 489.

7 This point is discussed at greater length in chapter 2.

8 J. M. Keynes (ed.), *Official Papers by Alfred Marshall* (London, 1926), p. 225.

9 C. Devas, *Political Economy*, 3rd edn (London, 1919), p. 1.

10 Devas, 'The Moral Aspect of Consumption', *International Journal of Ethics*, October 1899, p. 46.

11 *ibid.*, p. 53.

12 *ibid.*, p. 53.

13 Devas, *Political Economy.*

14 W. Smart, *Studies in Economics* (London, 1895), p. 332.

15 *ibid.*, p. 320.

16 *ibid.*, p. 263.

17 Smart, *The Distribution of Income* (London, 1899), p. 330n.

18 L. Robbins, 'Mr Hawtrey on the Scope of Economics', *Economica*, June 1927.

19 This information comes from the late Professor Philip Sargant Florence (pers. comm., 29 May 1981).

20 W. J. Ashley, *An Introduction to English Economic History and Theory*, 4th edn, London, 1906, vol. 2, p. 380.

21 'W.J.A.' *Oxford Magazine*, 1 February 1887, quoted by A. Kadish in *The Oxford Economists in the Late Nineteenth Century* (Oxford, 1983). It is also worth noting that Ashley, alone among his contemporaries, argued that even the economist's ability to make value-judgements was historically relative, claiming that the idea of the just price made sense in the thirteenth century (when a fair recompense which would allow a craftsman to live 'a decent life' was fairly readily identifiable),

but not in the twentieth (when value was 'something entirely subjective; it is what each individual cares to give for a thing') *An Introduction to English Economic History and Theory*, vol. 1, pp. 138–40.

22 L. L. F. R. Price, 'The Relation of Economic Science to Practical Affairs', Presidential Address, Section F, 1905, *Proceedings of the British Association for the Advancement of Science* (London, 1906).

23 J. S. Nicholson, *Principles of Political Economy*, vol. 1 (London, 1893), p. 14.

24 *ibid.*, p. 16.

25 *ibid.*, p. 232.

26 *ibid.*, p. 233.

27 Nicholson, Inaugural Address to the Scottish Society of Economists, 9 November 1897, published in the *Economic Journal*, December 1897, p. 540.

28 E. Cannan, *Political Economy and Socialism*, entry for Cobden Essay Prize, 1886, p. 86, Cannan Papers, L.S.E.

29 *ibid.*, p. 87n.

30 *ibid.*, p. 87.

31 Lecture notes, General Economic Theory, 1902–3, p. 4, Cannan Papers, L.S.E. There is no evidence that economists avoided political controversy because of fears that increased State interference in the universities would result. (This did happen in Germany; see J. Ben David and A. Zloczower, 'The Growth of Institutionalised Science in Germany' in J. Barnes (ed.), *The Sociology of Science* (London, 1972).) But after 1900 or thereabouts, British economists did become more sensitive to their public role. See the following articles by A. W. Coats: 'Sociological Aspects of British Economics *c.* 1880–1930', *Journal of Political Economy*, October 1967; 'The Origins and Early Development of the Royal Economic Society', *Economic Journal*, June 1968; 'Political Economy and the Tariff Reform Campaign of 1903', *Journal of Law and Economics*, April 1968.

32 See chapter 3.

33 *Dundee Advertiser*, 14 July 1914.

34 *Church Gazette*, 23 June 1900.

35 *Economic Review*, October 1894, p. 533.

36 Chiozza Money to Cannan, 27 May 1905, Cannan Papers, L.S.E. It is to be hoped Cannan did not reply to Chiozza Money in the vein he used on Fay: 'Equity . . . is a silly childish question, and the Americans ask it for that reason, they being in their infancy. Equitable! Why, if I had a lion's tail and a donkey's ears, I could make thousands a year and see the world by sitting in a show for an hour in the evening, what has equity to do with that?' Cannan to Fay, 7 February 1909, Cannan Papers, L.S.E.

37 Quoted by N. Annan, *Leslie Stephen* (London, 1951), p. 212.

38 H. Sidgwick, 'The Relation of Ethics to Sociology', *International Journal of Ethics*, October 1899, pp. 2–3.

39 L. T. Hobhouse, *Social Evolution and Political Theory* (New York, 1911), p. 8, quoted in P. Clarke, *Liberals and Social Democrats* (Cambridge, 1978), p. 148.

40 J. A. Hobson and M. Ginsberg, *L. T. Hobhouse* (London, 1932), p. 125.
41 A. Marshall, 'The Province of Political Economy', *Beehive*, 2 May 1874.
42 Third lecture on Henry George, reported in *Western Daily Press*, 6 March 1883.
43 Cannan, notes on Marshall's lectures, 11 November 1891. Cannan Papers, L.S.E.
44 *ibid.*, 11 November 1891.
45 *ibid.*, 18 November 1891.
46 *Principles*, 8th edn, pp. 714–15.
47 15 February 1886.
48 Marshall, 'The Poor Law in Relation to State-Aided Pensions', *Economic Journal*, March 1892.
49 *Official Papers*, pp. 202–3.
50 *Principles*, 1st edn, p. 81n.
51 *Principles*, 8th edn, p. 531.
52 Marshall, Preface to L. L. F. R. Price, *Industrial Peace* (London, 1887), p. xxv.
53 Some rough notes, undated, but apparently connected with the *Principles*. Marshall Papers, Marshall Library. My italics.
54 W. S. Jevons, *Methods of Social Reform* (London, 1883), p. 205.
55 E. Cannan, lecture notes, 1907–8, p. 9, Cannan Papers, L.S.E.
56 W. Cunningham, *Modern Civilisation in Its Economic Aspects* (London, 1896), p. 4.
57 *ibid.*, p. 6.

10. The ideology of marginalism

1 E. Cannan, *Political Economy and Socialism*, Cobden Essay Prize, 1886, p. 114. Cannan Papers, L.S.E.
2 J. A. Hobson, *Confessions of an Economic Heretic* (London, 1938), p. 24n.
3 (i) competition secured for workers the gains of all technical progress. (ii) Rich entrepreneurs, capitalists and shareholders were only receiving the rewards of ingenuity, industry and thrift. (iii) Capital (the product of thrift) was so mixed up with land values that even rent had no certain element of unearned increment. (iv) Workers as a class could only get higher wages by becoming more efficient. (v) Capital's and labour's interest coincided. (vi) Taxing the rich recoiled on the worker by reducing the demand for labour. (vii) Nationalisation was unjust and uneconomic. (viii) The remedy for all ills was improved individual character.
4 Hobson, *Veblen* (London, 1936), p. 104.
5 Hobson, *The Fight for Democracy* (London, 1917), p. 5.
6 M. Blaug, *Economic Theory in Retrospect*, 3rd edn (London, 1978), p. 317.
7 T. W. Hutchison *On Revolutions in Economics* (Cambridge, 1978), pp. 250–1.
8 Cannan, *Theories of Production and Distribution 1776–1848* (London, 1893), p. 310.

9 W. J. Ashley, 'The Present Position of Political Economy', *Economic Journal*, December 1907, p. 475.
10 Quoted by G. M. Koot in an unpublished article.
11 Cannan, *Theories of Production and Distribution 1776–1848*, p. 310.
12 Cannan, 'The use of estimates of aggregate capital and income as measures of the economic welfare of nations', ms. of conference papers. B.A.A.S. Section F, 1890, pp. 15–16. Cannan Papers, L.S.E.
13 *ibid.*, p. 17.
14 H. W. Blunt in the *Economic Review*, January 1891, p. 122.
15 The letter is quoted in Anne Ashley, *William James Ashley* (London, 1932), pp. 34–5.
16 See above, chapter 2.
17 J. Bonar, review of J. R. MacDonald's *Socialism and Society* (London, 1905), *Economic Review*, January 1906, p. 123.
18 Cannan, notes for lecture on Marshall's *Principles*, 1907–8, Supplement for 1911–12, p. 238. Cannan Papers, L.S.E.
19 See chapters 4 and 6 respectively.
20 And that Saint-Simon had more claim to be called a man of genius than Marx. H. Sidgwick 'The Economic Lessons of Socialism', *Economic Journal*, September 1895, pp. 337 and 338.
21 See chapters 2, 4 and 6 respectively.
22 'Nor could the impartial bystander, whether he were more dissatisfied with the economists or with the socialists, deny the sinister pertinence of much of Mr. Hobson's shrewd suggestive indication of defects crying for reform ...' L. L. Price, review of Hobson's *Work and Wealth* (paper unidentified; the review is in Hobson's press-cuttings book, now in Hull University Library).
23 C. S. Devas, 'Lessons from Ruskin', *Economic Journal*, March 1898, p. 36.
24 J. S. Nicholson, *Strikes and Social Problems* (London, 1896), p. 31.
25 F. Y. Edgeworth, review of Nicholson's *Strikes and Social Problems*, *Economic Journal*, June 1896, p. 247.
26 A. Marshall, *Preface* to L.L.F.R. Price, *Industrial Peace* (London, 1886), p. xi.
27 Marshall, 'Some Aspects of Competition', Presidential Address to Section, F. Leeds, 1890. Reprinted in A. C. Pigou (ed.), *Memorials of Alfred Marshall* (London, 1925), p. 282.
28 Marshall, discussion of A. L. Bowley's 'Changes in Average Wages (Nominal and Real) 1860–1891', *Statistical Journal*, vol. 58 (1895) p. 280.
29 Marshall to Westcott, 24 January 1900. Marshall Papers, Marshall Library.
30 Edgeworth, review of J.B. Clark's *The Distribution of Wealth* (London and New York, 1900), *Economic Journal*, December 1900, p. 537.
31 Smart, *The Distribution of Income* (London, 1899), p. 331.
32 *ibid.*, pp. 334–5.
33 P. H. Wicksteed, 'The Scope and Method of Political Economy in the

Light of the "Marginal" Theory of Value and Distribution', *Economic Journal*, March 1914, p. 11.

34 *ibid.*, p. 10.

35 P. H. Wicksteed, review of H. J. Davenport's *The Economics of Enterprise, Economic Journal*, September 1914, p. 422.

36 Wicksteed, 'The Scope and Method of Political Economy in the Light of the "Marginal" Theory of Value and Distribution', *Economic Journal*, March 1914, p. 11.

37 Marshall, 'The Old Generation of Economists and the New', *Quarterly Journal of Economics*, January 1897, reprinted in *Memorials*, p. 305.

38 Most of what we have said about paradigms applies also to the specific theories within those paradigms. Indeed in one respect it applies more strongly. Theories, unlike paradigms, are always consciously articulated so as to be understood and accepted. This leads economists into expository devices with a selective emphasis of their own. If Marx had simply listed the different factors affecting the rate of profit, his theory on the subject would be much harder to grasp. By picking out one of these factors – the rising organic composition of capital – and elevating its effect into a 'law' ruling among mere 'tendencies' (the effects of the other factors), he turned an amorphous set of hypotheses into an orderly skeleton with a backbone and five ribs. Yet who can deny that, had the tendency of the rate of surplus value to rise been given pride of place, many opinions about capitalism's life expectancy would have been altered?

39 Marshall, 'The Old Generation of Economists and the New', reprinted in *Memorials*, p. 305.

40 G. Myrdal, *The Political Element in the Development of Economic Theory* (London, 1953).

41 *ibid.*, p. 105.

42 J. Kornai, *Anti Equilibrium* (London, 1971), p. 153.

43 T. W. Hutchison, *On Revolutions in Economics* (Cambridge, 1978), p. 266.

11. The Marshallians and the Pigouese

1 Cannan Papers, L.S.E.

2 Marshall's opposition to Foxwell as his successor seems to have been partly based on the strong Protectionist stance Foxwell had taken in 1903. See A. W. Coats, 'Political Economy and The Tariff Reform Campaign of 1903', *Journal of Law and Economics*, April 1968; R. H. Coase, 'The Appointment of Pigou as Marshall's Successor', *Journal of Law and Economics*, October 1972, and A. W. Coats, 'The Appointment of Pigou as Marshall's Successor: A Reply', *Journal of Law and Economics*, October 1972.

3 Marshall quoted his own remarks to Higgs when he wrote to Neville Keynes on the subject. Marshall to Keynes, 13 December 1908. Keynes Papers, Marshall Library.

4 *ibid.*

5 *Cambridge Daily News*, 22 June 1916.
6 H. S. Foxwell, letter to the *Cambridge Daily News*, 25 May 1916.
7 This information came from the late Professor Philip Sargant Florence (pers. comm., 29 May 1981). Pigou's appeal had been preceded by an ugly exchange of letters in the *Morning Post*. It was started by Macleod's son, R. H. Macleod (a Fellow of Christ's College, though not in economics), who, in connection with Pigou's forthcoming appeal, asked whether the teaching of economics, 'at least of the particular brand in favour in Cambridge' was 'desirable, let alone indispensable' in wartime. Macleod quoted a Section F paper by Cunningham which had said there was 'some reason for believing' that Pigou's style of economics had helped prevent effective conduct of the war. Pigou angrily replied that Macleod had attacked not just him but the entire Faculty, all of whom but himself were in government departments or in the army. Pigou's letter mentioned neither Cunningham nor his paper, either directly or by implication; but this minor detail did not bother Cunningham, who promptly claimed that if Pigou had come across his paper 'he would have known that it does not consist of wholesale "insinuations" but that it is discriminating'. (This remarkable rejoinder to something Pigou had not said aroused even the placid Neville Keynes to write in his diary that Cunningham was 'beneath contempt'.) Pigou replied that he did not have to defend his abilities either against 'Dr Cunningham, who is an eminent authority on the economic history of England prior to 1846' or against 'Mr Macleod, of the subject-matter of whose eminence I am unfortunately unaware'. Cunningham leapt to the defence of 'the son of my old friend'; meanwhile 'a Member of the Senate' informed everyone that he had once been to a lecture of Pigou's and not thought much of it, and so was quite ready to let him 'use his talents in a wider sphere'. Pigou did not bother to reply to any of this, so a disappointed Macleod tried to start things up again. 'May I call the next witness?' The next witness was G. G. Coulton, who had apparently said Pigou had said the nation was 'morally bound' to try out his 'untested theories' etc. etc. etc. (*Morning Post*, 26 April–6 May 1916). Perhaps Macleod can be excused by heredity and Cunningham by failing health.
8 Foxwell to Keynes, 5 April 1881. Keynes Papers, Marshall Library.
9 Foxwell to Keynes, 25 January 1892. The 'guide' was a students' guide to economics teaching in Cambridge.
10 See p. 57n.
11 Foxwell to Keynes, 6 February 1912.
12 See C. E. Collet, 'Professor Foxwell and University College', *Economic Journal*, December 1936.
13 See chapter 2.
14 Marshall to Keynes, 15 June 1903. Keynes Papers, Marshall Library.
15 L. L. Price, review of Pigou's *Principles and Methods of Industrial Peace*, *Economic Journal*, September 1905, p. 386.
16 *ibid.*, p. 386.
17 *ibid.*, p. 386.
18 See p. 74.

19 Smith's article appeared in two parts: October 1913 and January 1914. Florence's reply was published in the *Review* in April 1914.
20 Except, of course, for the supremely important consideration that monetary instability threatens the social order – a fact which, however, is too big and uncontentious to generate the kind of intricate non-economic penumbra around monetary questions needed for specifically economic and less specifically economic styles of discourse to emerge and compete with one another.
21 Fraser to Cannan, 10 October 1896, Cannan Papers, L.S.E.
22 See p. 62.
23 C. R. Fay, 'Edwin Cannan: The Tribute of a Friend', ms., Cannan Papers, L.S.E., p. 10.
24 Strictly speaking, theories can only be brought face to face with other theories. By 'uncontested evidence' we mean theories which have been relegated to 'unproblematic background knowledge'.
25 A brief rebuke from the depths of a tent, it seems, was the nearest to an audience that even Fay (a cousin by marriage as well as a colleague) could expect (see p. 223). And Professor Sargant Florence, who was in Cambridge, either as an undergraduate or as a don, for most of Marshall's retirement, never met Marshall at all, seeing him but once – at King's Cross railway station.
26 J. M. Keynes, 'Alfred Marshall', *Economic Journal*, September 1924, reprinted in *Essays in Biography* (Royal Economic Society Edition, 1972), p. 223.

Select bibliography

A. Manuscript sources

Cannan Papers, London School of Economics and Political Science
Chapman Autobiography, London School of Economics and Political Science
J. N. Keynes Papers and diaries, University Library, Cambridge
J. N. Keynes papers, Marshall Library, Cambridge
Marshall Papers, Marshall Library, Cambridge

B. Printed Sources (primary)

Ashley, W. J., *An Introduction to English Economic History and Theory*, London 1888.

'On the Study of Economic History', inaugural lecture, Harvard University, 1893, reprinted in N. B. Harte (ed.), *The Study of Economic History*, London, 1971.

The Tariff Problem (1st edn 1903), 3rd edn, London, 1911.

'The Present Position of Political Economy', *Economic Journal*, December 1907.

Bastable, C. F., *Public Finance*, (1st edn 1892), 2nd edn, London, 1895.

'Ireland's Place in the Financial System of the United Kingdom', *Economic Journal*, June 1896.

Bonar, J., *Philosophy and Political Economy*, London, 1893.

British Association for the Advancement of Science, *Methods of Economic Training in This and Other Countries*, London, 1894.

Cairnes, J. E., *The Character and Logical Method of Political Economy* (1st edn 1854), 2nd edn, London, 1888.

Essays in Political Economy, London, 1873.

Some Leading Principles of Political Economy Newly Expounded, London, 1874.

Cannan, E., *A History of the Theories of Production and Distribution in English Political Economy from 1776 to 1848* (1st edn 1893), reprint of 3rd edn, London, 1953.

The Economic Outlook, London, 1912.

Wealth, London, 1914.

Money: Its Connection with Rising and Falling Prices, London, 1918.

An Economist's Protest, London, 1927.
A Review of Economic Theory (1st edn 1929), 2nd edn, London, 1964.
Clark, J. B., *The Distribution of Wealth*, London and New York, 1900.
Crozier, J. B., *My Inner Life*, 2 vols. (1st edn 1898), 2nd edn, London, 1908.
The Wheel of Wealth, London, 1907.
Cunningham, W., 'The Progress of Socialism in England', *Contemporary Review*, January 1879.
The Growth of English Industry and Commerce, Cambridge, 1882.
Politics and Economics, London, 1885.
Political Economy Treated as an Empirical Science, Cambridge, 1887.
'Nationalism and Cosmopolitanism in Economics', Presidential Address to Section F, 1891, published in the *Report of the Proceedings of the British Association for the Advancement of Science*, London, 1892.
'A Plea for Pure Theory', *Economic Review*, January 1892.
'The Relativity of Economic Doctrines', *Economic Journal*, March 1892.
'The Perversion of Economic History', *Economic Journal*, September 1892.
'Political Economy in Relation to Practical Life', *International Journal of Ethics*, January 1893.
'Economists as Mischief Makers', *Economic Review*, January 1894.
Strikes, Boston, Mass., 1895.
'The General Election – Prospects of Social Legislation', *Economic Review*, October 1895.
Modern Civilisation in Some of Its Economic Aspects, London, 1896.
'The Failure of the Free Traders to Realise Their Ideal', *Economic Review*, January 1904.
'Unconscious Assumptions in Economics', paper read to Section F, 1905, published in the *Report of the British Association for the Advancement of Science*, London, 1906.
The Wisdom of the Wise, Cambridge, 1906.
Christianity and Social Questions, London, 1910.
The Case Against Free Trade, London, 1910.
The Causes of the Labour Unrest, London, 1912.
Christianity and Economic Science, London, 1914.
Christianity and Politics, London, 1916.
Cunynghame, Sir H. H. S. *A Geometrical Political Economy*, Oxford, 1904.
Devas, C. S., *Political Economy* (1st edn 1892), 3rd edn, London, 1919.
'Lessons From Ruskin', *Economic Journal*, March 1898.
Edgeworth, F. Y., *Mathematical Psychics*, London, 1881.
'The Pure Theory of Taxation', *Economic Journal*, June 1897.
'The Theory of Distribution', *Quarterly Journal of Economics*, February 1904.
Papers Relating to Political Economy, 3 vols., London, 1925.
Fawcett, H., *Manual of Political Economy*, Cambridge, 1863.
Foxwell, H. S., *The Social Aspect of Banking*, London, 1886.
Irregularity of Employment and Fluctuations of Prices, Edinburgh, 1886.
Galton, F., 'Economic Science and the British Association', *Journal of the Royal Statistical Society*, September 1877.

George, H., *Progress and Poverty*, London, 1881.
Harrison, F., *Autobiographic Memoirs*, 2 vols., London, 1911.
Hewins, W. A. S., *The Apologia of an Imperialist*, 2 vols., London, 1929.
Hobhouse, L. T., *Social Evolution and Political Theory*, New York, 1911.
Hobson, J. A., *The Evolution of Modern Capitalism*, London, 1894.
John Ruskin, Social Reformer, London, 1898.
The Economics of Distribution, London, 1900.
The Social Problem, London, 1901.
Imperialism, London, 1902.
The Crisis of Liberalism, London, 1909.
The Industrial System (1st edn 1909), 2nd edn, London, 1910.
'Marginal Productivity', *Economic Review*, July 1910.
Gold, Prices and Wages, London, 1913.
Work and Wealth, London, 1914.
Free Thought in the Social Sciences, London, 1926.
Wealth and Life, London, 1929.
Veblen, London, 1936.
Confessions of an Economic Heretic, London, 1938.
Hobson, J. A. and Ginsberg, M., *L. T. Hobhouse, His Life and Work*, London, 1932.
Ingram, J. K., *A History of Political Economy* (1st edn 1888) 2nd edn, London, 1915.
Jevons, W. S., 'Notice of a General Mathematical Theory of Political Economy' read to Section F, 1862, and published in the *Report of the British Association for the Advancement of Science*, London, 1863.
The Coal Question, London and Cambridge, 1865.
The Theory of Political Economy (1st edn 1871), centenary edition, London, 1970.
The State in Relation to Labour, London, 1882.
Methods of Social Reform and other papers, London, 1883.
Letters and Journals, London, 1886.
Joseph, H. W. B., 'Karl Marx's Theory of Value', *Economic Review*, January 1910.
Keynes, J. M. (ed.), *Papers Relating to Political Economy*, London, 1926.
Keynes, J. N., *The Scope and Method of Political Economy*, London, 1890.
Leslie, T. E. C., *Essays in Political Economy*, Dublin, 1888.
Macleod, H. D., *The Theory and Practice of Banking*, London, 1855, 5th edn, London, 1892.
Thoughts on the Forthcoming Election of a Professor of Political Economy in the University of Cambridge, Cambridge, 1863.
A Dictionary of Political Economy, vol. 1, London, 1863.
The Elements of Economics, 2 vols., London, 1881 and 1886.
Bimetallism, London, 1894.
The History of Economics, London, 1896.
Mallock, W. H., *The New Republic* (1st edn 1877), Leicester, 1975.
Marshall, A., Review of Jevons' *The Theory of Political Economy*, *Academy*, 1 April 1872.
'The Future of the Working Classes', *Eagle*, 1874.

'On Mr. Mill's Theory of Value', *Fortnightly Review*, April 1876.
The Pure Theory of Foreign Trade (1st edn 1879), London, 1930.
The Pure Theory of Domestic Values (1st edn 1879), London, 1930.
'Where to House the London Poor', *Contemporary Review*, March 1884.
The Present Position of Economics, London, 1885.
'On the Graphic Method of Statistics', *Jubilee Volume of the Royal Statistical Society*, 1885.
Preface to Bagehot's *The Postulates of Political Economy*, London, 1885.
'Remedies for Fluctuations of General Prices', *Contemporary Review*, March 1887.
Preface to L. L. Price's *Industrial Peace*, London, 1887.
Presidential Address before the Co-operative Congress, Ipswich, 1889, Manchester, 1889.
Principles of Economics, London, 1890.
'Some Aspects of Competition', Presidential Address to Section F, 1890, published in the *Report of the British Association for the Advancement of Science*, London, 1891.
Elements of the Economics of Industry, London, 1892.
'The Poor Law in Relation to State-Aided Pensions', *Economic Journal*, March 1892.
'A Reply to "The Perversion of Economic History"', *Economic Journal*, September 1892.
'On Rent', *Economic Journal*, March 1893.
'The Old Generation of Economists and the New', *Quarterly Journal of Economics*, January 1897.
'Mechanical and Biological Analogies in Economics', *Economic Journal*, March 1898.
A Plea for the Creation of a Curriculum in Economics and Associated Branches of Political Science, Cambridge, 1902.
Economic Teaching at the Universities in Relation to Public Wellbeing, Cambridge, 1902.
The New Cambridge Curriculum in Economics, London, 1903.
Selections From Letters Recommending an Economics Tripos (flysheet), Cambridge, 1903.
Introduction to the Tripos in Economics and Associated Branches of Political Science, Cambridge, 1906.
'The Social Possibilities of Economic Chivalry', *Economic Journal*, March 1907.
'National Taxation After the War', in *After-War Problems*, ed. W.H. Dawson, London, 1917.
Industry and Trade, London, 1919.
Money, Credit and Commerce, London, 1923.
Marshall, A. and Marshall, M. P., *The Economics of Industry*, London, 1879.
Marshall, M. P., *What I Remember*, Cambridge, 1947.
Mill, J. S., *Essays on Some Unsettled Questions in Political Economy*, London, 1844.
Principles of Political Economy, 2 vols., London, 1848.

Money, Sir L. G. C., *Riches and Poverty*, London, 1905.
Mummery, A. F. and Hobson, J. A., *The Physiology of Industry*, London, 1889.
Nicholson, J. S., *The Effect of Machinery on Wages* (1st edn 1879), 2nd edn, London, 1892.
'A Plea for Orthodox Political Economy', *National Review*, December 1885.
A Treatise on Money and Essays on Present Monetary Problems, London, 1888.
Principles of Political Economy, 3 vols., London, 1893, 1897, and 1901.
Historical Progress and Ideal Socialism, London, 1896.
Strikes and Social Problems, London, 1896.
The Tariff Question, London, 1903.
A Project of Empire, London, 1909.
'The Economics of Imperialism', *Economic Journal*, June 1910.
War Finance, London, 1917.
Inflation, London, 1919.
The Revival of Marxism, London, 1921.
Palgrave, Sir R. H. I. (ed.), *Dictionary of Political Economy*, 3 vols., London, 1894–9.
Palgrave, Sir R. H. I. and Higgs, H. (eds.), *Dictionary of Political Economy*, 3 vols., 3rd edn, London, 1923–6.
Pigou, A. C., 'Some Remarks on Utility', *Economic Journal*, March 1903.
The Riddle of the Tariff, London, 1903.
Principles and Methods of Industrial Peace, London, 1905.
Wealth and Welfare, London, 1912.
The Economics of Welfare (1st edn 1920), 4th edn, London, 1932.
Alfred Marshall and Current Thought, London, 1953.
(ed.) *Memorials of Alfred Marshall*, London, 1925.
Price, B., *Practical Political Economy*, London, 1878.
Price L. L. F. R., *Economic Science and Practice*, London, 1896.
A Short History of Political Economy in England from Adam Smith to Alfred Marshall (1st edn 1891), 14th edn, London, 1937.
Report of the Industrial Remuneration Conference, London, 1885.
Ruskin, J., *Unto this Last* (1st edn 1860), Lincoln, Nebraska, 1967.
Fors Clavigera, London, 1872.
Seligman, E. R. A., *Progressive Taxation in Theory and Practice*, American Economics Association, 1894.
Sidgwick, H., *The Methods of Ethics*, London, 1874.
The Principles of Political Economy (1st edn 1883), 3rd edn, London, 1901.
Smart, W., *An Introduction to the Theory of Value on the Lines of Menger, Wieser and Bohm Bawerk*, London, 1891.
Studies in Economics, London, 1895.
The Distribution of Income, London, 1899.
Second Thoughts of an Economist, London, 1916.
Toynbee, A., *Progress and Poverty: A Criticism of Mr. Henry George*, London, 1883.

Lectures on the Industrial Revolution in England, London, 1884.
Walker, F. A., *Political Economy*, London, 1883.
Webb, B., *My Apprenticeship*, London, 1926.
Webb, S. and B., *Industrial Democracy*, 2 vols., London, 1897.
Wicksell, K., *Lectures on Political Economy*, translated by E. Classen, London, 1934.
Wicksteed, P. H., 'The Marxian Theory of Value', *To-Day*, October 1884.
An Essay on the Co-ordination of the Laws of Distribution (1st edn 1894), 2nd edn, London, 1932.
The Common Sense of Political Economy (1st edn 1910), 2nd edn, London, 1933.
'The Scope and Method of Political Economy in the Light of the "Marginal" Theory of Value and Distribution', *Economic Journal*, March 1914.

C. Printed sources (secondary)

Abrams, P., *The Origins of British Sociology, 1834–1914*, Chicago, 1968.
Annan, N., *Leslie Stephen*, London, 1951.
Ashley, A., *William James Ashley*, London, 1932.
Barker, C., *Henry George*, Oxford, 1955.
Black, R. D. C., *Economic Thought and the Irish Question*, Cambridge, 1960.
Introduction to Jevons' *The Theory of Political Economy*, centenary edition, London, 1970.
Blaug, M., *Economic Theory in Retrospect*, (1st edn 1962), 3rd edn, London, 1978.
Brailsford, H. N., *The Life-Work of J. A. Hobson*, London, 1948.
Burrow, J. W., *Evolution and Society*, Cambridge, 1966.
Clarke, P., *Liberals and Social Democrats*, Cambridge, 1978.
Coase, R. H., 'The Appointment of Pigou as Marshall's Successor', *Journal of Law and Economics*, October 1972.
Coats, A. W., 'The Historicist Reaction in English Political Economy, 1870–90', *Economica*, May 1954.
'The Politics of Political Economists: Comment', *Quarterly Journal of Economics*, November 1960.
'Value-Judgements in Economics', *Yorkshire Bulletin of Economic And Social Research*, November 1964.
'The Role of Authority in the Development of British Economics', *Journal of Law and Economics*, 1964.
'Sociological Aspects of British Economics c. 1880–1930', *Journal of Political Economy*, October 1967.
'Political Economy and the Tariff Reform Campaign of 1903', *Journal of Law and Economics*, April 1968.
'The Origins and Early Development of the Royal Economic Society, *Economic Journal*, June 1968.
'The Appointment of Pigou as Marshall's Successor: A Reply', *Journal of Law and Economics*, October 1972.

Coats, A. W. and S. E., 'The Social Composition of the Royal Economic Society and the Beginnings of the British Economics "Profession", 1890–1915', *British Journal of Sociology*, May 1970.
'The Changing Social Composition of the Royal Economic Society, 1890–1960, and the Professionalisation of British Economics', *British Journal of Sociology*, June 1973.
Coats, A. W., Black, R. D. C. and Goodwin, C. D., *The Marginal Revolution in Economics*, Durham, 1973.
Collett, C. E., 'Professor Foxwell and University College', *Economic Journal*, December 1936.
Collini, S., 'Idealism and "Cambridge Idealism"', *Historical Journal*, March 1975.
Cowling, M. J., *Mill and Liberalism*, Cambridge, 1963.
Religion and Public Doctrine in Modern England, Cambridge, 1980.
Cunningham, A., *William Cunningham, Teacher and Priest*, London, 1950.
Davenport, H. J., *The Economics of Alfred Marshall*, New York, 1935.
Dewey, C. J., '"Cambridge Idealism": Utilitarian Revisionists in Late Nineteenth-Century Cambridge', *Historical Journal*, March 1974.
Dobb., M., *Welfare Economics and the Economics of Socialism*, Cambridge, 1969.
Theories of Value and Distribution, Cambridge, 1973.
Eagly, R. V. (ed.), *Events, Ideology and Economic Theory*, Detroit, 1968.
Eshag, E., *From Marshall to Keynes*, Oxford, 1963.
Fay, C. R. 'Edwin Cannan, the Tribute of a Friend', ms., Cannan Papers, Printed with some alterations in the *Economic Record*, June 1937.
Freeden, M., *The New Liberalism*, Oxford, 1978.
Glassburner, B., 'Alfred Marshall On Economic History and Historical Development', *Quarterly Journal of Economics*, November 1955.
Halévy, E., *The Growth of Philosophic Radicalism* (1st edn 1901–4), London, 1972.
Harris, J. *Unemployment and Politics: A Study in English Social Policy 1886–1914*, Oxford, 1972.
Harte, N. B., *The Study of Economic History*, London, 1971.
Herford, C. H., *Philip Henry Wicksteed, His Life and Work*, London, 1931.
Houghton, W., *The Victorian Frame of Mind*, New Haven, 1967.
Howey, R. S., *The Rise of the Marginal Utility School*, Kansas, 1960.
Hunt, E. K. and Schwartz, J. G., *A Critique of Economic Theory*, London, 1972.
Hutchison, T. W., *The Significance and Basic Postulates of Economic Theory*, London, 1938.
Review of Economic Doctrines, 1870–1929, Oxford, 1953.
Positive Economics and Policy Objectives, London, 1964.
'Economists and Economic Policy in Britain after 1870', *History of Political Economy*, Fall 1969.
On Revolutions in Economics, Cambridge, 1978.
Inglis, K. S., *Churches and the Working Classes in Victorian England*, London, 1963.
Jha, N., *The Age of Marshall*, London, 1963.

Kadish, A., *The Oxford Economists in the Late Nineteenth Century*, Oxford, 1983.
Katouzian, H., *Ideology and Method in Economics*, London, 1980.
Kent, C., *Brains and Numbers*, Toronto, 1978.
Keynes, J. M., *Essays in Biography* (1st edn 1933), London, 1972.
Koot, G. M., 'T. E. Cliffe Leslie, Irish Social Reformer, and the Origins of the English Historical School of Economics', *History of Political Economy*, Fall 1975.
'English Historical Economics and the Emergence of Economic History in England', *History of Political Economy*, Summer 1980.
Kuhn, T. S., *The Structure of Scientific Revolutions*, Chicago, 1963.
Lakatos, I., and Musgrave, A. (eds.), *Criticism and the Growth of Knowledge*, Cambridge, 1970.
Little, I. M. D., *A Critique of Welfare Economics*, Oxford, 1950.
Mannheim, K., *Ideology and Utopia*, London, 1936.
Meek, R. L., *Economics and Ideology, and Other Essays*, London, 1967.
Minogue, K., *The Liberal Mind*, London, 1963.
Myint, H., *Theories of Welfare Economics*, London, 1948.
Myrdal, G., *The Political Element in the Development of Economic Theory*, London, 1953.
Parsons, T., *The Structure of Social Action*, New York, 1937.
Petridis, A., 'Bilateral Monopoly, Tariff Reform and the Teaching of Economics; the Neglected Contribution of Langford Price', *History of Political Economy*, Spring 1979.
Peel, J. D. Y., *Herbert Spencer: The Evolution of a Sociologist*, London, 1971.
Plamenatz, J., *Ideology*, London, 1971.
Popper, K. R., *The Logic of Scientific Discovery* (1st edn in German, 1934), London, 1959.
The Poverty of Historicism, London, 1957.
Conjectures and Refutations, London, 1963.
Richter, M., *The Politics of Conscience*, London, 1964.
Robbins, L., 'Mr Hawtrey on the Scope of Economics', *Economica*, June 1927.
An Essay on the Nature and Significance of Economic Science, (1st edn 1932), 2nd edn, London, 1935.
The Theory of Economic Policy in English Classical Political Economy, London, 1952.
Robertson, Sir D., *Utility and All That*, London, 1952.
Robinson, J., *Economic Philosophy*, London, 1962.
Robinson, J. and Eatwell, J., *An Introduction to Modern Economics*, London, 1973.
Rogin, L., *The Meaning and Validity of Economic Theory*, New York, 1956.
Roll, E., *A History of Economic Thought* (1st edn 1938), 4th edn, London, 1973.
Rothblatt, S., *The Revolution of the Dons*, London, 1968.
Routh, G., *The Origin of Economic Ideas*, London, 1975.

Russell, Earl, *The Autobiography of Bertrand Russell*, 3 vols., London, 1967–9.
Sanderson, M., *The Universities and British Industry, 1850–1970*, London, 1972.
Schneewind, J. B., *Sidgwick's Ethics and Victorian Moral Philosophy*, Oxford, 1977.
Schumpeter, J. A., *Ten Great Economists*, London, 1952.
History of Economic Analysis, Oxford, 1954.
Semmel, B., 'Sir William Ashley and the Socialists of the Chair', *Economica*, November 1957.
Imperialism and Social Reform, London, 1960.
Shove, G. F. 'The Place of Marshall's Principles in the Development of Economic Theory', *Economic Journal*, December 1942.
Sidgwick, A. and E. M., *Henry Sidgwick: A Memoir*, London, 1906.
Smyth, R. L. (ed.), *Essays in Economic Method, 1860–1913*, London, 1962.
Stephen, L., *Life of Henry Fawcett*, London, 1885.
The English Utilitarians, 3 vols., London, 1900.
Stigler, G. J., *Essays in the History of Economics*, Chicago, 1965.
Viner, J., 'Marshall's Economics in Relation to the Man and his Times', *American Economic Review*, June 1941.
Whitaker, J. K., 'Alfred Marshall, the Years 1877 to 1885', *History of Political Economy*, Spring 1972.
Winch, D., *Economics and Policy*, London, 1969.

Index

For Product Safety Concerns and Information please contact our
EU representative GPSR@taylorandfrancis.com Taylor & Francis
Verlag GmbH, Kaufingerstraße 24, 80331 München, Germany